Survival and Development
of Language Communities

MULTILINGUAL MATTERS
Series Editor: John Edwards, *St. Francis Xavier University, Canada*

Multilingual Matters series publishes books on bilingualism, bilingual education, immersion education, second language learning, language policy, multiculturalism. The editor is particularly interested in 'macro' level studies of language policies, language maintenance, language shift, language revival and language planning. Books in the series discuss the relationship between language in a broad sense and larger cultural issues, particularly identity related ones.

Full details of all the books in this series and of all our other publications can be found on http://www.multilingual-matters.com, or by writing to Multilingual Matters, St Nicholas House, 31–34 High Street, Bristol BS1 2AW, UK.

Survival and Development of Language Communities

Prospects and Challenges

Edited by
F. Xavier Vila

MULTILINGUAL MATTERS
Bristol • Buffalo • Toronto

Library of Congress Cataloging in Publication Data
A catalog record for this book is available from the Library of Congress.
Survival and Development of Language Communities: Prospects and Challenges/Edited by F. Xavier Vila.
Multilingual Matters: 150
Includes bibliographical references and index.
1. Language policy—Europe--History—21st century. 2. Language policy—Europe, Central—History—21st century. 3. Language policy—Europe, Eastern—History—21st century. 4. Language planning—Europe—21st century. 5. Language planning—Europe, Central—21st century. 6. Language planning—Europe, Eastern—21st century. 7. Language and languages—Variation—Europe. I. Vila, F. Xavier. II. Vila, F. Xavier.
P119.32.E85S87 2012
306.44'94–dc23 2012036455

British Library Cataloguing in Publication Data
A catalogue entry for this book is available from the British Library.

ISBN-13: 978-1-84769-835-3 (hbk)
ISBN-13: 978-1-84769-834-6 (pbk)

Multilingual Matters
UK: St Nicholas House, 31-34 High Street, Bristol BS1 2AW, UK.
USA: UTP, 2250 Military Road, Tonawanda, NY 14150, USA.
Canada: UTP, 5201 Dufferin Street, North York, Ontario M3H 5T8, Canada.

Copyright © 2013 F. Xavier Vila and the authors of individual chapters.

All rights reserved. No part of this work may be reproduced in any form or by any means without permission in writing from the publisher.

The policy of Multilingual Matters/Channel View Publications is to use papers that are natural, renewable and recyclable products, made from wood grown in sustainable forests. In the manufacturing process of our books, and to further support our policy, preference is given to printers that have FSC and PEFC Chain of Custody certification. The FSC and/or PEFC logos will appear on those books where full certification has been granted to the printer concerned.

Typeset by Techset Composition Ltd., Salisbury, UK.

Contents

	Tables and Figures	vii
	Contributors	ix
1	The Analysis of Medium-Sized Language Communities F. Xavier Vila and Vanessa Bretxa	1
2	The Main Challenges Facing Czech as a Medium-Sized Language: The State of Affairs at the Beginning of the 21st Century Jiří Nekvapil	18
3	Challenges Facing Danish as a Medium-Sized Language J. Normann Jørgensen	38
4	Slovene, Between Purism and Plurilingualism Maja Bitenc	58
5	Challenges Faced by a Medium-Sized Language Community in the 21st Century: The Case of Hebrew Anat Stavans	81
6	Challenges for the Estonian Language: A Poststructuralist Perspective Delaney Michael Skerrett	105
7	A Small National Language and its Multilingual Challenges: The Case of Latvian Uldis Ozolins	130

8 Is Catalan a Medium-Sized Language Community Too? 157
   Emili Boix-Fuster and Jaume Farràs i Farràs

9 Challenges and Opportunities for Medium-Sized Language
   Communities in the 21st Century: A (Preliminary) Synthesis 179
   F. Xavier Vila

   Index 201

Tables and Figures

List of Tables

2.1 Number of inhabitants in the Czech Republic based on 'mother tongue' (2001) — 20

2.2 Number of inhabitants in the Czech Republic based on ethnicity (2001) — 21

2.3 Foreigners in the Czech Republic (30 April 2009) — 22

2.4 Number of students in primary and secondary schools learning foreign languages in the Czech Republic between 1995/1996 and 2008/2009 (numbers in thousands) — 23

5.1 Comparison of ethno-linguistic vitality between the study groups: Russian and Ethiopian immigrants of the early 1990s — 96

7.1 Non-titulars in the Baltic states claiming proficiency in the titular language — 137

7.2 Use of language by sociolinguistic domains and institutions in Latvia — 142

7.3 Changing proficiency in Latvian of persons whose mother tongue is not Latvian — 147

7.4 What is your attitude towards the teaching of subjects in Latvian in minority schools? — 148

9.1 Numbers of speakers of languages analysed in the MSLCs project (in millions)   180

9.2 Multilinguals in the EU: 'Which languages do you speak well enough in order to be able to have a conversation, excluding your mother tongue?'   185

List of Figures

2.1 The Czech Republic and its main regions   19

5.1 Jewish population and Hebrew around the world (April 2010)   85

5.2 Street signs in Tel Aviv   88

5.3 The local branch of the Ministry of Immigrant Absorption in Rehovot   89

5.4 Hebrew–Russian bilingual store sign in Rehovot   90

5.5 Poster announcing a concert in Amharic and Hebrew in Rehovot   90

5.6 Shopping bags from Israel labelled with two alphabets   95

7.1 Latvia: Changes in national compostion of inhabitants 1935–1989   136

7.2 Latvian language environment 1935–2000   144

7.3 Latvians knowing Russian and Russians knowing Latvian, by age group   145

Contributors

Maja Bitenc is a postgraduate student, researcher and assistant in the field of Slovene studies and sociolinguistics at the Faculty of Arts of the University of Ljubljana. Her research interests include language and identity, language attitudes, variationist sociolinguistics, dialectology and corpus linguistics. She studied Slovene and English at the University of Ljubljana and at Eberhard Karls Universität Tübingen, Germany. She has conducted research on Slovene emigrants in Germany for her diploma thesis, which was awarded the Prešeren Prize of the Faculty of Arts and the prize offered by the Government's Office for Slovenians Abroad. She has worked at the Centre for Slovene in Second/Foreign Language and has taught Slovene and English at primary and grammar school.

Emili Boix-Fuster is a full Professor in Sociolinguistics at the Department of Catalan Philology, University of Barcelona, Catalonia, Spain. He regularly teaches sociolinguistics and language planning. In conjunction with Miquel Strubell, he has recently edited *Democratic Policies for Language Revitalisation: the Case of Catalan* (Palgrave Macmillan, 2011). He has been awarded the 'Serra i Moret' prize by the Catalan government for his essay, 'Civic responsibility against cynicism. Languages to live and to coexist' (Generalitat de Catalunya, 2011, in Catalan). He is editor of the academic journal *Treballs de Sociolingüística Catalana* and a member of the steering committee of the University of Barcelona's University Centre of Sociolinguistics and Communication (CUSC).

Vanessa Bretxa is an Assistant Professor at the University of Barcelona and a researcher at the University Centre for Sociolinguistics and Communication (CUSC). She has participated in several large-scale sociolinguistic projects regarding language use and competence in the Catalan-speaking areas, and in the practices of cultural and media consumption of young speakers of

Catalan and Spanish in the Barcelona metropolitan area. She is the co-editor of the journal *Llengua, societat and comunicació* (LSC), a publication of CUSC.

Jaume Farràs i Farràs is Associate Professor in Sociology at the Department of Sociology and Organizational Analysis, University of Barcelona. He obtained his PhD in Sociology at UCM and the École des Hautes Études en Sciences Sociales de la Sorbonne in Paris. He has been a researcher at the University of Michigan and the University of Essex. He is a member at the University Centre for Sociolinguistics and Communication at the University of Barcelona (CUSC). He conducts research on various American, European and national programmes, as well as for different Catalan institutions. His research interests are the sociology of leisure, consumption and sociolinguistics.

J. Normann Jørgensen is a Professor, dr.pæd., at the University of Copenhagen (1995–) and was previously at the University of Texas (1978–1979) and the Danish University of Education (1980–1995). He is the Leader of the University of Copenhagen Center for Danish as a Second Language and a co-leader of the Center for the Study of Language Change in Real Time. He was the Leader of the Køge Project in bilingualism (1987–2007), and he is currently the leader of the Amager Project in Polylanguaging (2009). He has conducted studies in sociolinguistics, particularly in polylingualism, language change and youth language. His publications include books, articles and reviews, among them *Languaging. Nine Years of Polylingual Development of Turkish–Danish Grade School Students*, Copenhagen, 2010. He has won several Danish and Nordic championships in sabre fencing.

Jiří Nekvapil teaches sociolinguistics, pragmatics, discourse analysis and general linguistics in the Department of General Linguistics at Charles University, Prague. He has published extensively in these areas. His current research focuses on multilingual practices in companies and universities, history and theory of language planning, including Language Management Theory, and history as used and produced in biographic narratives. In 2009, he founded the book series Prague Papers on Language, Society and Interaction (Peter Lang Publishing Group).

Uldis Ozolins is a past Australasian President of the Association for the Advancement of Baltic Studies and an active researcher and commentator on contemporary Baltic issues. He gained his PhD from Monash University, has taught at the University of Melbourne, Deakin University, La Trobe University Royal Melbourne Institute of Technology and University of Western Sydney in several disciplines (politics, philosophy, education, interpreting/translating). He also runs his own consultancy on areas of language, interpreting and translating, and multicultural communication. He has taught and conducted research on Baltic issues at several universities in Latvia and has collaborated with scholars in Estonia and Lithuania.

Delaney Skerrett recently completed his PhD in Applied Linguistics at The University of Queensland, where he is also Associate Lecturer. He also has a Bachelor of Business and a Master of Education from the Queensland University of Technology and an Honours degree in Spanish from The University of Queensland. He has an MA in Baltic Studies from the University of Tartu, a Postgraduate Diploma in Applied Linguistics from Monash University, a Graduate Diploma in Social Science from the University of New England, and a Graduate Diploma of Psychology from Central Queensland University. Skerrett also lectures part time at the Centre for Baltic Studies and the Department of English at the University of Tartu and is a part-time Senior Research Assistant at the Australian Institute for Suicide Research and Prevention at Griffith University.

Anat Stavans, PhD is a Senior Lecturer in Applied Linguistics in the English Department and Director of the Research Authority at Beit Berl Academic College, as well as researcher at the Institute for Innovation in Education at the Hebrew University in Jerusalem. Her research focuses on developmental and educational linguistics, trilingual acquisition and development, and cross-cultural and cross-linguistic literacy development. She is the author of numerous articles on code-switching, narrative input and development, immigrant bilingualism, educational language policy, parent–child interaction, and multiliteracy development. Recently, she edited the volume *Studies in Language and Language Education: Essays in Honor of Elite Olshtain* (with Irit Kupferberg, 2008) and *Linguistic and Developmental Analysis of Child-Directed Parental Narrative Input* (in Hebrew). Dr Stavans has led several projects concerning early language and literacy development among educators and parents and has served as consultant to several international agencies.

F. Xavier Vila is an Associate Professor at the University of Barcelona. He obtained an Extraordinary Degree Award in Catalan Philology in Barcelona and a PhD in Linguistics at the Vrije Universiteit Brussel. He was the first director of the CRUSCAT Research Network on sociolinguistics of the Institut d'Estudis Catalans, the Catalan National Academy of Sciences, and is the current Director of the University Centre for Sociolinguistics and

Communication at the University of Barcelona (CUSC). He is also the director of the Master's programme in Language Consultancy, Multilingual Language Management and Editorial Services at the UB's Catalan Philology Department. He has published a wide range of books and specialist articles in the areas of sociolinguistics, demolinguistics and language policy of Catalan and other medium-sized and minority languages, among them *New Immigrations and Languages*, in press, Barcelona (in Catalan).

1 The Analysis of Medium-Sized Language Communities

F. Xavier Vila and Vanessa Bretxa

Looking at Languages in Between

It may come as a surprise to many that sociolinguistics, understood in a broad sense as the discipline that studies the relation between language and society, has so far been unable to agree on a basic typology of linguistic communities. More than half a century ago, Ferguson's *Diglossia* (1959) established the outlines of what was expected to be the first step towards a more general classification (Ferguson, 1991). However, in spite of the paper's huge success, and also the calls made by other authors in this direction (e.g. Einar Haugen's (1971: 25) advocacy of a 'typology of ecological classification', as well as Gumperz, 1962, or Kloss, 1966), the truth is that the efforts to establish a clear, systematic and comprehensive sociolinguistic classification of languages and linguistic communities around the world have been relatively unsuccessful. In other words, sociolinguistics has still not produced a typology that classifies language communities and/or their linguistic ecologies according to a widely accepted set of features. Also, to put it in in Peter Mühlhäusler's terms, 'To understand why so many individual languages are disappearing requires an understanding of the ecological conditions that sustain complex language ecologies' (Martí et al., 2005: 45).

One of the reasons for this failure may lie in the complex relation of sociolinguistics with the language construct, and with some of the main concepts associated with it. The main focus of research of sociolinguistics as a discipline is linguistic diversity (Coulmas, 2005), and most introductions to the field make clear from the very beginning that the notion of language itself is polysemic, ambiguous, difficult to define and even 'a fallacy' (Simpson, 2001: 31). It is indeed commonplace that every introductory course to sociolinguistics reminds the novice that language borders are often impossible to delineate in purely linguistic terms; that languages show very disparate degrees of internal structural difference; that mutual intelligibility is not a safe indicator of the 'language' versus 'dialect' divide; and that, in actual terms, the distinction between a language and a dialect is a contingent sociohistorical compromise rather than an immutable structural fact, to the extent that some scholars propose rejecting the notion of language altogether (Blommaert, 2010).

In such a context, it is not surprising that many of the existing typologies of linguistic situations have not adopted languages or language communities as their analytical frame, but rather polities, and especially sovereign states (cf. Bastardas & Boix, 1994; Laitin, 2000; Spolsky, 2004). These typologies attempt to classify polities according to the number of languages spoken in each country and the official status and function of each, and thus have a strong legal, politological approach to the analysis of sociolinguistic situations. Indeed, one does not have to subscribe whole-heartedly to the oft-quoted saying that 'a language is a dialect with an army and a navy' to consider that (sovereign) states constitute one of the main factors to be taken into account when analysing any given sociolinguistic ecosystem. In fact, states play such a central, decisive role in language policy in contemporary times that any classification that ignores their existence and impact is doomed to failure. Besides this, empirical quantitative analyses are often impossible across state borders, for the basic statistical data crucially needed for sociolinguistic analysis are usually provided by public administrations, and therefore depend strongly on existing political and administrative borders. Consider Europe, for instance. Comparative analysis of the sociolinguistic reality of the European languages has become much easier since the Union – a *sui generis* political entity, but a polity at the end of the day – decided to take on the task of obtaining comparable data in all of its Member States by means of the Eurobarometers. Before then, sociolinguistic comparisons across countries had to deal with the arduous task of putting side by side the results from disparate data-collecting methods based on vastly different premises (cf. Extra & Gorter, 2008). It is no coincidence that the root of the term 'statistics' is 'state'.

Important as they undoubtedly are, politologically oriented classifications of languages and language groups and situations do not in themselves exhaust the possibilities of classifying languages and linguistic situations. On the one hand, they do not necessarily capture some crucial aspects of a particular language community such as the degree of intergenerational transmission, language use in socioeconomic spheres, cultural production and consumption, and the ideological positioning of its speakers vis-à-vis other languages. On the other hand, almost by definition, research structured on the basis of political borders finds it difficult to deal with phenomena that go beyond them, and languages do go beyond borders at least in three different senses. First, the borders of the almost 200 independent states in the world do not coincide with those of the 5000 to 6000 languages (still) spoken. Second, even if nation states have striven to make their citizens linguistically homogeneous, people move around and take their linguistic repertoires with them. Finally, people communicate more and more across borders. A glance at Fischer's (2011) map of the world language communities of Twitter should suffice to convince the reluctant that next to the politologically oriented classifications, we need more refined sociolinguistically oriented comparative analyses, that is, analyses that pay attention not only to sovereign states, but also to people(s) and communities.

In fact, there are a number of classifications that are more community oriented, and therefore link themselves, in a more or less ambiguous way, with the historical meaning of language community mentioned above. Most of these classifications (although not all – think of the concept of ethnolinguistic vitality; Ehala, 2010; Giles *et al.*, 1977; Harwood *et al.*, 1994) tend to focus on one of the ends of an imaginary 'majority–minority' continuum, basically understood in demographic terms. Several among them focus on the weakest extreme of this continuum, analyse in detail the challenges and prospects of weak and weakened languages, and provide refined analyses and classifications of more or less severely endangered language communities (cf. Edwards, 1992, 2010; Euromosaic; Fishman, 1991; Grenoble & Whaley, 1998; Moseley, 2010). Others, in contrast, such as those produced by de Swaan (2001), Calvet (1999) or Graddol (2006), focus particularly on the most spoken languages of the world, and pay little attention to the rest, packing 98% of them together in the lowest, clearly undifferentiated category of 'peripheral' languages. Thanks to these and many other initiatives, sociolinguistics has made remarkable progress in understanding the dynamics at both ends of the continuum. However, between these two extremes the situation is rather different. Languages in 'intermediate' positions, those that can be regarded simultaneously as the head of a dog and the tail of a lion, are less often taken as the explicit object of comparative analyses. Indeed, there is much to be learned from comparing the communities placed between the big ones (i.e. those with many millions of speakers) and the small ones (i.e. those with only a few thousand).

Certainly, the languages included in this intermediate group are far from homogeneous. They range from fully standardized languages, with a long record of written literature, to varieties that have rarely transcended the status of oral vernaculars and tend to be regarded as dialects of other languages. Many of these languages enjoy some sort of official status in one or more countries and even in supranational institutions, while others have no legal protection at all. Some are widely used on the internet and for software facilities; others have only a marginal presence in the virtual world. Some of these communities are universally literate in their language, whereas in others literacy is universally provided in a different language. Others are far away from literacy in any language at all. Many of these languages are used as a means of instruction in higher education; others do not even enter kindergartens. Some of these languages are hegemonic in their communities' press, radio and television, but others only rarely enter these domains. In general terms, the majority of these languages are not considered to be in immediate danger of extinction, thanks to their demography and the advantages it provides, but some are severely at risk. In fact, it would be erroneous to think that all these languages lead a placid life. Debates about the long-term sustainability of many of these languages, even those that enjoy full support from developed nation states, are not rare, although the continuation of such strongly endangered languages may often be regarded as unrealistic by specialists and speakers alike. Nevertheless, in spite of all these debates, many of these languages, especially but not only those that have gained the status of nation state official language, constitute vivid examples of linguistic sustainability in virtually all domains of social life. This makes them appropriate subjects for analysis in order to make progress in the field of language policy.

It is within this framework that, in 2007, the University Centre for Sociolinguistics and Communication at the University of Barcelona (CUSC–UB)[1] launched a project sponsored by Linguamón (House of Languages),[2] focusing on what could provisionally be described as 'medium-sized language communities' (MSLCs). Both institutions shared a concern about the sustainability of linguistic diversity, as well as the conviction that language management theory in general would benefit from also paying attention to the many linguistic communities in a demographically intermediate position between the really big languages and the smaller ones. The main research questions addressed by the project were the following. What was to be learnt from comparing the sociolinguistic ecologies of MSLCs, especially those that were doing relatively well in the 21st century? Were these MSLCs facing particular challenges? Were these challenges different from those experienced by smaller languages, but also different from those experienced in the major linguistic communities? What lessons could be learnt from their experiences in order to help other language communities to progress towards a situation of viability in the 21st century? This approach was felt to be of major interest, initially, to the MSLCs themselves. It was thought that a cross-comparative view might help speakers and language managers of these languages to understand their position, individually and collectively, in the language system of an increasingly globalized world. Learning from others may give a clear sense of what is viable and what is not in comparable cases. In this respect, it was felt that many language communities, especially in postcolonial scenarios, might benefit from a comparison with fully developed languages. This was the starting point of the project 'The Sustainability of Medium-Sized Language Communities (MSLC) in the age of globalization: new trends, new solutions?'[3]

The Medium-Sized Language Communities Project: Some Methodological Decisions

Among the first decisions that had to be taken were those that defined the methodology to be used and the object of the research. Current sociolinguistics seems uneasy with the notion of a 'language (linguistic or speech) community', understood as '(...) those who use a given language for part, most or all of their daily existence' (Baker & Jones, 1998: 96). This term, which parallels the German *Sprachgemeinschaft*, the Dutch *Taalgemeenschap* or the Spanish *comunidad lingüística*, did enjoy some currency in English, particularly a few decades ago (cf. Bloomfield, 1933: 42; Kloss, 1966). However, the success of the alternative 'speech community' notion in the 1970s displaced it in at least two different senses. On the one hand, the term 'language community' became (at best) a less favoured synonym for speech community (e.g. Baker & Jones, 1998; Kachru, 2001; Madera, 1996; Trudgill, 2003). At the same time, the very meaning of the term speech community was thoroughly modified after the objections of Labov (1972) and Hymes (1974). Indeed, today, in most specialized contexts, this term has lost its original connection with the totality of speakers of one given language, and has become understood basically as a (smaller) group of individuals in habitual contact with each other, with shared norms of speaking and interpretation of speaking performance, and/or shared attitudes and values, irrespective of the monolingual or multilingual composition of their linguistic repertoire (cf. Kachru, 2001; Swann *et al.*, 2004).

It should be noticed that this process of conceptual replacement and reduction was not necessarily followed by all authors. In fact, the use of 'language community' to include all customary speakers of a given language pops up from time to time in the literature. It also may well be that the term is more commonly used in sociolinguistic traditions other than the anglophone one (see Moreno Fernández (1998), Mollà (2002) or Berruto (2003) for three introductions to sociolinguistics in Spanish, Catalan and Italian, respectively). Both the 1996 Universal Declaration of Linguistic Rights[4] and the United Nations Educational, Scientific and Cultural Organization (UNESCO)-supported World Languages Review (Martí et al., 2005) used the concept as a cornerstone. In fact, this wide understanding of language community even enjoys some legislative translation. The current Belgian constitution enshrines the existence of three linguistic communities (Dutch-speaking, French-speaking and German-speaking) made up by the totality of their respective speakers living in Belgium. In any case, the conceptual merger of the two sorts of communities is an unfortunate development, for it leaves both the specialist and the layperson without a term for the whole set of speakers of a language. Irrespective of the many problems of practical operationalization – already identified by Bloomfield (1933) or, *mutatis mutandi*, Dorian (1982) or Le Page and Tabouret-Keller (1985) – a term is needed to refer to those groups formed by individuals who speak French, Portuguese, Arabic, Kiswahili, but also Albanian, Quechua, Tamazight and so on, and who are scattered across several independent countries, in different continents even. Indeed, some of them have their own name, such as *la francophonie* or *la lusofonia*. In other words, because we need a social correlate of the term 'language' to analyse linguistic situations, in this book we will be using the term 'language community' in this sense.

Given the exploratory nature of this project, it was agreed that a number of specialists from different language communities would be invited to present the situation and the main challenges that, in their opinion, the MSLCs they were familiar with would have to face in the increasingly globalized world of the 21st century, and to discuss them with both international and local colleagues in a round of workshops held in Barcelona in late 2009.[5] The drawback of this approach was that the visions of each particular linguistic community might be biased in some way by the personal (although obviously legitimate) perspective of each individual researcher. Nevertheless, this procedure offered an invaluable advantage: it would make accessible to a wider audience a bulk of data, research results and even academic discussions that would otherwise have been available only to those proficient in each of the languages involved in the research. Furthermore, the workshop format would allow the participants to discuss their points of view, establishing comparisons and challenging preconceptions when needed. The presentations and discussions that ensued form the basis of the current volume.

Given that resources were limited and only a small number of communities would be analysed, it became essential to establish a number of theoretical and practical criteria that could guide the selection of cases. First, the very notion of MSLCs had to be narrowed down to make it operational. As noted above, the organizers used the term 'language community' to refer to the social correlate of language, that is, a human group defined by the primary use and intergenerational transmission of a set of varieties usually identified as the same language. Although the declared goal of the project was to compare the situation of linguistic communities ranked between the biggest and the smallest, the precise definitions of this intermediate space were virtually infinite, and no definitive theoretical arguments could be advanced in favour of one solution or another. Nevertheless, it was obvious that some sort of tentative demographic limits were needed in order to select the cases. Accordingly, after some discussion, a bracket for the category was provisionally set on the basis of both theoretical and practical criteria, with a lower limit of one million speakers and an upper limit of 25 million. This upper limit was applied because it guaranteed that – to use de Swaan's (2001) terminology – all 'hypercentral' and 'supercentral' languages, but also most very big 'central' languages, would be automatically excluded from the selection. In practical terms, for instance, this limit for the MSLCs includes all the official languages of the European Union that are traditionally considered to be small. At the other end, the lowest threshold of one million speakers was adopted to make sure that most of the smallest 'peripheral' linguistic groups – again, in de Swaan's terms – would not feature in the comparison. In fact, these two limits were at the same time sufficiently restrictive, but also sufficiently broad for our exploratory task. A quick glance at Ethnologue (http://www.ethnologue.com/) shows that there are more than 300 languages between these limits around the world. Of course, both limits were provisional and neither should be regarded as a fixed boundary giving a strict definition of the notion of an MSLC. Indeed, many good reasons could be put forward for either raising or lowering either limit and, in fact, subsequent workshops of this project included sessions about linguistic communities that are classified outside this category. However, in practical terms, although the limits established may not include all MSLCs, they were reasonably effective for identifying a large number of communities that were medium-sized, and this was a good starting-point for a comparative approach.

During the preliminary phase, a second important decision was made, in the sense that the workshops in 2009 would focus on languages spoken in socioeconomically developed societies. Given that the goal of these workshops was to provide insights into the challenges facing MSLCs, it was felt that exploring languages already fully involved in the process of globalization would be of help not only to their communities, but also to all other communities that are currently lagging behind in the process of integration in the globalized world. To study sustainability, the focus had to be not on the most traditional societies and socioeconomic institutions, but rather on formulae that look to the future.

Finally, a third significant decision was made in relation to the sociolinguistic vitality of the MSLCs. At least since Joshua Fishman's (1991, 2000) *Reversing Language Shift*, a consensus has existed in sociolinguistics and language policy theory about the crucial relevance of intergenerational transmission to the long-term viability of a language. Although it would have been relatively easy to include in our selection of case studies a number of communities affected by severe problems of intergenerational language transmission, given the goals of this project, the organizers rejected this possibility, and an effort was made to focus on cases that could be described as relatively successful in terms of linguistic survival. To guarantee this point, and because the goal of this project was to learn about good practices, it was decided to concentrate on communities that were not experiencing large-scale processes of language shift.

These three criteria – demographic dimension, socioeconomic development and sociolinguistic vitality – were the main rationales used to select the handful of communities to be analysed. Other criteria were also used precisely to avoid restricting the selection. The organizers were aware that restricting the analyses to languages spoken in ethnolinguistically homogeneous societies would unnecessarily limit the scope of their work, so decided to study both homogeneous and heterogeneous societies. Correspondence between language community and nation state was not a prerequisite for selection, so a variety of political situations were included in the sample. Some communities coincided with one nation state, others were divided among different states, some were dominant in a state that was shared with other languages spoken by a smaller number of speakers, and one was in a minority position vis-à-vis another language within a composite nation state. Political regime was not adopted as a criterion for selection, although it transpired that all MSLCs fulfilling the rest of the criteria were spoken in liberal democratic countries. Of course, other more practical considerations, such as the amount of information about each case at the disposal of the organizers, or the availability of specialists, were also taken into account.

After defining the universe to be explored, the research team identified potential candidates, and a number of contacts were made during the first half of 2009. Finally, the organization invited eight linguistic experts (in Dutch, Finnish, Danish, Estonian, Latvian, Hebrew, Czech and Slovene) to Barcelona to discuss the situation and the challenges experienced by these MSLCs at the start of the 21st century in the company of researchers from CUSC–UB and Linguamón.

This Volume

This volume contains the results from the workshops organized in 2009 in Barcelona regarding the main challenges faced by MSLCs.[6] The book has three major objectives. First, it aims to provide new data and reflections regarding the current state of language practices, ideologies and public debates in a number of MSLCs in order to develop a comparative framework of analysis for these languages. Second, the chapters in the volume aim to identify the attainable goals in connection with MSLC language management and language policy, by providing a consideration of the language domains being served in each language. Finally, the volume aims to reevaluate the opposition between 'majority' and 'minority' languages, a simplistic, dichotomist approach that hinders an adequate understanding of how the world's language system is being reconstructed under the pressure of glocalization. Although the chapters were written for publication after the workshops had been held, they express the personal view of each author on each particular subject and therefore do not necessarily share the same analytical framework of interpretation. Nevertheless, the reader will identify a number of coincidences and shared assumptions among them that transcend a simple description.

The volume starts with a chapter by Jiří Nekvapil (Charles University, Prague) titled 'The Main Challenges Facing Czech as a Medium-Sized Language: The State of Affairs at the Beginning of the 21st Century', which focuses on the main challenges faced by Czech as a medium-sized language, and starts by wondering to what extent the challenges are felt by the general population, by intellectual elites and by linguists. After providing a detailed account of the demolinguistic and ethnolinguistic composition of the Czech Republic, he deals with one of the characteristic features of the Czech linguistic ideologies: the ideology of language threat associated with the 'language of a small nation' complex, which may lead Czech speakers to regard it as a minor language. One of the consequences of this ideology for Czechs is the historical need to reassure themselves that the language is not really in danger. Another consequence is the widespread expectations that Czech will only be spoken by Czechs; that is, foreigners are not expected to learn it. It is interesting to see that these ideologies seem to be well rooted in spite of the fact that, in comparative terms, foreign languages have a smaller presence in the Czech Republic than in many other central and Western European medium-sized language communities, as they are mostly limited to multinational companies and scientific and university scenarios. Nevertheless, they exert their influence when it comes to designing language policies, especially in connection with language promotion beyond its borders, that appear to be quite weak, or when dealing with the teaching of Czech as a second language to recent immigrants. Still in the language ideologies arena, Nekvapil refers to a debate connected with language corpus, namely the debate on the effects of the *destandardization* of Czech, that is, the increase in variability of standard Czech due to the introduction of non-standard features in domains that require the standard language. A final and very important point is made by Nekvapil with regard to the relationship between Czech and Slovak. In the past, both varieties were mutually comprehensible, and therefore there was a common market for both languages. However, since the end of Czechoslovakia, this fluidity seems to be in retreat, with young Czechs reporting a decreasing ability to understand Slovak.

The chapter by J. Normann Jørgensen (University of Copenhagen) entitled 'Challenges Facing Danish as a Medium-Sized Language' begins by describing the general sociolinguistic situation for this Scandinavian language, which is not only fully established as the main vehicle of social interaction in virtually all domains in Denmark, but also enjoys the benefits of being thoroughly described and firmly standardized. Although in a position that many may regard as idyllic from the point of view of linguistic sustainability, Danish faces a number of challenges that are the object of explicit language policies and ideological controversies in at least two different dimensions. First, there is the encroachment of English in a number of domains, including higher education, science, business and as a linguistic marker of smartness and cosmopolitanism. This trend is perceived by some sectors as threatening the Danish language and is triggering a number of defensive reactions against alleged 'domain loss', among them the *parallelsproglighed* (i.e. 'language parallelism' policy) – systematic use of both languages in these delicate domains. Scarce as it is, the research on the matter nevertheless suggests that Danish is not in danger of being pushed aside by English in these domains, but draws attention to another danger – that of depending exclusively on English-speaking sources to understand the rest of the world due to the decreasing familiarity with other major languages. Second, the general push towards egalitarianism and uniformity in all aspects of Danish society has a number of unexpected consequences in linguistic terms, such as the dissolution of traditional dialects and the progressive loss of familiarity with linguistic diversity among Danes. Jørgensen analyses this trend in connection with political and educational practices, and claims that this reduction of contact with internal diversity is at the root of the decreasing ability of Danes to understand other Scandinavian languages. In his view, lack of tolerance towards (linguistic) heterogeneity is also strongly related to widespread reluctance to accept immigrants, their heritage languages and their ways of speaking Danish. In short, Danish faces two challenges: uniformity, with its practical and attitudinal implications, and isolation.

The position of Slovene, one of the smallest communities dealt with in this volume, and the challenges it faces in the near future, are analysed by Maja Bitenc (University of Ljubljana) in the chapter 'Slovene, Between Purism and Plurilingualism'. Since the independence of Slovenia from the former Yugoslavia, Slovene has increased both its domains of use and its value in Slovene society, and economic prosperity has attracted a significant percentage of immigrants who seem to be learning Slovene as the means to communicate with the local population. In general terms, the language is used in all areas of contemporary society, both public and private, from all governmental procedures to press, mass media, popular culture and education. Higher education and scientific activities appear to be the major challenge in this respect, because the demands for internationalization seem to be promoting the use of English at the expense of Slovene in some cases, a move that is not necessarily welcomed by all sectors. Broadly speaking, however, in terms of language practices (and despite the fact that the use of foreign languages for international purposes seems to be widespread), the use of Slovene seems to be fairly sustainable, if not on the increase. The situation is rather different for the Slovene-speaking minorities in Italy, Hungary and Austria, where the language is used, at best, as a means for internal communication. As far as Slovenia is concerned, it is on the internal front (i.e. in the corpus) that this language seems to be facing the most serious challenges. Slovene is a rather diverse language, and linguistic ideologies predominant in Slovenia place great importance on the use of a *correct*, standardized form of the language, which leads speakers to depend heavily on linguistic consultants, and urge the educational system to equip pupils with the linguistic competence required. Another area of concern is the growing need for materials to cater for newcomers who need to learn Slovene as a second language.

The chapter by Anat Stavans (Hebrew University, Jerusalem) introduces the reader to the challenges faced by Hebrew as a medium-sized language, both as the majority language of a multilingual Israel and as the (sacred) language that unifies the Jewish diaspora. The most successful case of language revival has increased its demographic basis exponentially in the 20th century thanks to a process of intergenerational language shift away from the languages of the Jewish immigrants. This process remains under way today, although significant differences are recorded between different immigrant communities; for example, Ethiopians adopt Hebrew much faster than Russian Jews. Hebrew remains, nonetheless, the most widely used language in Israel in virtually all domains. It is used not only in administrative affairs, across the whole educational system and in daily interpersonal communication, but also in the written and audiovisual media, cinema, theatre, music, the book industry and popular culture. This is not to say that Israel is a monolingual society. Next to Hebrew, Arabic is a *de jure* official language of Israel, and Palestinian Arabic remains the everyday language of the Arab community, but the clear communitarian gap makes Arabic a rather distant language for many Jews. In contrast, English occupies a pivotal position as the country's major language of communication with the rest of the world, both virtually and face to face. English is the major second language learnt by Israelis. Many other languages, from Russian to Circassian and from Yiddish to French, are also used to a greater or lesser degree, mostly (though not always) among the older immigrant generations. Although it is a revived language, the Hebrew language system does not seem to offer many reasons for concern, although some voices have been raised warning of the dangers of anglification. The chapter reviews in some detail the complexities of Israel's dual educational system, and its efforts both to integrate children with varied linguistic backgrounds and to prepare them for a multilingual society. It ends by noting some of the challenges facing Hebrew in the future. One of them, shared with all other MSLCs, will be that of establishing their need, legitimacy and essentiality as cultural vehicles of their speakers in the framework of a globalized world. Another one, specifically related to Hebrew, will be 'whether the educational system will make linguistic allowances and accept other minority languages as legitimate heritage languages[?] This will only be possible when the "organic" multilingualism of Israel will outlive the "synthetic" need to mainstream both linguistically and culturally its people.'

'Challenges for the Estonian Language: A Poststructuralist Perspective' by Delaney Skerrett (University of Queensland) examines the specific challenges faced as part of the process of promoting Estonian as the language of wider societal, interethnic use in Estonia from a historical-structural approach that strives to contextualize this process in the framework of the changing power balances in Estonia in recent times. Most of the chapter is devoted to the intricate relationships between the two major languages spoken in the country, Estonian and Russian. Skerrett's review of the available research shows that Estonian appears to be reaffirming its position as the national language, by slowly gaining ground as the default language in interethnic communication, in a general framework of slow intergenerational decrease in competence in Russian and an increase in competence in Estonian. According to Skerrett, a process of social integration across the ethnolinguistic gap is under way, with Russian speakers redefining their identity and feeling increasingly part of Estonian society, even though they have retained their language. Nevertheless, a number of factors, including some attitudes among ethnic Estonians and the Russian authorities, may be hindering this process. In this context, Skerrett argues that a reconstruction of Estonianness is vital to overcoming the challenges posed to Estonia(n) in the near future. This reconstruction should aim at promoting 'the solidarity between all residents of Estonia, regardless of ethnicity, by emphasizing the commonalities they share in inhabiting the same physical and, in many ways, social space. At the same time, respect for diversity, promoted through continued minority language maintenance in the case of "Estonian Russian" and by strengthening revivals efforts of Võro, would, it is hoped, see a queerer, more equitable sense of what it means to be "Estonian".' In a context of an increasing societal need for Estonian, this more inclusive approach to Estonian identity would enhance the potential for positive outcomes for all residents of Estonia through the Estonian language.

Uldis Ozolins (University of Western Sydney, Australia) presents the second case of post-Soviet MSLC, Latvian. As for the case of Estonian, most of its discussion of the challenges for the language revolves around the position of Russian and Russian speakers in the country. After reviewing the process whereby Russian became widely spoken in Latvia during the Soviet period, Ozolins offers a panoramic view of current language use in all domains, which shows a predominance of Latvian in most sectors except for the private sector – namely in businesses owned by non-citizens – where Russian is prevalent, and in science and international affairs, where English is the most common language. Ozolins shows also that since independence, some domains such as the Latvian language publication industry have expanded substantially. However, the author places special emphasis on demolinguistic evolution, using a range of surveys to show that, in contrast to Soviet times, bilingualism is no longer reserved to Latvian L1 speakers. Instead, a new generation of Russians who know Latvian is emerging. Nevertheless, the habit of Latvian speakers of addressing Russian speakers in Russian, even if the latter can also speak Latvian, remains quite widespread, and is a reason for concern with regard to the future. In Ozolins's view, the future of Latvian remains uncertain and depends on a number of internal (the recruitment of more L2 speakers, interplay between linguistic tolerance and insistence on the use of Latvian in critical sectors, refinement of the language in view of new demands) and external factors (basically, being able to operate between Russia and Europe).

'Is Catalan a Medium-Sized Language Community Too?' by Emili Boix-Fuster and Jaume Farràs i Farràs (University of Barcelona) analyses the case of Catalan in the framework of the other MSLCs and focuses on its main differential features. Except in Andorra, Catalan is not the language of a sovereign state. This lack of a nation state apparatus means, on the one hand, that Catalan does not have the support of a state administration, or of other institutions such as the European Union, which are primarily supported by Member States. On the other hand it also dramatically reduces the autonomy of the Catalan language community in many aspects that are important for language survival. Boix-Fuster and Farràs i Farràs point out some of the most significant risks for Catalan in the long run, such as those deriving from political subordination, massive immigration and globalization. However, the authors argue that, in spite of the extreme pressure exerted on the language, Catalan remains a powerful vehicle of formal and informal communication that is not only passed on from one generation to another, but also recruits thousands of speakers in what is probably the most deeply bilingualized community in current Europe.

The last chapter, 'Challenges and Opportunities for Medium-Sized Language Communities in the 21st century: A (Preliminary) Synthesis' by F. Xavier Vila (University of Barcelona), summarizes some of the most important similarities and differences between the communities analysed here. Indeed, the MSLCs selected for this volume differ in many respects, but also have a number of conspicuous similarities that suggest that the notion itself is worth taking into consideration. For instance, all these communities show a considerable degree of institutional completeness, with a significant presence in virtually all spheres of life, from home to university and business, and from book production to the internet. Indeed, the only domains that were consistently described as beyond the scope of these MSLCs were science and research. All the communities also coincided in having a standard variety that is hegemonic in formal and written domains, although the degree of homogeneity of this variety differs markedly. An interesting feature of this issue was the strong connection between administrative limits and cultural and linguistic exchanges. Contrary to expectations, globalization does not appear to be blurring state borders, in one sense at least – whereas speakers of neighbouring, related languages used to learn the language of one another, or at least acquire a passive understanding, this no longer appears to be the case. On the contrary, state borders seem to exert a powerful influence, and intercommunication with neighbouring communities increasingly takes place in a lingua franca. All in all, the notion of an MSLC seems to be useful in at least suggesting that languages in this category may aspire to have institutional completeness.

Some Final Remarks

One of the main conclusions arising from the Barcelona workshops was that, although it would be unrealistic to compare MSLCs to the big, hyper- or supercentral languages, MSLCs at least have the potential not to be regarded as minority groups with no political power and/or low levels of techno-economic development. MSLCs must be addressed and dealt with in a different way from more subordinate minorities. They have specific problems, quite often deriving from techno-economic interdependence and other levels of the globalization process. It is quite probable that MSLCs will need a specific theoretical focus that differs from the prevailing conceptualization of 'majority' and 'minority' communities or 'greater' and 'lesser' used languages. This volume is a first attempt to break down this simplistic, dichotomous pattern and to analyse the characteristics of these communities, their problems and their future prospects.[7]

Notes

(1) See http://www.ub.edu/cusc/
(2) See http://www10.gencat.cat/casa_llengues/AppJava/en/index.jsp
(3) See http://www.ub.edu/cusc/llenguesmitjanes/?lang=en
(4) See http://www.culturalrights.net/descargas/drets_culturals389.pdf
(5) Participants were first asked to produce a general description of the situation for their particular language, and these descriptions were posted on the internet for consultation by the general public. The next morning, most participants took part in a seminar with other guests and local researchers, aiming to analyse the similarities and differences between the various linguistic communities under scrutiny. Finally, once the comparative discussion had taken place, researchers were invited to present their papers about the main challenges experienced by their MSLC (see http://www.ub.edu/cusc/llenguesmitjanes/). These seminars took place on 8–9 October, 5–6 November and 3–4 December 2009, and were followed by other more specialized workshops in 2010 and 2011.
(6) It was not possible to include chapters on Dutch and Finnish in this volume, although there are some references to these cases, especially in the concluding chapter.
(7) Readers specifically interested in the legal aspects of these challenges may find it interesting to consult Milian-Massana (ed.)(2012).

References

Baker, C. and Jones, S.P. (1998) *Encyclopedia of Bilingualism and Bilingual Education.* Clevedon: Multilingual Matters.
Bastardas, A. and Boix, E. (1994) *¿Un Estado, una Lengua? La Organización Política de la Diversidad Lingüística.* Barcelona: Octaedro.
Berruto, G. (2003) *Fondamenti di Sociolinguistica.* Roma, Bari: Laterza.
Blommaert, J. (2010) *The Sociolinguistics of Globalization.* Cambridge: Cambridge University Press.
Bloomfield, L. (1933) *Language.* London: George Allen & Unwin.
Calvet, L-J. (1999) *Pour une Écologie des Langues du Monde.* Paris: Plon.
Coulmas, F. (2005) *Sociolinguistics. The Study of Speakers' Choices.* Cambridge, New York: Cambridge University Press.

de Swaan, A. (2001) *Words of the World. The Global Language System*. Malden, MA: Polity Press.
Dorian, N. (1982) Defining the speech community to include its working margins. In S. Romaine (ed.) *Sociolinguistic Variation in Speech Communities* (pp. 25–33). London: Edward Arnold.
Edwards, J. (1992) Sociopolitical aspects of language maintenance and loss: Towards a typology of minority language situations. In W. Fase, K. Jaspaert and S. Kroon (eds) *Maintenance and Loss of Minority Languages* (pp. 37–54). Amsterdam/Philadelphia: John Benjamins.
Edwards, J. (2010) *Minority Languages and Group Identity. Cases and Categories*. Amsterdam, Philadelphia: John Benjamins.
Ehala, M. (2010) Refining the notion of ethnolinguistic vitality. *Journal of Multilingualism* 7, 363–378.
Euromosaic, accessed 10 April 2012. http://www.uoc.edu/euromosaic/index.html.
Extra, G. and Gorter, D. (2008) The constellation of languages in Europe: An inclusive approach. In G. Extra and D. Gorter (eds) *Multilingual Europe: Facts and Policies* (pp. 3–62). Berlin: Mouton de Gruyter.
Ferguson, C.A. (1959) Diglossia. *Word* 15 (2), 325–340.
Ferguson, C.A. (1991) Diglossia revisited. *Southwest Journal of Linguistics* 10 (1), 214–234.
Fischer, E. (2011) *Language Communities of Twitter/Flickr – Photo Sharing!*, accessed 10 April 2012. http://www.flickr.com/photos/walkingsf/6277163176/in/photostream/
Fishman, J.A. (1991) *Reversing Language Shift. Theoretical and Empirical Foundations of Assistance to Threatened Languages*. Clevedon: Multilingual Matters.
Giles, H., Bourhis, R. and Taylor, D.M. (1977) Towards a theory language in ethnic group relations. In H. Giles (ed.) *Language, Ethnicity and Intergroup Relations* (pp. 307–348). London: Academic Press.
Graddol, D. (2006) *English next. Why global English may mean the end of 'English as a Foreign Language'*. British Council. Online document: http://www.britishcouncil.org/learning-research-englishnext.htm
Grenoble, L.A. and Whaley, L.J. (1998) Toward a typology of language endangerment. In L.A. Grenoble and L.J. Whaley (eds) *Endangered Languages. Current Issues and Future Prospects* (pp. 22–54). Cambridge: Cambridge University Press.
Gumperz, J.J. (1962) Types of linguistic communities. *Anthropological Linguistics* 4 (1), 28–40. Reprinted in Fishman. J. (ed.) (1968) *Readings in the Sociology of Language* (pp. 460–472). The Hague: Mouton.
Harwood, J., Giles, H. and Bourhis, R.Y. (1994) The genesis of the Vitality Theory: Historical patterns and discoursal methods. *International Journal of the Sociology of Languages* 108, 167–206.
Haugen, E. (1971) The ecology of language. *Linguistics Reporter Supplement* 25, winter: 19–26. Reprinted in: Haugen, E. (1972) *The Ecology of Language. Essays by Einar Haugen*. Selected and introduced by Anwar S. Dil. Standford, CA: Stanford University Press, 325–339.
Hymes, D. (1974) *Foundations in Sociolinguistics: An Ethnographic Approach*. Philadelphia: University of Pennsylvania Press.
Kachru, B.B. (2001) Speech community. In R. Mesthrie (ed.) *Concise Encyclopedia of Sociolinguistics* (pp. 105–107). Amsterdam, New York, Oxford, Shannon, Singapore, Tokyo: Elsevier.
Kloss, H. (1966) Types of multilingual communities: A discussion of ten variables. *Sociological Inquiry* 36 (2), 135–145.

Labov, W. (1972) *Sociolinguistic Patterns*. Philadelphia: University of Pennsylvania Press.
Laitin, D.D. (2000) What is a language community? *American Journal of Political Science* 44, 142–155.
Le Page, R.B. and Tabouret-Keller, A. (1985) *Acts of Identity. Creole-based Approaches to Languages and Ethnicity*. Cambridge: Cambridge University Press.
Madera, M. (1996) Speech community. In H. Goebl, P. Nelde, Z. Starý and W. Wölk (eds) *Kontaktlinguistik – Contact Linguistics – Linguistique de contact. Ein Internationales Handbuch zeitgenöissischer Forschung/An International Handbook of Contemporary Research/Manuel International des Recherches Contemporaines* (Vol. 1) (pp. 169–175). Berlin: Mouton de Gryter.
Martí, F., Ortega, P., IIdiazabal, I., Barreña, A., Juaristi, P., Junyent, C., Uranga, B. and Amorrortu, E. (2005) *Words and Worlds: World Languages Review*. Clevedon: Multilingual Matters.
Milian-Massana, A. (ed.) (2012) *Language and Legal Challenges in Medium-Sized Language Communities*. Barcelona: Institut d'Estudis Autonòmics.
Mollà, T. (2002) *Manual de Sociolingüística*. Alzira: Bromera.
Moreno Fernández, F. (1998) *Principios de Sociolingüística y Sociología del Lenguaje*. Barcelona: Ariel.
Moseley, C. (ed.) (2010) *Atlas of the World's Languages in Danger*, 3rd edn. Paris: UNESCO Publishing. Online version: http://www.unesco.org/culture/languages-atlas/
Simpson, J.M.Y. (2001) Language. In R. Mesthrie (ed.) *Concise Encyclopedia of Sociolinguistics* (pp. 31–34). Amsterdam, New York, Oxford, Shannon, Singapore, Tokyo: Elsevier.
Spolsky, B. (2004) *Language Policy*. Cambridge: Cambridge University Press.
Swann, J., Deumert, A., Lillis, T. and Mesthrie, R. (2004) *A Dictionary of Sociolinguistics*. Edinburgh: Edinburgh University Press.
Trudgill, P. (2003) *A Glossary of Sociolinguistics*. New York, Oxford: Oxford University Press.

2 The Main Challenges Facing Czech as a Medium-Sized Language: The State of Affairs at the Beginning of the 21st Century

Jiří Nekvapil

Introduction

The title of this chapter, as is usually the case, is little more than an identifying abbreviation and raises a number of questions. The first of these is whether it is actually the Czech language that faces these challenges, or rather, its speakers. The next question is this: Who is aware of these challenges? Is it the intellectual elite (or merely the linguists) or is it also the everyday users of the language? Finally, in what sense of the word can Czech be considered a medium-sized language? What kind of classifying category is this (or, more precisely, *whose* category is it)? This chapter will address all these questions. However, let me start by presenting some 'raw data' concerning the Czech language and the country where it is predominantly used – the Czech Republic.

Raw Data

The Czech Republic came into existence as an independent state quite recently, in 1993. In that year, the former Czechoslovakia, with a population of approximately 15 million, ceased to exist, and the Czech Republic and Slovakia became the successor states. Four years before that, in 1989, the

Communist regime had collapsed and the then pro-Soviet society began its transformation into an open democratic society of the western type. This development formally culminated in 2004 with the entry of the Czech Republic into the European Union.[1]

The Czech Republic occupies an area of 78,866 km² in the centre of Europe, and is approximately the same size as Austria or Portugal. Its longest borders are those with German-speaking countries, Germany and Austria. It also borders Poland and Slovakia (Figure 2.1),[2] where the Slavic languages Polish and Slovak are spoken.

According to the census carried out in 2001, the population of the Czech Republic is 10,230,000, approximately the same as that of Belgium or Portugal. Of this number, about 95% are speakers of the Czech language, and approximately 5% use languages other than Czech. Czech is spoken predominantly in the Czech Republic, and the number of speakers of Czech abroad does not exceed two or three hundred thousand (living mostly in North America). Table 2.1, based on the results of the 2001 census, indicates the other languages used in the territory of the Czech Republic.

The data regarding the declared mother tongue do not indicate directly how (or whether) the speakers use the declared language in their daily lives. Nevertheless, the information provided is significant (even more so if other aggregate data regarding language use are not available).

Czech is used predominantly by ethnic Czechs, but also by people who declare their ethnicity to be Moravian or Silesian. Czech is also spoken by tens of thousands of Roma/Gypsies and Slovaks, and by thousands of Poles,

Figure 2.1 The Czech Republic and its main regions

Table 2.1 Number of inhabitants in the Czech Republic based on 'mother tongue' (2001)

Mother tongue	Population	%
Czech	9,707,397	94.9
Slovak	208,723	2.0
Polish	50,738	0.5
German	41,328	0.4
Romani	23,211	0.2
Russian	18,746	0.2
English	3791	<0.1
Other	99,258	1.0
Not declared	76,868	0.8
Total	10,230,060	100.0

Source: The Czech Statistical Office (http://www.czso.cz) and the Centre for Information in Education (www.uiv.cz).

Vietnamese and others. Although members of non-Czech ethnic groups are willing to acquire Czech and tend to do so quite quickly, a number of them also use their first language. Thus, a certain (albeit rather imprecise) idea of the linguistic diversity of the Czech Republic can be obtained from the results of the census concerning declared ethnicity (Table 2.2).

The table includes not only Czech citizens but also foreigners with permanent or long-term residence (i.e. more than 90 days) in the Czech Republic. It is in this category that the increase has been most dramatic, as recent data show (Table 2.3).[3]

A comparison of Tables 2.2 and 2.3 reveals an increase in the number of Ukrainians or Russians, Vietnamese, Moldovans and Mongolians, as well as other ethnic groups living in the Czech Republic. Note, however, that this is another case where ethnicity cannot be viewed as equivalent to the respective ethnic language. Accordingly, when looking at the tables, one has to exercise due caution. For example, on the one hand, citizens of Ukraine may not be ethnic Ukrainians, but on the other hand, even the ethnic Ukrainians coming from Ukraine do not always use the Ukrainian language – they are often speakers of Russian or are bilingual. In any case, the increase in the number of foreigners, and members of some ethnic groups in particular, enhances the linguistic diversity of the Czech Republic, raising the question of how these foreigners make themselves understood in the Czech Republic. Do they communicate using their own languages? Do they acquire Czech quickly? Do they rely on the Czechs' knowledge of an international language?

This brings us to Table 2.4, which lists the foreign languages (i.e. excluding Czech) taught in Czech schools.

Table 2.2 Number of inhabitants in the Czech Republic based on ethnicity (2001)

Ethnicity	Number	Percent	Change from 1991
Czech	9,249,777	90.4	↑
Moravian	380,474	3.7	↓
Slovak	193,190	1.9	↓
Polish	51,968	0.5	↓
German	39,106	0.4	↓
Ukrainian	22,112	0.2	↑
Vietnamese	17,462	0.2	↑
Hungarian	14,672	0.1	↓
Russian	12,369	0.1	↓
Roma	11,746	0.1	↓
Silesian	10,878	0.1	↑
Bulgarian	4363	<0.1	↑
Greek	3219	<0.1	↓
Serbian	1801	<0.1	?

Source: The Czech Statistical Office (http://www.czso.cz) and the Centre for Information in Education (www.uiv.cz).

The data indicate that there has been a marked increase in the number of students of English, accompanied by a decrease in the number of those studying German. Although this is a significant phenomenon, it should not be overestimated nor overgeneralized. First, it does not directly reveal the communicative competence acquired, and second – and most importantly – it has to be considered relative to different generations of people. Roughly speaking, the younger generation tends to learn English and the older one has mostly acquired German. In any case, the extent of knowledge of German in the Czech Republic is high compared with the rest of Europe. The situation regarding Russian is similar. The teaching of Russian is insignificant in comparison with English and German, but some knowledge of the language (passive at least) is widespread among older and middle generations because it was once a compulsory subject at school under the Communist regime. It has also recorded a slight increase in recent years.

Language Ideologies and Discourses

The current language ideologies and discourses in the Czech Republic are related not only to the 'raw data' presented above, but also to the history of

Table 2.3 Foreigners in the Czech Republic (30 April 2009)

Citizenship	Total	Permanent residence (%)
Total	443,870	39
Ukraine	133,548	31
Slovakia	78,024	33
Vietnam	60,986	58
Russia	27,988	44
Poland	21,942	50
Germany	16,567	27
Moldova	11,183	20
Mongolia	7120	21
Bulgaria	6076	50
United States	5968	45
China	5224	62
United Kingdom	4656	26
Serbia and Montenegro	4219	74
Belarus	4101	54
Romania	3762	58
Kazakhstan	3638	49
Austria	3413	35
Italy	2689	44
Netherlands	2643	23
France	2529	29
Bosnia and Herzegovina	2379	62
Croatia	2349	83
Macedonia	2168	41
Armenia	1920	65
Japan	1593	12
Other	27,185	44

the Czech nation and state. We do not have enough space here to present a detailed account of Czech history; however, we should mention at least one of the decisive factors determining today's ideologies, discourses and attitudes – the period of the Czech National Revival under the Austrian monarchy in the first half of the 19th century. It was during this period that the modern Czech nation was constituted in the struggle against the dominant German-speaking culture, and systematic efforts were made to restore and

Table 2.4 Number of students in primary and secondary schools learning foreign languages in the Czech Republic between 1995/1996 and 2008/2009 (numbers in thousands)

	School year					
Language	1995/96	2004/05	2005/06	2006/07	2007/08	2008/09
English	632.3	886.5	902.7	991.6	1020.6	1047.1
German	734.7	486.2	454.7	425.0	389.1	364.1
French	39.4	48.0	47.6	50.3	50.8	51.2
Russian	8.1	16.4	20.0	23.5	27.6	35.6
Spanish	6.8	13.8	16.1	18.6	21.2	23.7
Italian	1.9	1.6	1.4	1.6	1.4	1.3
Latin	15.6	13.5	12.6	12.8	13.8	13.7
Classical Greek	0.1	0.1	0.1	0.1	0.1	0.1
Other European languages	0.1	0.3	0.1	0.1	0.1	0.1
Other languages	0.5	0.3	0.4	0.4	0.3	0.3
Total no. of students*	Unavailable	1197.2	1162.5	1207.5	1192.7	1181.5

*Some students were learning more than one foreign language.

develop the cultural functions of the Czech language after centuries of neglect. The next landmark was the establishment of Czechoslovakia in 1918, when the Czech and Slovak nations obtained their 'own' state (although, from the ethnic point of view the state was a very heterogeneous one, having inherited inter-ethnic tensions that twice led to its disintegration, most recently in 1993). Not surprisingly, the National Revival was accompanied by an intensive purism aimed at countering the influence of the German culture and language. This purism retained a firm position in the first quarter of the 20th century and was only removed by the theory of standard language and linguistic culture formulated by the Prague Linguistic Circle in the 1930s, when Czechoslovakia (and Bohemia in particular) had already adopted the characteristics of a modern (western) European state. Nevertheless, although the purist ideology was theoretically replaced, some of its features can still be traced in the linguistic behaviour of today's speakers of Czech (for more detail, see Neustupný & Nekvapil, 2003).

The Czechs – the main speakers of Czech – have felt their language to be under threat several times throughout their history. This feeling was strongest during the Nazi occupation (1939–1945), when it was not only the Czech language and culture that were in danger, but also the very existence of the Czech people. Generally, the feeling of language threat grows in intensity in times of social upheaval and with the insecurity that follows.

The last instances of such upheavals were the fall of the Communist regime (1989) and the break-up of Czechoslovakia (1992). This period saw the beginning of a debate among Czech linguists, which we shall deal with briefly below.

In 1993, Čmejrková and Daneš published an article, or rather an essay, with the symptomatic title 'the language of a small nation' (Čmejrková & Daneš, 1993).[4] The analysis focuses particularly on the position of the language of a small nation – Czech – in the new social circumstances. The essay points out that, historically, Czech was not always a small language (cf. its restricted expansion during the late Middle Ages). Nevertheless, the general tone of the article may be characterized more by the claim that 'the language of a small nation pursues mainly the goals of self-preservation' (Daneš, 2009: 7). The authors deal with the practical reasoning and categories shared by the majority of the society (concerning the concept of the small nation or language in particular). Consequently, they underestimate the relational aspects of the concept of the small nation/language, namely the fact that from the synchronous point of view a particular entity may be small with respect to one entity, and yet large with respect to another. This argument pertains to the more recent, more assertive reflections on the position of Czech (cf. Nekvapil, 2007b).

During the mid-1990s, three articles were published on the feeling of language threat. Characteristically, this debate was stimulated by an impulse from Slovenia. An article by Stich, 'Is there a feeling of language threat in the Czech Republic?' (Stich, 1995) was first published in Slovenian and in Slovenia (Stich, 1994). It was written at the request of Slovenian specialists and, as Stich himself states in the introduction, 'it therefore entered the stormy and dramatic discussions on the threat to the Slovenian language' (Stich, 1995: 61). In contrast to Čmejrková and Daneš (1993), Stich concludes by saying that 'today's Czech society is, and considers itself to be, linguistically stabilised, unthreatened and confidently self-assured' (p. 69). In his view, 'in the Czech Republic there is hardly any feeling of Czech being considerably affected or threatened by linguistic Anglo-Americanisation' (p. 69). Although, according to the author, these claims are generally true, there is 'a certain disconcertment' that can be traced in Czech society concerning the state of Czech itself (p. 70). In other words, there is a feeling of internal threat to, or devaluation of, the Czech language (p. 72).

The dichotomy of internal and external threat to the Czech language is further developed by Kraus (1996), who refers back to Čmejrková and Daneš (1993), making them, retrospectively, a part of the ongoing debate. Drawing on empirical research, Kraus shows that the feeling of a decrease in the quality of Czech not only exists, but is also prevalent in Czech society. He agrees with Stich that 'today there is no substantial reason for the feeling of the threat to the very existence of the Czech language' (p. 1). Nevertheless, he warns against unfavourable tendencies in its development that could result from not deflecting the problems arising from the following factors: (1) immigration into the Czech Republic; (2) new contacts among people and languages; (3) teaching foreign languages and teaching Czech as a foreign (as well as native) language; and (4) using Czech in multinational institutions.

The dialogue initiated by Stich was also taken up by Šaur (1996) in the very title of his article: 'The feeling of the threat to the Czech language does exist!' Šaur supports his claim by pointing out that the programmes of several political parties and social organizations indeed include the defence of the mother tongue. He also notes that the intensity of the feeling of language threat in the Czech Republic varies not only in relation to the social stratum but also according to the region.

More than 10 years later, the debate was revived by Nejedlý (2008). In his view, the existence of Czech is not in danger, for the speakers of the language presently enjoy a reasonable degree of political, economic and cultural power. In addition, the current development of the Czech language in contact with other languages does not differ substantially from situations in the past, with which it coped successfully. In this context, he points out the aptitude of Czech as an inflectional language to absorb elements of foreign languages (especially English) in an organic way, in other words, to adapt them to its own system. What he considers a certain threat to Czech is the fact that the speakers of the language are losing their ability to use some traditional grammatical forms (e.g. to distinguish between the perfective and imperfective aspect), and that they use some foreign language elements without the inflectional adaptation.[5] Generally, he regards the 'non-cultivated use' of the language system, that is, what Stich called the devaluation of Czech, as the 'real threat to the Czech language' (p. 233). Nejedlý explicitly declares his agreement with Stich's and Kraus's conclusions, and rejects those drawn by Šaur, clearly underestimating the regional and temporal contextualization of the feeling of language threat.

So far, we have traced the discourse of the 'threat to the Czech language' as developed by prominent Czech linguists in prominent Czech academic journals. Although the discourse was initiated in Slovenia and contained a great deal of expert knowledge, it will have reflected, at least to a certain extent, the feelings and practical reasoning of the common speakers of Czech, in other words, their language ideologies.[6] We shall continue along these lines, focusing on a language ideology that can be formulated in brief as 'Czech is a small language used only by Czechs' (we have already encountered a certain manifestation of the ideology in Čmejrková & Daneš,

1993). The ideology, shared by a large number of ethnic Czechs, has a considerable bearing on their linguistic behaviour and on their approach to communication with westerners.[7] The first consequence of this ideology is that Czechs readily accept that they have to adapt linguistically in communication with westerners – they do not expect the foreigners (tourists and expatriates, in particular) to be able to communicate in Czech. Consequently, Czechs find it difficult to communicate with foreigners who are trying to use the Czech language. Indeed, Czechs can barely use 'foreigner talk' (i.e. 'speaking one's mother tongue with a foreigner'). More precisely, this variety of Czech has not been developed so far. They do not feel that they should communicate in Czech with foreigners, offering them (or even forcing upon them) their English or German, however poor it may be. In the last instance, this means that Czechs indirectly discourage foreigners from learning their language, something that is occasionally noted by the foreigners themselves. This situation may be caused by several factors, one of them being the fact that speaking Czech is a constitutive feature of Czech identity, a social fact of relevance ever since the period of the Czech National Revival. Czech appears to be a highly valued (and often perhaps the only) possession of the people, which explains their close ties with their language.

Let us turn now to the category of a 'medium-sized language', as mentioned in the title of the present chapter. As suggested above, as far as the size or power of languages is concerned (for more detail see Nekvapil, 2007b), the emic categories are 'a large language' and 'a small language'. The term 'a medium-sized language', used to refer to a language of one to 20–25 million speakers(Bastardas & Vila, personal communication), is not an emic category (at least not with respect to the Czech cultural environment). Nevertheless, it offers an interesting comparative perspective.

Czechs and the Czech Language in the International Context

Towards the end of the 20th century, especially after the fall of the Communist regime in 1989, the contact between Czechs and the members of other ethnic groups and between the Czech language and other languages grew at an unprecedented rate. In spite of this, Czech has remained the dominant language in almost all communicative domains, ranging from official to everyday communication. English has had a considerable influence (see above), but it has failed to penetrate extensively into the communicative domains and genres where Czech is used owing to the fact that knowledge of English is relatively limited among the Czech population in comparison with Scandinavian countries, for example. To a certain extent, this may also be due to the fact that the differences between English and Slavic languages are greater than between English and, for instance, Swedish; that is, the languages of the same language group (viz. Germanic languages). Another relevant factor is that the spread of English in the Czech Republic is still hindered by competition from German, which is taught widely in Czech schools. To a lesser extent, English also has to compete with French and Russian (Table 2.4).

The general communicative dominance of Czech is somewhat weakened in multinational companies, in some genres of academic communication and in university education (see below). However, this certainly does not mean that Czech is absent in these domains.

Multinational Companies

Let us first consider the multinational companies that have established their branches in the Czech Republic, such as Siemens. These branches use 'corporate' languages – typically English – even in companies with headquarters in Germany. The corporate language is used in particular for reporting, at branch meetings attended by expatriates or in communication with headquarters or with customers, which means that it is used by top management (some of whom may be Czech) and to a certain extent by the lower management (usually completely Czech). Our research has revealed that in a branch producing car components, approximately 500 of a total of 2000 employees are expected to have some knowledge of the corporate language (this being the ideal state, although not fully in correspondence with reality). It is also significant that even the Czech members of top management can sometimes spend an entire day without using a language other than Czech (for more details, see Nekvapil & Sherman, 2009a, 2009b; Nekvapil & Nekula, 2006; Nekula *et al.*, 2009).

The University Sphere

Whereas the language situation in multinational companies operating in the Czech Republic has been the subject of systematic research, communication in the university and academic sphere has not received much attention.[8] Czech clearly prevails, but the university sphere is to some extent linguistically diverse and rather chaotic due to the liberal conditions present there since the social change in 1989. Foreign languages are brought into the university domain by numerous foreign students, visiting academics, foreign examiners of dissertations and by academic literature that is not available in Czech (although a large number of translations are published, particularly in the humanities). Thus, at Czech universities one finds lectures given in Czech as well as in foreign languages. It is by no means unusual that foreign languages are used during the defence of dissertations. Professors giving lectures in Czech may use slides in English or German. Students read not only Czech academic books but also foreign ones, and they write their bachelor's and master's theses not only in Czech but, for example, also in English. There may be differences between different types of universities or faculties (technical universities, medical faculties, faculties of arts and humanities, of natural sciences, and so on); however, as mentioned above, systematic research is needed in order to draw firmer conclusions.

Academic and Scientific Communication

Because there is a lack of systematic research in the area of academic and scientific communication, I carried out a small examination (drawing predominantly on internet resources) of the languages currently used in journals in mathematics (and natural sciences) published in the Czech Republic. There are four prominent top-ranking mathematical journals, two of which have English titles (*Applications of Mathematics*, *Czechoslovak Mathematical Journal*) and two Latin ones (*Mathematica Bohemica*, *Commentationes Mathematicae Universitatis Carolinae*).[9] According to the instructions to authors, identical for the three journals published by the Institute of Mathematics, 'the English language is preferred, but German and French are also accepted'. It may be of interest to find out to what extent this option is actually used; nevertheless, the key point is that Czech is not included among the languages. Why is this, and what are the consequences? Generally, the first part of the question can be answered by saying that having reached a high international standard, the field would like to retain it in order to remain in contact with the international mathematical community, which is why it prefers academic communication in international languages. It seems crucial from the point of view of the development of the Czech language to establish whether the mathematical language for special purposes (LSP) is constituted only in these journals. This does not appear to be the case. In the Czech Republic there are several other journals, operating at various levels of expertise, that are published only in Czech (or also Slovak). They can be arranged as follows, with the first ranking highest from the scientific point of view and the last lowest:

- *Pokroky matematiky, fyziky a astronomie* (*Advances in Mathematics, Physics and Astronomy*). This publishes (in Czech and in Slovak) both original and translated reviews and articles dealing with the history, current development and teaching of mathematics, physics and astronomy.
- *Matematika – fyzika – informatika* (*Mathematics – Physics – Informatics*), a journal aimed at teaching in primary and secondary schools.
- *Učitel matematiky* (*The Teacher of Mathematics*), a journal for primary and secondary school teachers.
- *Rozhledy matematicko fyzikální* (*The Mathematical and Physical Review*), a journal for talented students at primary and secondary schools.

Thus, although mathematics journals are published predominantly in English, there nevertheless exist a number of journals that can contribute to the constitution of the Czech language of mathematics. This language has reached such a level of development that the teaching of mathematics at primary and secondary schools (as well as the majority of universities) is carried out in Czech without any difficulty, as is demonstrated by the numerous Czech textbooks being written for all types of schools.

In the context of primary and secondary schools, the situation in mathematics can also be extrapolated into other fields. However, not all top scientific journals published in the Czech Republic share the same language policy as the top mathematical journals listed above. For instance, *Chemické listy* (*Chemical Review*), published since 1876 (with an impact factor since 1997), publishes articles in Czech and Slovak, and only invited papers are in English. Further research may reveal other strategies.

It would also be worth examining whether the transfer of certain mathematical expressions from the theoretical language of science to the professional language and the language used in schools manifests itself also in common everyday language. The example of mathematics could thus serve as an instantiation of Nejedlý's (2008: 225) general claim that 'the current trend toward unilingual global communication (English) in highly specialised branches (science, military affairs, astronautics, cybernetics) is compensated for by the rich metaphorical feature of technical terms used in a non-terminological way by the whole population'.

Czech as a Second Language and Lingua Franca

The last 15 or 20 years have seen an unprecedented increase in the teaching of Czech as a foreign language. The reason for this is that the Czech Republic has become an attractive location for tens of thousands of foreigners, from within the EU and beyond (Table 2.3). The teaching of Czech as a foreign language has thus become a pedagogical challenge faced by hundreds of Czech teachers, especially in Prague and the region of Karlovy Vary, the places with the highest concentration of foreign pupils (mainly from Vietnam, Ukraine, Slovakia and Russia). According to the Centre for Information in Education, in the school year 2008/2009 there were 13,583 foreign pupils attending Czech primary schools, 3691 of whom were from EU countries (including 2729 from Slovakia), 4945 from other European countries and 4947 from elsewhere. Every year the number of foreign pupils increases slightly and, in some schools, particularly in Prague, the concentration of foreigners is quite conspicuous. The integration of the children of foreigners is therefore an issue that is frequently discussed in the Czech public sphere. In my opinion the trend should be assessed realistically; in the school year 2008/2009 there were 802,432 pupils of Czech nationality at Czech primary schools, meaning that foreign pupils account for only 1.6%. Nonetheless, it appears to have been a step in the right direction that, after a long period of preparation, the teaching specialization 'Czech as a foreign language' was finally opened at one Czech university.

Considering the fact that there are at least half a million foreigners in the Czech Republic, a more fundamental question is to what extent adult foreigners in the Czech Republic communicate using the Czech language and how they acquire the language. Do they learn it spontaneously at work, or do they acquire it on the street? Do they learn Czech in language courses, either before they arrive in the Czech Republic or after their arrival? And in the Czech Republic, can all groups of foreigners afford these courses, and are enough courses offered? There are no aggregate data available to answer these questions, because Czech as a foreign language is taught predominantly at private language schools (recently, courses have also been organized by some non-governmental organizations). Since 2009, foreigners applying for a permanent residence permit have had to pass an examination in the Czech language at least at level A1 of the Common European Framework of Reference for Languages. According to the information available, the number of Czech courses they can attend is still not sufficient, even in urban centres.

The language behaviour of foreign communities has not been researched systematically. Based on informal observation of the members of these communities, it seems that western foreigners such as Americans or Germans are able to communicate in Czech only exceptionally (probably because they can use their mother tongues, English or German). On the other hand, foreigners whose mother tongue is a Slavic language (e.g. Ukrainian) rely on the relative closeness of their mother tongue and Czech and try to communicate with

Czechs by modifying their mother tongue to approximate Czech and to make themselves understood better (the passive knowledge of Russian among the middle and older generations of Czech seems to play a positive role here).

Moreover, there has been an unprecedented increase in the use of Czech as a means of communication among foreigners from different ethnic groups, in other words, as a lingua franca. There is no information available concerning this function of the language.

Czech as a Foreign Language Abroad

The spread of the Czech language abroad is promoted to a certain extent by the Czech state. On the basis of international agreements, teaching positions have been established in 25 countries of the world (at several universities in some countries, totalling 52 official lecturer positions).[10] As pointed out by Hasil (2005), this support, although often relying on a relatively long tradition, has proved quite insufficient today. There is no specialized institution concerned with the propagation of the Czech language, such as the Goethe Institute for German or Polonicum for Polish (a more suitable inspiration for Czech), and the teaching positions mentioned above have been established in only 14 EU countries. Unlike the Czech Republic, Poland, Slovenia and Croatia all finance lecturers and even professors of the respective languages at prestigious foreign universities. This rather lax approach to the propagation of Czech corresponds to a certain unwillingness on the part of the Czech representatives in the EU to use the Czech language, as they are themselves at a loss to see how Czech could be propagated (Hasil, 2004: 60; Dovalil, 2007). This, in turn, corresponds with the fact that many Czechs who grew up under the influence of the ideology 'Czech is a small language used only by Czechs' (see above) find it difficult to imagine that foreigners might speak the Czech language.

Drawing on an analysis of the current state of the teaching of Czech abroad, I proposed some time ago that the propagation of the Czech language in the Member States of the EU should focus on the following parameters and goals:

- In the cross-border areas of neighbouring countries, the Czech language should be at least offered as a subject at primary schools and there should be follow-up Czech courses at secondary schools.
- In neighbouring countries, leaving aside the cross-border areas, one should aim at establishing at least one bilingual/foreign-language (Czech)

secondary grammar school in the capital or another centre of the neighbouring country.
- In other EU states, Czech should be taught adequately within the framework of Slavic or even independent Czech studies at university level (for more details, see Nekvapil, 2003).

It may be worth considering to what extent and under what circumstances a system of language propagation of this kind might be applicable to other official languages of the EU.

The Relationship Between Standard and Common Czech

A number of problems that I have mentioned above are considered marginal by Czech linguists (and partly also by Czech society). Even the above-mentioned debate on language threat did not evoke much response, which attests to the fact that the feeling of a threat to the Czech language is not significant, or from a different point of view, reflects the linguistic confidence of Czech speakers.

The problem discussed most by Czech linguists is the standard form of the language. The starting point is that a process of 'destandardization of standard Czech' is under way in Czech society, manifested in a fall in the use of standard Czech in some spheres of communication or in the penetration of features of the (so far) non-standard (especially colloquial) Czech language into standard Czech, which increases its variability.[11] Language destandardization can of course also be found in other European languages, but in the Czech Republic some specific historical factors come into play. It is significant that the standardization of Czech carried out at the beginning of the Czech National Revival (in the first half of the 19th century) separated standard Czech from the supra-local colloquial standard, known as common Czech. Common Czech differs from standard Czech, especially in the system of inflectional endings (cf. the standard Czech instrumental case *s dívkami* [with girls] versus the common Czech form *s dívkama*). The controversial issues are which features of common Czech in particular (e.g. the above plural feminine form of the instrumental case) should be incorporated into standard Czech and at what speed, or whether an 'intermediate standard' between standard and common Czech should be formed and acknowledged.[12]

What I would like to stress here is that this problem not only concerns ethnic Czechs and the Czech language but also has an inter-ethnic dimension, viz. which form of Czech will be taught as a foreign language, which form should be supported as a lingua franca and – as an empirical problem – which form of the Czech language indeed functions currently as a lingua franca. It may be suggested that a higher degree of variability of standard Czech could make this variety more widely accessible, even to foreigners, a number of whom fall into the lower strata of Czech society. Whether (or to what extent) this hypothesis is valid, however, can only be decided by thorough research.

The Relationship Between Czech and Slovak

The division of Czechoslovakia in 1993 placed the relationship between Czech and Slovak in an international context. As is well known, Czechs and Slovaks each used their own language in mutual communication and understood each other quite well. This could also be described as receptive bilingualism or, following Haugen (1966), as semicommunication, the term often used in the Czech and Slovak specialized literature. This model of communication, which also made it possible for Czechs to communicate with the Hungarian minority in Slovakia, which numbered half a million, became one of the leading principles of the Czechoslovak language policy adopted during the last two decades of the existence of the state. Receptive bilingualism still exists in communication between Czechs and Slovaks – we have seen above that it is assumed, for instance, by some scientific journals published in the Czech Republic. Moreover, it has been embodied in more recent Czech laws, which state explicitly that in certain areas of official communication Slovak can be used on a par with the Czech language (see, for example, the Administrative Code issued in 2004). The mutual intelligibility of Czech and Slovak is not based solely on their structural and lexical proximity. It also involves the speakers' attitudes and a certain degree of communicative practice, in other words, factors that can be influenced – positively or negatively – by the language policy in various strata of society. In this respect, the younger generation, whose receptive competence is sometimes doubted, should receive particular attention.[13] Generally, the Czech language and culture are more well and more broadly received in Slovakia than the Slovak language and culture in the Czech Republic (many Slovaks have an active knowledge of Czech). In any case, it holds true for both states that receptive bilingualism not only enriches them culturally but also pays off economically. It is not much of an overstatement to say, for example, that owing to the understanding and prestige of the Czech language and culture in Slovakia, the Czech culture market does not have just 10 million consumers (i.e. the population of the Czech Republic) but rather 15 million (including the Slovak population). This, certainly, has a positive influence on the development of the Czech language itself.

Conclusions

In this chapter, I have dealt with the linguistic, communicative and sociocultural situation in the Czech Republic and pointed out several pertinent problems. Dealing with these problems is a demanding and stimulating task, which may change the current state of affairs or, in contrast, may prevent any radical change.

I consider meeting the following challenges (listed in a generalized form of slogans and formulated as recommendations) to be of the utmost importance:

(1) Increasing awareness of the fact that Czech does not necessarily have to be a small language (and consideration of the consequences of this).
(2) Increasing awareness of the fact that the Czech language is not used only by Czechs (and consideration of the consequences of this).
(3) Retention of receptive bilingualism between the Czechs and Slovaks.
(4) Coping with the relationship between standard and common Czech.
(5) Maintenance of the inflectional type of the Czech language.

Can these recommendations be arranged hierarchically with respect to their relevance? Linguists seem to consider the problem addressed in (5) to be of particular importance. This problem, however, appears to be a relatively marginal issue from the point of view of everyday users of the language, who may not have noticed it at all. My personal belief is that the future development of the Czech language is most closely tied to recommendations (2) and (3). My insistence on recommendation (3) may seem quite surprising at first glance; nevertheless, we should realize that receptive bilingualism between Czechs and Slovaks increases the demand for Czech cultural products, thus contributing significantly to the everyday reproduction of the Czech language.[14]

Whom these recommendations are primarily intended for is yet another question. There is no single answer to this question that is applicable to all the recommendations. Although (4) and (5) are quite inconceivable without the assistance of linguists, (2) and (3) are addressed in particular to societal institutions, including state institutions at the highest level. Recommendations (1) and (2) relate to language ideologies of the population in general, and are therefore the concern of *every* speaker of Czech, whether a linguistic specialist or a layman.

I have stressed throughout this chapter that some conclusions may not be entirely reliable because the particular problem, language area or genre is still under-researched. My final recommendation is therefore intended primarily for linguists:

(6) The systematic study of linguistic behaviour in all varieties of domains, situations or genres.

Acknowledgements

Thanks are due to Marián Sloboda and Tamah Sherman for their valuable comments on various aspects of the text.

Notes

(1) For the consequences of this process, see Nekvapil (2007a). The article also contains additional data that cannot be presented here for reasons of space.
(2) Figure 2.1 has been taken from Nekvapil *et al.* (2009); its author is M. Sloboda.
(3) Asylum seekers, foreigners with a visa up to 90 days, EU citizens without residence permits and foreigners in the country illegally are not included in Table 2.3.
(4) A Russian version of the article was published as Daneš – Čmejrková (1994). Daneš also included it as an introduction in a comprehensive collection of his works (Daneš 2009). Moreover, keeping in mind that Daneš was one of the most prominent members of the Prague School in the latter half of the 20th century, this rather obscurely written essay can be expected to play a significant role in the discussions on the position of the Czech language.
(5) Drawing on my own data I can provide examples of the non-inflected use of the word 'wellness' (the highlighting is mine): the headline *Lázeňské a* **wellness** **pobyty** *jako dárek* [Spa and wellness stays as a gift] (Metro 11.12.09, p. 02, commercial supplement) and, in the text of the same article, *Portál Spa.cz nabízí desítky lázeňských balíčků a* **wellness programů** *v českých, slovenských, maďarských, rakouských, polských a slovinských hotelech* [Port Spa.cz offers tens of spa packages and wellness programs in Czech, Slovak, Hungarian, Austrian, Polish and Slovene hotels]. The expression 'wellness' could be integrated into the traditional system of Czech by being used as a postmodifier ('pobyty wellness') or by adopting an inflected suffix ('wellnessové pobyty'). Lack of inflectional adaptation is typical of the language of advertising and of the media (and partly also of academic language), written as well as spoken. Further examples can be found in Daneš (2000).
(6) Language ideologies have various definitions. I shall mention at least a classical one defining them as 'sets of beliefs about language articulated by users as a rationalisation or justification of perceived language structure and use' (Silverstein, 1979, cited in Kroskrity, 2004: 497).
(7) It is to be noted that the following discussion deals not with foreigners in general, but only with 'western foreigners'. Regarding this category, see Sherman (2001).
(8) On the priorities of Czech sociolinguistics, see Kontra *et al.* (2009).
(9) The first three journals are published by the Institute of Mathematics of the Czech Academy of Science. They are considered to be the successors of journals formerly published under Czech titles: *Aplikace matematiky*, published since 1956 (succeeded by

the journal *Applications of Mathematics*), and *Časopis pro pěstování mathematiky a fysiky*, published since 1872 (succeeded both by *Czechoslovak Mathematical Journal* and by *Mathematica Bohemica*). The fourth journal has been published by the Faculty of Mathematics and Physics of Charles University, Prague, since 1960 (always in foreign languages, currently only in English).
(10) The situation in August 2008.
(11) For more details, see Nekvapil (2008).
(12) For example, see Nekvapil (2000), Neustupný and Nekvapil (2003) and, most recently, Wilson (2010).
(13) See a recent discussion of the relationship of Czechs and the Slovak language based on a large survey in Dickins (2009).
(14) It should also be pointed out that from the logical point of view (3) is partly included in (2).

References

Čmejrková, S. and Daneš, F. (1993) Jazyk malého národa [Language of a small nation]. *Slovo a slovesnost* 54, 19–30.

Daneš, F. (2000) People, nations, and languages in contact: the drifting of Czech in the present-day flood of English. *Journal of Asian Pacific Communication* 10, 228–238.

Daneš, F. (2009) *Kultura a struktura českého jazyka* [Cultivation and structure of the Czech Language]. Praha: Karolinum.

Daneš, F. and Čmejrková, S. (1994) Экология языка малого народа [Language ecology in a small nation]. In Язык – Культура – Этнос. Москва: Наука, pp. 27–39.

Dickins, T. (2009) Češi a slovenština [The Czechs and the Slovak language]. *Naše společnost* 7 (1), 12–26.

Dovalil, V. (2007) Sprachenpolitik in der Tschechischen Republik (unter besonderer Berücksichtigung der Beziehungen zur EU und zum Europarat). In D. Blanke and J. Scharnhorst (eds) *Sprachenpolitik und Sprachkultur* (pp. 139–161). Frankfurt am Main: Peter Lang.

Hasil, J. (2004) Čeština v proměnách 20. století [Czech in the 20th century changes]. In *Přednášky z XLVII. běhu Letní školy slovanských studií* (pp. 53–62). Praha: Univerzita Karlova v Praze, Filozofická fakulta.

Hasil, J. (2005) Český jazyk po vstupu Česka do Evropské unie [Czech language after the accession of the Czech Republic to the European Union]. In *Přednášky z XLVIII. běhu Letní školy slovanských studií* (pp. 25–33). Praha: Univerzita Karlova v Praze, Filozofická fakulta.

Haugen, E. (1966) Semicommunication: The language gap in Scandinavia. *Sociological Inquiry* 36, 280–297.

Kontra, M., Nekvapil, J. and Kiełkiewicz-Janowiak, A. (2009) Sociolinguistics in Hungary, the Czech Republic and Poland. In M.J. Ball (ed.) *The Routledge Handbook of Sociolinguistics Around the World* (pp. 359–371). London and New York: Routledge

Kraus, J. (1996) Několik poznámek k pocitu jazykového ohrožení [Some remarks on the feeling of language threat]. *Naše řeč* 79, 1–9.

Kroskrity, P.V. (2004) Language ideologies. In A. Duranti (ed.) *A Companion to Linguistic Anthropology* (pp. 498–517). Malden, Oxford, Carlton: Blackwell Publishing.

Nejedlý, P. (2008) Je čeština jako menší jazyk v ohrožení? (Pohled očima historika jazyka) [Is Czech as a minor language endangered? (From the viewpoint of a language historian)]. *Naše řeč* 91, 225–234.
Nekula, M., Marx, Ch. and Šichová, K. (2009) Sprachsituation in Unternehmen mit ausländischer Beteiligung in der tschechischen Republik. *Sociolinguistica* 23, 53–85.
Nekvapil, J. (2000) Language management in a changing society: Sociolinguistic remarks from the Czech Republic. In B. Panzer (ed.) *Die sprachliche Situation in der Slavia zehn Jahre nach der Wende* (pp.165–177). Frankfurt am Main: Peter Lang.
Nekvapil, J. (2003) On the role of the languages of adjacent states and the languages of ethnic minorities in multilingual Europe: The case of the Czech Republic. In J. Besters-Dilger, R. de Cillia, H-J. Krumm and R. Rindler Schjerve (eds) *Mehrsprachigkeit in der erweiterten europäischen Union/Multilingualism in the Enlarged European Union/ Multilinguisme dans l'Union Européenne élargie* (pp. 76–94). Klagenfurt: Drava Verlag.
Nekvapil, J. (2007a) On the language situation in the Czech Republic: What has (not) happened after the accession of the country to the EU. *Sociolinguistica* 21, 36–54.
Nekvapil, J. (2007b) On the relationship between small and large Slavic languages. *International Journal of the Sociology of Language* 183, 141–160.
Nekvapil, J. (2008) Language cultivation in developed contexts. In B. Spolsky and F. Hult (eds) *The Handbook of Educational Linguistics* (pp. 251–265). Oxford: Blackwell.
Nekvapil, J. and Nekula, M. (2006) On language management in multinational companies in the Czech Republic. *Current Issues in Language Planning* 7, 307–327.
Nekvapil, J. and Sherman, T. (2009a) Czech, German and English: Finding their place in multinational companies in the Czech Republic. In P. Stevenson and J. Carl (eds) *Language, Discourse and Identity in Central Europe* (pp. 122–146). Basingstoke: Palgrave MacMillan.
Nekvapil, J. and Sherman, T. (2009b) Pre-interaction management in multinational companies in Central Europe. *Current Issues in Language Planning* 10, 181–198.
Nekvapil, J., Sloboda, M. and Wagner, P. (2009) *Mnohojazyčnost v České republice. Základní informace. Multilingualism in the Czech Republic. Basic Information.* Praha: Nakladatelství Lidové noviny.
Neustupný, J.V. and Nekvapil, J. (2003) Language management in the Czech Republic. *Current Issues in Language Planning* 4, 181–366. Reprinted in R.B. Baldauf and R.B. Kaplan (eds) (2006) *Language Planning and Policy in Europe, Vol. 2.: The Czech Republic, The European Union and Northen Ireland* (pp. 16–201). Clevedon: Multilingual Matters.
Šaur, V. (1996) Pocit ohrožení českého jazyka existuje! [The feeling of the threat to the Czech language does exist!]. *Naše řeč* 79, 10–14.
Sherman, T. (2001) The experience of Czech–English bilingualism for Czech–American families. In O. Šrajerová (ed.) *Otázky národní identity – determinanty a subjektivní vnímání v podmínkách současné multietnické společnosti* (pp. 268–274). Opava, Praha: Slezský ústav SZM, Dokumentační a informační středisko Rady Evropy při EIS UK.
Stich, A. (1994) Preživetje jezikovne dominacije: Primer češčine [Surviving linguistic dominance: The case of the Czech language]. *Javnost* 1 (3), 11–20.
Stich, A. (1995) Existuje u nás pocit ohrožení jazyka? [Is there a feeling of language threat in the Czech Republic?]. *Naše řeč* 78, 61–73.
Wilson, J. (2010) *Moravians in Prague. A Sociolinguistic Study of Dialect Contact in the Czech Republic*. Frankfurt am Main: Peter Lang.

3 Challenges Facing Danish as a Medium-Sized Language

J. Normann Jørgensen

The Status of Danish

Danish is a language spoken by somewhere between 5–6 million people, the vast majority of whom are citizens of the nation state of Denmark and native speakers of the language. Danish is taught as a foreign language in grade schools in Iceland, the Faroe Islands and Greenland. In addition, it is taught at university level in a range of European nations and a few other places such as China, Japan, North America and Australia. There are no indigenous minorities anywhere who speak Danish as their mother tongue, as the Danish minority in northern Germany mostly speak German as their first language (Pedersen, 2000). Danish is closely related to Norwegian and Swedish, and it takes little adjustment for speakers of these languages to understand each other.

Danish is the language used for all public functions in Denmark, including the entire range of educations, politics, public administration and the armed forces. It is a language with an army, a navy, a parliament, an educational system from cradle to the grave via high school and university to adult education, a business life, an extensive library system and many other facilities.

Danish is furthermore one of the world's most thoroughly described languages, with a number of authoritative scholarly grammars (Diderichsen, 1946; Hansen, 1967; Mikkelsen, 1911), a 28-volume dictionary published between 1918 and 1956, with a five-volume supplementary dictionary and a six-volume dictionary covering the language since 1950. Modern Danish is blessed with two pronunciation dictionaries. One is prescriptive, and therefore of less scholarly interest, but the other, larger one is a descriptive account of all non-classical dialects' pronunciations, including national standards and a range of regional standards. The sociolinguistics of Danish is also described in Kristiansen and Jørgensen (1998, 2003).

In the educational system, Danish is a central and high-profile subject at all levels from kindergarten through high school. The number of hours Danish is taught may vary, but in school curricula and syllabi it uniformly takes a prominent position. Danish is the medium of instruction in the vast majority of educational institutions. The exceptions are the International Baccalaureate, a few experimental schools and some parts of university education. All of these exceptions use English as a medium of instruction, sometimes alongside Danish. A very small number of schools use other languages as a medium for teaching, including Japanese, Turkish or Arabic, but the numbers of students are negligible.

In business life in Denmark, the use of Danish is predominant, although in a few major companies English is (at least on paper) the company language. There are functions in the private sector one can perform without speaking Danish if one knows English, primarily in the IT sector, but the vast majority of jobs require Danish or one of the other Scandinavian languages. In everyday life and in the media Danish is ubiquitous. In the capital, Copenhagen, which is connected to southern Sweden by a bridge, several thousand Swedes are employed, most of whom speak an adjusted form of Swedish in their jobs, and all understand Danish.

The local media broadcast in Danish, although many television productions on the national channels are bought from English-language producers. All non-Danish productions broadcast on the major local television stations, including the public-service mastodont Radio Denmark TV, are subtitled in Danish. Even Swedish and Norwegian productions are subtitled in Danish. Most homes have access to the national television channels as well as channels covering a wide range of languages from abroad.

In schools, Danish is not universally used, but the vast majority of teaching is carried out in Danish. Even the teaching of English occurs predominantly through Danish. The teaching of English is obligatory from the age of 9 (grade 3), and at the age of 13 (grade 7) the students choose between German and French. In some high schools students may select Russian, Spanish and a few other languages. University students and business school students may take their degrees in many different languages, including, as a matter of course, English, German, Spanish, Russian and French.

Against this background it is evident that the linguistic or sociolinguistic challenges faced by the speakers of Danish are not as threatening as the problems confronting the speakers of many other languages. In addition to its secure place in the administration, politics, education and public life in Denmark, the Danish language is – at least for the time being – further supported by EU language policies, according to which Danish can be used for all purposes, and according to which rules and regulations do not take effect until they are also available in a Danish version.

The safeguards set up to manage and protect the Danish language are not particularly strong. A language commission, *Dansk Sprognævn* (www.dsn.dk), is charged with the registration of new developments in the Danish language, but not with prescribing them. The only prescriptive function of the Sprognævn is the task of issuing the orthographic dictionary, *Retskrivningsordbogen*, which by law sets the orthographic norms for all texts issued by public authorities and institutions, including schools. Otherwise, the Sprognævn has no regulating powers.

Nonetheless, the Sprognævn has sometimes been the object of controversy. In 1985 its presentation of a proposal for a (very modest) change in the spelling of a few dozen words led to a heated media debate that raged for months, with two cabinet ministers taking opposing sides. This so-called 'Mayonnaise war' (named after one of the controversial words for which a new spelling was proposed) is regularly cited by the Sprognævn as a reason for taking all possible precautions when suggesting changes. The thought of a real reform is not even mentioned. As a consequence, the low level of regulation of Danish that is carried out is conservative.

Over the past decade or so there has been an increasing tendency for politicians (and some linguists) to want to introduce political measures to 'protect' the Danish language. This has led to a relatively new phenomenon in Denmark: an explicit language policy.

Language Policy and Language Ideologies

Denmark has had a right-wing government between 2001 and 2011, a fact that has had an effect on official language policy. The Ministry of Culture has issued two language reports (Kulturministeriet, 2003, 2008), both of which deal with the relationship between Danish and other languages, English in particular. The first report was issued at a time when there was no formulated official language policy. It raised a range of issues that could be regarded as relevant for a language policy and proposed some principles for a Danish language policy. The report was the work of a commission composed of scholars, including the president of the Dansk Sprognævn, and bureaucrats. This combination of members had a curious effect on some of the recommendations offered by the report, as we shall see. The second report proposed concrete language political measures based on a concept introduced as *parallelsproglighed* – language parallelism.

The main point of both reports was the relationship between Danish and English. The idea that English is a 'threat' to Danish runs through the texts. The understanding is that certain areas of public life are conducted – or may be on their way to being conducted – more in English, at the cost of Danish. Certain businesses, a number of areas of higher education, and sciences are regarded as being taken over by English. The phenomenon is labelled 'domain loss' by those who believe that this development is dangerous. The 2008 report proposes the concept of 'parallel languages' as a reaction to the perceived threat. The idea is that all public functions and documents must be available in Danish as well as in English. Education, scientific reports, business documents and so on should, according to this policy, be carried out in both Danish and English. The policy can be viewed as an attempt at compromising between those who see a spread of English throughout society and dislike it, and those who enthusiastically argue for the increased use of English as a means of globalizing and internationalizing Danish businesses.

Cultural variation, particularly linguistic deviation from the norm, is usually not very well received in Denmark, as many observers have noticed (e.g. Thomas, 1990: 7). The background is historical. From the mid-1600s through to the mid-1800s, the state of Denmark suffered a range of military defeats that cut the geographical size of Denmark proper (not including the North Atlantic parts) down to its present size, while a self-image developed that sees the country as a small, homogeneous, but peaceful country in which 'few have too much and fewer too little' (Grundtvig, 1820: 148). Also, the defeats in 1659, 1721, 1805, 1864 and even in 1940 led to an understanding of Denmark as a small country surrounded by dangers and threats, including cultural ones. This is the thinking behind the fear of English as a 'threat' to the Danish language.

While the country was diminishing in size a process of homogenization was also going on with respect to language variation within the population. A near-complete defeat by the Swedes in 1659 led to a coup in which the king, supported by the Copenhagen bourgeoisie, deprived the traditional landed nobility of its powers. This nobility was local, to a certain extent also linguistically, in that it spoke the local dialects of its home areas. It was replaced by a new elite educated at the university in Copenhagen who did not belong to the locality, but referred to the king in Copenhagen. The Copenhagen dialect became the prestige variety, a national standard developed in the 1700s on the basis of Copenhagen Danish, which has been the standard since then and has gradually spread to all corners of Denmark. In the second half of the 1900s this development accelerated, and the classical dialects all but disappeared (Pedersen, 2003).

The ideological representation of Danishness, a self-image reproduced in many types of discourse in Denmark, has developed against this background into one of peaceful, relaxed, homogeneous equality. The emphasis on equality and homogeneity is strong. The Times *Handbook of European Peoples* found this deeply characteristic of the Danes in 1997. Although the handbook finds that 'high living standards, classlessness, sexual equality and excellent state provisions for education, health and welfare' are important qualities in Denmark, there is also a flip side:

> ... there is a distinct levelling tendency in Danish society which has been satirised as the 'Jante Law' (*Jantelov*), after a fictional village in a novel by Axel Sandemose. In Jante people don't like to draw attention to themselves and don't like it when others rock the boat or get too ambitious: Danes tend to conform. (Fernández-Armesto, 1997: 33)

One consequence of this conformity is the particularly xenophobic reaction to post-World War II immigration. Although the high living standards contributed to giving Denmark the international image as relaxed, open, egalitarian and hospitable, as observed by the handbook, things were already changing by the end of the 20th century.

> The Danes have a not altogether deserved reputation for tolerance: immigration from the Third World has sparked some racial tensions and the right wing anti-tax Progress party adopted a 'send them back' policy in the early 1980s, with some electoral success. Support for the Progress Party has declined in the 1990s, but the problem of integrating a diverse immigrant population remains. (Fernández-Armesto, 1997: 33)

Since 2000, the political heir to the Progress Party, an openly xenophobic, anti-Moslem party, has regained all the votes lost by the Progress Party, and has even increased its share. This party has supported the right-wing government since 2001, with the result that the minority policies of Denmark have become increasingly tougher, and Denmark has become a European leader in preventing immigration and refusing asylum to refugees. Among the policies are the abolition of mother tongue teaching of minority languages in the public school system, and stiffer sanctions against immigrants who do not learn Danish.

Minorities are expected to learn Danish, and it must be a form of Danish that is indistinguishable from the native standard language. Danish with a foreign accent is routinely debased as 'bad' Danish. This is true of the Turkish-accented Danish used by working-class immigrants, but it is also true of the Danish used by the royal family. Prince Henrik, the husband of Queen Margrethe II, has a command of Danish that by most foreign language assessment standards would be considered good, but he has an easily detectable French accent, and after more than 40 years he has never really been accepted by the population. His pronunciation is usually given as the argument for this, and he is routinely ridiculed in the yellow press and elsewhere for his accent. The same is beginning to happen to his daughter-in-law, who was born and raised with English as her mother tongue.

It is not only Danish with a foreign accent but also local speech that carries very low prestige. Kristiansen (1990: 13) who was born and raised in Norway, explicitly wonders why Danes do not understand or appreciate local dialects. He notes that classical dialect speech is subtitled like foreign movies on Danish television. As a consequence of the de-dialectalization of Denmark in the second half of the 20th century, the younger generations have no experience with classical dialects, and they need translations. With his Norwegian background, Kristiansen (1990) finds this surprising. He also observes that in public discussion the disappearance of classical dialects is often regretted by politicians and decision makers, but nothing is done to prevent this development. On the contrary, given the way curricula are built up and the educational system oriented through teaching guidelines issued by the ministry of education, all efforts are contributing to the eradication of variation and to making the Danish language uniform.

In addition to the tendency to avoid and regulate against variation, there is a long-running discourse in Denmark that Danish is a particularly difficult language to learn because of its unique linguistic qualities. One book aimed at language teachers is titled 'Why is it so hard to learn Danish?' (Skovholm, 1996). Another example is provided by Grønnum (2003), who argues that the pronunciation of Danish is more difficult than the pronunciation of (at least certain) other languages.

These two works present Danish as a particularly difficult (you may sometimes think advanced and sophisticated – but not say so) language with difficult pronunciation and difficult words. This is presented as the reason why substandard speakers and foreigners fail to learn and use the language 'properly'. The linguistic minorities (with the exception of sign language users) are considered either unable or unwilling to learn Danish properly. Less gifted immigrants or refugees are believed to be prevented by 'their culture' from learning a language fit for a technologically advanced, democratic society. Unwilling minority members are suspected of wishing to change Danish society in unwanted directions – in more extreme cases to abolish Christianity and let Islam take over. Points of view of this kind often emerge in discussions about identity and nationality (see section 'Language in Politics').

Immigrants are often thought to learn Danish so poorly that their speech is 'incomprehensible' and their words must be translated into proper Danish. This is sometimes done by television subtitles.

There is an alternative explanation. Kristiansen (1990) has carefully read all teaching guidelines and other documents that govern the teaching of pronunciation in the Danish grade school. He documents that the teaching, more than anything, uniforms the students' pronunciation according to a conservative Copenhagen norm. He also shows that students learn that deviation from this norm is unworthy and unacceptable to the school. The school system has unequivocally chosen one norm as the only acceptable way of pronouncing Danish, and no deviation from this norm is permitted. Poor language skills are considered the responsibility of the individual student. Understandably, non-standard speakers may lose confidence and think of themselves as inadequate.

A series of verbal guise tests (Kristiansen, 1991, 1999; Kristiansen *et al.*, 2002) found that people who speak Danish with even a slight local influence are evaluated negatively along all parameters. Traditionally, guise tests find that high-prestige varieties are associated with intelligence, power, high education and efficiency (status dimensions), while low prestige varieties are associated with dependability, friendliness and trustworthiness (sociability dimensions). However, in Denmark, low-prestige speakers are evaluated more negatively than high-prestige speakers in all dimensions, including sociability dimensions. Similar findings are presented in H.J. Ladegaard (1992) and U. Ladegaard (2002), who also report that Danish with a foreign accent is systematically given low ratings. Kirilova (2004) performed a more refined study that found that it matters *what* foreign accent a speaker uses. Kirilova found that the majority of Danes are very positive when they evaluate speakers with a German accent (or more precisely, speakers who appear to the Danes to have a German accent), and more generally accents relating to Germanic languages. When native Danish speakers believe that they hear somebody with an accent from non-Germanic European languages, they are somewhat more negative. When the speakers are taken to be Middle Eastern or African, the evaluations are the most negative.

This means that there is very strong pressure on those citizens who do not speak the Copenhagen standard. The more local the Danish a Dane speaks, the greater the pressure to adapt to the Copenhagen standard. Even stronger pressure is applied on minority language speakers. Second language users with very little accent may find themselves subtitled on television. This, together with the fact that Danes are not trained in hearing and understanding Danish spoken in different ways, increases the distance between standard speakers and other speakers.

The educational system is not geared to expand the linguistic experience of majority standard Danish speakers. Variations in spoken Danish are all but absent from the grade school. There is a large market for teaching materials for the school subject of Danish at all levels of the educational system – literally hundreds of different textbooks – but there is only one textbook (Pedersen & Adriansen, 1993) that aims to familiarize students with Danish spoken in different ways, including regional variations. Interestingly, it is mandatory in English classes that students hear several different varieties of English. In other words, the students are led to understand that English is a rich and varied language, while Danish may be spoken in one, and only one, way.

Public discussions about variation are reflected in political life. Over the past decades politicians have routinely demanded tightened orthography and punctuation in order to eliminate variation. The 'Mayonnaise war' of 1985 is an extreme example of this. Several cabinet ministers, and their ministries and every corner of the media world were involved in a discussion about the spelling of a couple of dozens of words, because the editors of the orthographic dictionary had suggested changes and – worst of all – that a few words could have two correct forms. The indignation among politicians and newspaper editors was so strong that the editors gave up proposing double spellings in almost every case (Hansen, 1985).

The lack of tolerance of variation is widespread, both among the elite, including politicians, and among the population in general, and it has been carefully supported and developed through the educational system. Apart from the negative attitudes to regional Danish it has also led to negative consequences with respect to intercultural understanding and ethnic integration. The low degree of tolerance is not only a phenomenon of certain limited parts of the population; it has also been explicitly expressed by leading politicians (see the examples above) and is carefully built up through the public school and educational system as such (Kristiansen, 1990, 2001).

In addition to the negative attitude towards non-standard Danish, there is very little tolerance of Danish spoken with a non-native accent. Such accents are simply not accepted in society at large. This holds for everybody, ranging from the Turkish-born unskilled worker to the royal family.

Language in Politics

The understanding that Danish should not be spoken with a non-native accent is widely held by politicians all across the political spectrum. The negative attitude to the identities reflected in accented Danish is not restricted to right-wing politicians. Leading Social Democratic politicians can make statements like the following: 'If one is born and raised in Denmark and intends to stay here, then one's mother tongue is Danish.' (Lene Jensen, deputy party chairperson, in a press release in September 2000, my translation). Another even more precise statement is 'We have neither time nor place for Danish as a second language in our part of the world' (Svend-Erik Hermansen, Social Democrat, education commission chairman, press release 14 September 2000, my translation). On this issue the major political parties agree, and there is a massive rejection of the thought of allowing languages such as Arabic, Turkish, Punjabi, Hindi, Cantonese, Mandarin and Tagalog any place in the educational system through mother tongue education of the children from these minorities. These children meet with a strong rejection of important parts of their resources, particularly if their Danish is not exactly as that of their native peers.

The mother tongues of Denmark's linguistic minorities are the object of a great deal of negative politics. The negative attitudes to English expressed by some opinion makers are nothing compared to the pressure on minority languages. Until 2001, Danish local communities were obliged to offer minority language mother tongue teaching in accordance with EU Council Directive 77/486, which was extended to also cover non-indigenous minorities. One of the first acts of the present government after taking over the ministries was to abolish the mother tongue teaching of minority children in the public school system. Reflecting the statements cited above, this decision was celebrated by a broad range of politicians.

Even linguists who know better have been affected by the widespread tendency to regard the minority languages as useless. The 2003 Ministry of Culture report quotes the scientific and educational arguments for teaching minority children their mother tongues. These arguments are juxtaposed with political arguments against allowing the minorities access to their mother tongues in the school system (arguments along the same lines as the one just mentioned). The surprise here is that the experts let the political arguments outweigh the scientific arguments in a text that claims to be based on scholarly research. The report describes its conclusions with respect to this issue in bland words:

> The commission has not, with the time allotted and its combination of expertise, considered itself able to propose on a sufficiently qualified basis any recommendations regarding the problem and therefore suggests that the issue be closely observed. (Kulturministeriet, 2003: 59, my translation)

Among the linguists who wrote this, at least two had earlier argued for mother tongue teaching of minority languages in grade schools. One was the chairman of the language commission and had, a few months earlier, published a language policy document with a range of specific recommendations:

> It is important that immigrant languages such as Turkish, Arabic, Farsi, and Urdu be taught in Denmark. Knowledge of these languages is an important resource, and at a time when strong powers influence us in the direction of less linguistic and cultural variation, it is crucial to be attentive to the value of linguistic pluralism and to try to maintain this pluralism (Dansk Sprognævn, 2003: 5, my translation)

This is an unequivocal recommendation from the language commission – there is no hesitation with respect to lack of time or ability. However, between the Sprognævn publication and the commission publication some months later, the professional expertise of the chairman of the Sprognævn had evaporated.

One of the other linguists in the commission has published a description of some of the commission's work, and he tries to give an explanation of why the linguists in the commission suddenly forgot everything they knew about bilingualism.

> About this, Education Minister Ulla Tørnæs states (without having seen the report): 'It has not been unequivocally proven that mother tongue teaching leads to better integration. I believe that it is the task of the public school to teach people Danish.'

> Ulla Tørnæs has said so many times, and this is probably the reason why there is nothing in 'Sprog på spil' [the 2003 report] about teaching of minority languages in the Danish school. (Togeby, 2003: 15, my translation).

The explanation given here is as follows. The linguists knew that scientific evidence clearly favours mother tongue teaching of minority children. The bureaucrats who represented the Ministry of Education on this Ministry of Culture commission pursued the political agenda of the Minister of Education, who did not even bother to read the report before making statements about it, and the bureaucrats succeeded in making the linguists foreswear their professional knowledge.

What obviously happened is that the linguists who were appointed to be members of the commission were well aware of the unanimity in their profession regarding the benefits of mother tongue teaching, and to the extent that they had any professional opinion, they shared the general view. At least two of them have publicly expressed this. In the course of the commission's work, however, they agreed to change their view to 'not having the resources' to form an opinion. If Togeby's description is correct, the linguists were cajoled by bureaucrats (see also Jørgensen, 2005). This is an illustrative example of the way professionalism and scholarly work become marginalized if their conclusions go against the neo-national romantic ideologies shared by a wide range of politicians and bureaucrats. Kristjánsdóttir (2006) is a detailed documentation of how this has happened systematically in and through the Ministry of Education between the 1970s and 2001. Big, expensive projects aimed to develop education for linguistic minorities have seen their conclusions scrapped or shelved when they did not fit the reigning ideology. For many years EU Council Directive 77/486 was a source of irritation and aggression, but because previous governments were dependent on parties who supported the directive, they could not abolish minority language mother tongue teaching. This lasted until the right-wing government took over in 2001 with the support of an extremist party.

The atmosphere and public debate about minorities sharpened considerably during the first decade of the 2000s. The extreme right-wing, xenophobic party gained an increasing number of votes in elections, and regulations openly introduced to discourage immigration and to encourage asylum seekers to leave were commonplace. The abolition of minority language mother tongue teaching is an important aspect of a continuous development away from the open and egalitarian society described by the Times handbook.

Another consequence of the low tolerance of variation in Danish society has been the rapid disappearance of the classical dialects, which accelerated during the second half of the 1900s. This is a development that Denmark shares with at least the rest of Europe as it urbanizes, but it has happened faster and more completely in Denmark, as argued and documented by Pedersen (2003). Kristiansen (1996) analyses how two societies that have gone through practically the same structural developments (urbanization, industrialization, mobility, and so on), namely Norway and Denmark, have developed in exactly opposite directions with respect to language variation. Kristiansen ascribes this to the different ideologies – Danish society being characterized by an ideology of equality bordering on sameness, in which variation is being substituted by uniformization. And so it is – practically everybody speaks a version of Copenhagen Danish, some with a distinctly different intonation pattern, but by and large the same vocabulary, morphology, syntax and so on. In Norway the sense of localness is stronger, and the general understanding of the duty of the public is that variation should be maintained. Media are obliged to broadcast in different varieties of Norwegian, and students are obliged to read and understand all kinds of Norwegian. The causes of uniformization in Denmark, argues Kristiansen, are not structural, but ideological.

A combined effect of the government-issued 'parallel language' policy and intolerance of variation in present-day Denmark is the decreasing knowledge of language among the population. The intended defence of Danish against English through a 'parallel language' policy only works to isolate Danish speakers from all those other people who do not speak English. The number of high school students taking more language classes than the absolutely mandatory ones has dropped dramatically from 40% to less than 10% over a period of three years (Sproglæreren okt. 2009). The business school of Copenhagen plans to completely cut out education in languages other than Danish and English, because they have been abandoned by the students. We predict that the command of languages, which could ease communication between Danish citizens, politicians, businesses and people in Germany, France, Italy, Spain and Latin America, will decrease dramatically over the coming decades. The language policy that was intended to defend Danish against English will work directly against its purpose, because it isolates Danish speakers and English speakers. This can lead to an even more narrow-minded pattern of public discourse, because reporters have access only to English-medium international sources and politicians understand only what is said in Danish or English.

English

English has been held in awe in Denmark for at least a couple of decades: 'We must be bilingual in Denmark: English as a global language – Danish as a local one. Both children and old people must be taught English and taught through English.' This statement was quoted in a Ministry of Education publication in 1991, credited to Paul Hammerich, a journalist and author. The view is common – many people believe that it is crucial for Danes to know English. The Minister of Education at the time, Bertel Haarder, is quoted as saying 'The teaching of English must have a higher priority.'

The arguments behind this view are many, and they vary considerably. Sometimes it is argued that English is a 'big' language and a 'cultivated' language (Shakespeare and so on), and that English is 'the language of computers'. All of these congeal into one argument: English is 'the language of globalization'. This rather primitive understanding of globalization is evident in much of the public debate, and it is to a large extent reflected in the behaviours of students in the educational system. The educational system today offers traditional high school education entirely in English; for example, Danish-speaking teachers teach physics to Danish-speaking students, but in English. In addition there are high schools that offer an international baccalaureate in English and attract students from outside Denmark.

In the dominant circles in Denmark the fact that English is an important language is undisputed. Its importance indicates several things. First, it means that it is considered useful for society and for the nation, and that many individuals should have a good command English. Second, it means that it is considered useful for the individual person to know English. Society as such and individuals in other words share an interest in increasing the knowledge of English. As we have seen, quite a few individuals consider English to be so important that they discard Danish as their educational language.

The status of English in Denmark, particularly in the educational system, is the object of intense discussion, both in society at large and among linguists (e.g. Andersen, 2002; Davidsen-Nielsen *et al.*, 1999; Holmen & Jørgensen, 2001, 2010; Jørgensen, 1991; Kulturministeriet, 2008; Preisler, 1999). It is usually taken for granted that Danes and Danish society as such is more positive towards English influence, and that young Danes tend to import English material more liberally than young people in the rest of the Nordic countries. An extensive pan-Nordic research project has studied different perspectives of imported linguistic material in Iceland, the Faroe Islands, Norway, Finnish-speaking Finland, Swedish-speaking Finland, Sweden and Denmark. One important aspect concerns attitudes. A sample of Nordic citizens (6000 people) were asked directly about their attitude to English influence, and to the use of English instead of their national language in certain situations (Kristiansen & Vikør, 2006). The overall result is no surprise. The most negative attitudes were found in Iceland and the Faroe Islands. The Norwegians and both groups of Finns were in the middle with no significant differences between them. The Swedes came next, and the most positive overt attitudes were expressed by the Danes. However, when people are asked more surreptitiously about their attitudes, as happens with matched guise tests or semi-matched guise tests, the result is different (Kristiansen, 2006). The Danes have the most negative covert attitudes to the influence of English, while the Finnish-speaking Finns are slightly less negative, followed by the Swedes, and the Norwegians are the most positive (the project could not carry out a guise test in Iceland and the Faroe Islands, because people there are immediately aware that the test is to do with the use of English). This may indicate that the fear of English as a 'threat' to the Danish language is a purely political issue, and in a few cases an academic issue – but in any case, it is an elitist thing.

The high status of the English language in Denmark means that a certain measure of borrowing takes place. Danes are importing more words from English than ever before – and Danish has a history of heavy borrowing, from Low German, French, Latin and so on. Danes borrow words such as *shit* and *software*, but also fixed expressions and chunks such as *fuck you* and *see you*. Even an occasional orthographic principle, such as the spelling of composite nouns in two words instead of the official norm of one word, is increasingly seen. All these loans are being integrated into the Danish of everyday speech. This is also an issue in the debates. Some people, including linguists, see a danger in this – another threat to the Danish language (e.g. Davidsen-Nielsen & Herslund, 1999). These are not the same people as those who see a danger of 'domain losses'. Generally, linguists find that Danish is not threatened because of its importing of English items. Danish has survived this far in spite of long periods of mass importing, particularly from German. In fact, Danish has benefited from its ability to integrate loans and to adapt them to its needs. A good example is the Danish word *speeder*, which has all the orthographic signs of an English loanword (and indeed is a relatively old English loanword), but which is phonetically and morphologically Danish: *speederen, speedere, speederne* (singular definite, plural indefinite, plural definite). However, the word means something completely different from its meaning in English – in Danish it means *accelerator*. In other words, it was imported for a very practical purpose, to fill a gap in the Danish vocabulary where no obvious Danish equivalent offers itself as an alternative, and it was dealt with accordingly.

A point that is made in some parts of the debate is that English loans comprise only a small part of, for instance, everyday newspaper articles (Brink, 2001), and that there is no particular danger in that. Sometimes English loanwords serve an entirely different function, namely that of identity marking. By using newer English loanwords one can signal *smartness*, youth, sophistication or other positively valued aspects of identity. This irritates some people, including linguists who argue that using English for these purposes is in reality provincial and superficial. Against this view stands the observation that if English did not serve these purposes, something else would. Currently it is English, but this will probably change at some time.

The most frequently expressed fear for the Danish language is the idea of 'domain losses'. The increasing use of English in society, at the cost of Danish, is criticized. There are references to the airline industry, advertising, negotiations in the EU, and – as mentioned above – science. In the long run, Danish may, according to this view, become the lesser part of a diglossic relationship, reduced to private relations and the home. This development actually happened with the local classical dialects that eventually disappeared from society.

Madsen (2008) is the only empirical study of the use of English and Danish among natural scientists in Denmark. She finds that their self-reporting of their practices, as well as their attitudes, lend very little support to the accusations of Anglicization and deserting Danish. They all report that they write their technical and scientific reports in English. Writing them in Danish would be absurd, because there would be nobody to read them. Nevertheless, they also report that they write textbooks and popularizations in Danish, and express a strong preference for the use of Danish in professional situations. Preisler (2010) and Haberland (2010) both present strong conceptual and theoretical arguments against the weakly supported concept of 'domain loss' (see also both authors' contributions to Holmen & Jørgensen, 2010). This does not alter the fact that English is seen as a very important factor in Denmark, and to some people as a threat. This gives English a special status in Danish society.

In public discussions on issues in education, language planning and politics at different levels in Denmark we observe considerable differences in attitudes to other languages among native speakers in the country. This is reflected in the results of Kirilova's study (2004), and in many other ways. The major opinion makers seem to share a view of languages that can be compared to a hierarchy, with English on top, followed by French, German and perhaps Spanish. The Scandinavian languages follow soon after that, and at the bottom we find languages such as Turkish, Urdu, Arabic, Berber, Punjabi, Tagalog and Swahili. This hierarchy is the hidden foundation of much argumentation in public debates, in official documents, in educational practices and elsewhere; although rarely expressed openly, it is often evident. In 1992 the Ministry of Education issued a report on the quality of language teaching in the educational system, focusing on language awareness and knowledge. In this report, a 'language view' was defined that emphasized the importance of language to humanity, stating that 'linguistic insight increases the students' understanding of mankind as a linguistic creature with a need to express itself, means of expression, and with the language as an important personal basis for experience, thinking, and other mental processes' (Undervisningsministeriet, 1992: 19, my translation). This statement emphasizes the nature of language as a human phenomenon. Without openly shifting the perspective of language as a human phenomenon, the report gradually begins to make statements like: [first a child hears the language of its immediate surroundings] 'later the child meets and perceives language from surroundings a little further away. The child hears the shared language – regional Danish and standard Danish – through the media and in the contact with people outside the home and the institution... New perspectives are added when the child is ready to perceive and take an interest in languages other than the mother tongue. Through the media the child will, at a young age, meet English, German and the neighboring languages [i.e. Swedish and Norwegian], just as most of the children will have opportunities to hear more distant languages, e.g. immigrant languages' (Undervisningsministeriet, 1992: 19–20, my translation). In this view, it is an integrated part of life as a human being to grow up with a variety of Danish, then to meet English and German, later the other Scandinavian languages, and finally the (exotic) immigrant languages such as Turkish, Urdu, Arabic and Mandarin. The fact that around 10% of school beginners in the country have immigrant languages as their primary means of communication does not make any impression here.

Another report (Bacher *et al.*, 1992) on the foreign language knowledge of Danes documents that English, German and French dominate the Danes' idea of foreign languages. No other language is spoken sufficiently to register significantly in the statistical data of the report.

Lip service is routinely paid to bilingualism as an asset when the languages involved are Danish and English, and this is no new phenomenon (e.g. Karker, 1993: 73). When immigrant minority languages are concerned, however, the more radical purists even refuse to recognize bilingualism. A few linguists even reject the idea of bilingualism as an asset altogether:

> I do not believe that children when starting school can develop a set of associations for two significantly different languages at a time when their vocabulary grows rapidly, and when they are about to make the great leap connected to understanding the mysteries of literacy. (Lund, 1993: 95–96)

The 'significantly different' languages referred to are English and Danish. These two languages are, by almost all accounts, very similar. One could think this was meant ironically, but it is not. At that time the author was a professor of Danish, and he remains an influential opinion maker in educational circles. He also happens to be a member of the commission that wrote the 2008 Ministry of Culture report, and he was the main author of the 1992 Ministry of Education report. In conclusion: English is very important, for some maybe too important. The English language, even in bilingual coexistence with Danish, is considered a threat to Danish children. There is very little mention of a possible threat posed by Danish language to minority languages (an exception is Kristjánsdóttir, 2010), and very little mention of bilingualism involving these languages; they are only cited as exotic phenomena occasionally encountered by increasingly aware Danish-speaking children. This hierarchy of languages is of course no secret to the linguistic minorities, including the immigrant groups.

Uniformity and Isolation – The Two Challenges Facing Danish as a Medium-Sized Language

The hierarchization of languages has the two negative effects I have described here. First, it leads to a decrease in the combined knowledge of language in the population of Denmark. Second, it leads to an increased isolation of Danes from non-English speakers.

The first effect is documented by the tendency among young people that I mentioned above to deselect education in other languages. It further combines with the increasing uniformization of the Danish language (the disappearance of the classical dialects) to decrease the comprehension potential of young Danish speakers. Increasingly, young Danes are unable to understand forms of Danish other than their own, and they understand Norwegian and Swedish even less (Delsing & Åkesson, 2005). This means that Danish is on its way out of the Scandinavian community – and Danes are therefore becoming linguistically isolated from other Scandinavians.

In contrast to the rest of the EU, the language policy of the Danish government leads to a *limitation* of the linguistic resources available to Denmark's citizens. Not only does the policy encourage young people to give up studying French, German, Russian, Spanish and so on, but the government (supported by the Social Democrats, so all the big parties agree on this issue) also strongly urges the minorities to give up their mother tongues and embrace Danish. Interestingly, although speakers of Arabic and Pashto are pressed to give up their languages, relatively old majority Danes are taught the very same languages so they can become soldiers or spies.

The inner development of Danish leads to isolation from the other Scandinavian languages. The government policy towards minority languages isolates minority Danes from other members of their diaspora, not to mention their relatives who, two or three generations back, chose to stay and not emigrate. The connection between citizens in Afghanistan and Denmark becomes much more difficult if the citizens of Denmark are prevented from maintaining their knowledge of language for communication with Afghans.

The explicit language policy of 'parallel languages' further leads to the isolation of Danish citizens from speakers of German, French and Spanish (and of course Russian, Italian, Dutch and so on). This affects cultural, political and economic life. No Danes will have direct access to, say, Russian culture. Danish journalists and reporters will not be able to study and evaluate Russian sources or Russian media. Danes and Denmark make themselves dependent on speakers of English.

Danish as a mid-sized language, and Denmark as a language community, are facing two serious challenges at the beginning of the 2000s. The uniformity of the development of Danish, together with very negative attitudes and direct intolerance of variation, reduces the people's comprehension skills. This, together with intolerant government policies, leads to the linguistic isolation of the people and the country.

References

Andersen, M.H. (2002) *Engelsk i dansk: Helt vildt sjovt eller wannabeagtigt og ejendomsmæglerkækt?* København: Dansk Sprognævn.
Bacher, P., Clemmensen, N., Mørch Jacobsen, K. and Wandall, J. (1992) *Danskerne og fremmedsprog. En undersøgelse om den voksne befolknings sprogfærdigheder.* København: Udviklingscenteret for folkeoplysning og voksenundervisning.
Boyd, S., Holmen, A. and Jørgensen, J.N. (eds) (1994) *Sprogbrug og sprogvalg blandt indvandrere i Norden. Bind I-II. Københavnerstudier i tosprogethed, bind 22-23.* København: Danmarks Lærerhøjskole.
Brink, L. (1991) Nordens folkesprog i fare? In J.N. Jørgensen (ed.) *Det danske sprogs status år 2001 - er dansk et truet sprog? Københavnerstudier i tosprogethed bind 14* (pp. 107-110). København: Danmarks Lærerhøjskole.
Bugge, K.E. and Jørgensen, J.N. (1995) *Tre år efter. En punktvis efterundersøgelse af Folkeskolens Udviklingsråds projekter vedrørende indvandrerelever. Københavnerstudier i tosprogethed, bind 26.* København: Danmark Lærerhøjskole.
Dansk Sprognævn (2003) Forslag til retningslinjer for en dansk sprogpolitik. http://www.dsn.dk/Sprogpolitik-DSN.htm.
Davidsen-Nielsen, N. and Herslund, M. (1999) Dansk han med sin tjener talte. In N. Davidsen-Nielsen, E. Hansen and P. Jarvad (eds) *Engelsk eller ikke engelsk? That is the question. Engelsk indflydelse på dansk* (pp. 11-18). København: Gyldendal.
Davidsen-Nielsen, N., Hansen, E. and Jarvad, P. (eds) (1999) *Engelsk eller ikke engelsk? That is the question. Engelsk indflydelse på dansk.* København: Gyldendal.
Delsing, L-O. and Lundin Åkesson, K. (2005) *Håller språket ihop Norden? En forskningsrapport om ungdomars förståelse av danska, svenska och norska.* København: Tema Nord.
Diderichsen, P. (1946) *Elementær dansk grammatik.* København: Nordisk Forlag.
Fernández-Armesto, F. (ed.) (1997) *The Peoples of Europe.* London: Times Books.
Grønnum, N. (2003) Why are the Danes so hard to understand? In H.G. Jacobsen, D. Bleses, T.O. Madsen and P. Thomsen (eds) *Take Danish - For Instance* (pp. 119-130). Odense: University Press of Southern Denmark.
Grundtvig, N.F.S. (1820) Danmarks trøst - langt højere bjerge. In *Sange til den 10de april 1820* (p. 148). DIH Kildebind.
Haberland, H. (2008) Domains and domain loss. In B. Preisler, A. Fabricius, H. Haberland, S. Kjærbeck and K. Risager (eds) *The Consequences of Mobility: Linguistic and Sociocultural Contact Zones* (pp. 227-237). Roskilde: Roskilde University.
Haberland, H. (2010) Noget om, hvem der ejer det danske sprog, og hvem der truer det - om domænebegrebets storhed og fald. In A. Holmen and J.N. Jørgensen (eds) *Sprogs status*

i Danmark 2021. Københavnerstudier i tosprogethed (Vol. 58, pp. 77–86). Københavns Universitet.

Hansen, A. (1967) *Moderne Dansk 1–3*. København: Det Danske Sprog- og Litteraturselskab.

Hansen, E. (1985) Tolv ord der rystede Danmark. *Nordisk Tidsskrift för vetenskap, konst og industri, 61. Årg* (pp. 420–425). Stockholm: Föreningen Norden.

Holmen, A. and Jørgensen, J.N. (1994) Forældreholdninger til skole og sprogbrug. In S. Boyd, A. Holmen and J.N. Jørgensen (eds) *Sprogbrug og sprogvalg blandt indvandrere i Norden. Bind I-II. Københavnerstudier i tosprogethed* (pp. 91–115). København: Danmarks Lærerhøjskole.

Holmen, A. and Jørgensen, J.N. (eds) (2001) *Sprogs status i Danmark år 2011. Københavnerstudier i tosprogethed bind 32*. København: Danmarks Pædagogiske Universitet.

Holmen, A. and Jørgensen, J.N. (2010) Skærpede holdninger til sproglig mangfoldighed i Danmark. In A. Holmen and J.N. Jørgensen (eds) *Sprogs status i Danmark 2021. Københavnerstudier i tosprogethed* (Vol. 58, pp. 121–135). Københavns Universitet.

Jørgensen, J.N. (ed.) (1991) *Det danske sprgos status år 2001 – er dansk et truet sprog? Københavnerstudier i tosprogethed bind 14*. København: Danmarks Lærerhøjskole.

Jørgensen, J.N. (2005) Hvorfor er det så svært for danskerne at forstå dansk? In A. Hauksdóttir, J. Lund and É. Skyum-Nielsen (eds) *Ordenes slotte. Om sprog og litteratur i Norden* (pp. 148–156). Reykjvík: Stofnun Vigdísa Finnbogadóttur í erlendum tungamálúm.

Karker, A. (1993) *Dansk i EF – en situationsrapport om sproget*. København: Nordisk Sprogsekretariat.

Kirilova, M. (2004) Danskernes holdninger til fremmed accent – et uerkendt lillebrorkompleks? In C.B. Dabelsteen and J.S. Arnfast (eds) *Taler de dansk? Aktuel forskning i dansk som andetsprog. Københavnerstudier i tosprogethed bind 37* (pp. 77–98). København: Københavns Universitet.

Kristiansen, T. (1990) *Udtalenormering i skolen. Skitse af en ideologisk bastion*. København: Gyldendal.

Kristiansen, T. (1991) *Sproglige normidealer på Næstvedegnen. Kvantitative sprogholdningsstudier*. København: Københavns Universitet.

Kristiansen, T. (1996) Det gode sprogsamfund: det norske eksempel. In *NyS, Nydanske studier and Almen Kommunikationsteori 21* (pp. 9–22). København: Dansklærerforeningen.

Kristiansen, T. (1999) Unge sprogholdninger i Næstved 89 og 98. In *Danske Fokemål bind 41* (pp. 139–162). København: C.A. Reitzel.

Kristiansen, T. (2001) Normering og holdninger. In A. Holmen and J.N. Jørgensen (eds) *Sprogs status i Danmark år 2011. Københavnerstudier i tosprogethed bind 32* (pp. 21–58). København: Danmarks Pædagogiske Universitet.

Kristiansen, T. (ed.) (2006) *Nordiske sprogholdninger. En masketest*. Oslo: Novus.

Kristiansen, T. and Jørgensen, J.N. (1998) Sociolinguistics in Denmark. *Sociolinguistica* 12, 230–250.

Kristiansen, T. and Jørgensen, J.N. (eds) (2003) The sociolinguistics of Danish. *International Journal of the Sociology of Language* 159.

Kristiansen, T. and Vikør, L. (ed.) (2006) *Nordiske språkhaldningar. Ei meiningsmåling*. Oslo: Novus.

Kristiansen, T., Bruun Clausen, T. and Havgaard, M. (2002) Sprogholdninger hos unge i Nakskov. In *Danske talesprog bind 3* (pp. 17–70). København: C.A. Reitzel.

Kristjánsdóttir, B. (2006) *Evas skjulte børn. Diskurser om tosprogede elever i det danske nationalcurriculum*. København: Danmarks Pædagogiske Universitet.

Kristjánsdóttir, B. (2010) Kan dansk være et dræbersprog? In A. Holmen and J.N. Jørgensen (eds) *Sprogs status i Danmark 2021. Københavnerstudier i tosprogethed* (Vol. 58, pp. 17–33). Københavns Universitet.

Kulturministeriet (2003) *Sprog på spil. Et udspil til en dansk sprogpolitik.* København: Kulturministeriet. http://www.kum.dk/graphics/kum/downloads/Publikationer/Sprog_paa_spil.pdf

Kulturministeriet (2008) *Sprog til tiden, rapport fra Sprogudvalget.* København: Kulturministeriet.

Ladegaard, H.J. (1992) Sprogholdninger i Danmark. En socialpsykologisk analyse af stereotype holdninger til sprog og sprogbrugere i fire danske lokaliteter. *Nordisk Psykologi* 44 (3), 173–189.

Ladegaard, U. (2002) *Sprog, holdning og etnisk identitet. En undersøgelse af holdninger over for sprogbrugere med udenlandsk accent.* Odense Universitetsforlag.

Lund, J. (1993) *Med sproget som indsats.* København: Gyldendal.

Lund, J. (1998) *Sidste udkald.* København: Gyldendal.

Madsen, M. (2008) *Der vil altid være brug for dansk.* København: Københavns Universitet, Humanistisk Fakultet.

Mikkelsen, K. (1911) *Dansk Ordföjningslære med sproghistoriske Tillæg. Haandbog for viderekomne og Lærere.* København: Hans Reitzels Forlag.

Pedersen, I.L. (2003) Traditional dialects of Danish and the de-dialectalization 1900–2000. *International Journal of the Sociology of Language* 159, 9–28.

Pedersen, K.M. (2000) *Dansk sprog i Sydslesvig 1-2.* Aabenraa: Institut for Grænseregionsforskning.

Pedersen, K.M. and Adriansen, I. (1993) *Vi bor i Sønderjylland. Sprog og kultur i lokalsamfundet – et materiale til dansk og tværfaglig undervisning. Tekstmappe & båndmappe.* Aabenraa: Institut for grænseregionsforskning.

Preisler, B. (1999) *Danskerne og det engelske sprog.* Frederiksberg: Roskilde Universitetsforlag.

Preisler, B. (2008) Deconstructing 'the domain of science' as a sociolinguistic entity in EFL societies: The relationship between English and Danish in higher education and research. In B. Preisler, A. Fabricius, H. Haberland, S. Kjærbeck and K. Risager (eds) *The Consequences of Mobility: Linguistic and Sociocultural Contact Zones* (p. 238). Roskilde: Roskilde University.

Preisler, B. (2010) Engelsk og dansk: funktioner og status – nu og i nærmeste fremtid. In A. Holmen and J.N. Jørgensen (eds) *Sprogs status i Danmark 2021. Københavnerstudier i tosprogethed* (Vol. 58, pp. 106–120). Københavns Universitet.

Skovholm, J. (ed.) (1996) *Hvorfor er det så svært at lære dansk?* København: Dansk Flygtningehjælp og Special-pædagogisk forlag.

Thomas, F.R. (ed.) (1990) *Americans in Denmark.* Carbonville: Southern Illinois University Press.

Togeby, O. (2003) Sprogpolitik. *Mål & Mæle* 26 (3), 10–16.

Undervisningsministeriet (1992) *Sproglig viden og bevidsthed, KUP-rapport.* København: Undervisningsministeriet.

Undervisningsministeriets nyhedsbrev (1991) 5. årgang, nummer 13, 12th August. København: Undervisningsministeriet.

4 Slovene, Between Purism and Plurilingualism

Maja Bitenc

Introduction[1]

As the westernmost South Slavic language, the Slovene language is spoken today by around 2.4 million people. The majority live in Slovenia, a country at the crossroads of the Romance, Germanic, Ugro-Finnic and Slavic worlds. In addition, there are Slovene autochthonous minorities in neighbouring Italy, Austria and Hungary, as well as Slovenes living in other European countries and overseas.[2] In the last two decades, Slovenia has faced two historic steps that seem to have marked its sociolinguistic situation: the achievement of independence in 1991, when Slovene became the official language of the Republic of Slovenia, and integration into the European Union (EU) in 2004, which made Slovene one of the official languages of the EU.

Looking back to the past,[3] the history and language status of Slovene in the Slovene territory have been shaped by strong connections with other languages, especially the languages of the multilingual political entities in which the Slovene-speaking community has existed (German in the Austro-Hungarian Monarchy and Serbo-Croatian in the Yugoslav states), as well as neighbouring languages. With the inception of the Slovene national movement in the 19th century the language became 'an eminently political question, the most powerful symbol, the strongest unifying force' (Stabej, 2007a: 14) in the Slovene community, which wished to establish itself as an autonomous political entity. It was intellectuals – often linguists and writers – who, through their vision, led the Slovene people through its eventful past, and independence was finally achieved in 1991. Although the status of Slovene is, at least formally, more secure now than ever before, the ideologies of 'guardianship' (cf. Stabej, 2007b) and purism, connected with a feeling of smallness, are still present and often determine the processes of language planning and political decisions. However, default opinions about the language situation, the feeling that the language is endangered and the emphasis on the need for Slovene language preservation and cultivation seem to be insufficient for effective language policy, especially with regard to the complex linguistic, social and political situation in today's Europe, as well as the vertiginous technological developments.

Immediately after Slovenia achieved independence from the former Yugoslavia, the Slovene language was introduced into all domains where Serbo-Croatian had previously served as the main language. In Slovenia, the languages of the former Yugoslavia lost prestige and speakers of these languages increasingly began to use Slovene. Accordingly, and also because of the greater number of foreigners coming to Slovenia for economic and political reasons (including war refugees), the number of those who wished or needed to learn Slovene as a second/foreign language increased[4] (cf. Stabej, 2007a). Following EU membership, Slovenia became an attractive destination for various groups of immigrants, and a knowledge of Slovene gained additional value because of its new status. Slovene has become increasingly present in the international setting, both in the institutional and non-institutional framework. Globalization and the free flow of people and labour are also reflected in the sociocultural and communication spheres. On the one hand, Slovenia is becoming more diverse, and there are more and more learners/ speakers of Slovene as a second/foreign language. On the other hand, Slovenes learn other foreign languages more, and plurilingualism is on the increase in Slovenia. It seems that as well as an earlier, more widespread and functional mastery of English as a lingua franca, a more varied competence in other foreign languages is also increasing (cf. Stabej, 2006).

One of the main challenges facing the Slovene language community seems to be the question of how to retain the vitality of the Slovene language so that it remains the dominant language in the Republic of Slovenia, without violating (and in fact promoting) democratic principles and the basic human rights of those whose mother tongue is not Slovene but who reside in the Slovene territory. As far as native speakers of Slovene are concerned, it appears that they sometimes need more self-confidence in using different varieties of Slovene in different situations. Furthermore, their needs for relevant reference books about their mother tongue should be met, and learning English and other foreign languages should be made more efficient and more widely accessible.

This chapter presents an overview of the current sociolinguistic situation, pointing out the challenges in some more or less specific fields that seem to be most relevant to the Slovene situation and that are often discussed in relevant (Slovene) publications.

The Sociolinguistic Situation in Slovenia

For the debate on the current sociolinguistic situation, the census data from 1991 and 2002, especially on the population of Slovenia by mother tongue and ethnic affiliation, can be taken as the basis.[5] In 1991, 88.3% of the population (equivalent to 1,690,388 people) declared Slovene to be their mother tongue, but in 2002 the figure was 87.8% (1,723,434 people).[6] Although the proportion of native speakers of Slovene decreased by 0.6%, their number actually increased by 33,046,[7] which can be explained in a wider context. There was a significant drop in the proportion of inhabitants whose mother tongue was Serbo-Croatian[8] (from 4.2% to 1.8%), the proportion of Croatian and Serbian native speakers was slightly higher in 2002 than in the 1991 census (2.8% compared to 2.6%, and 1.6% compared to 0.9%, respectively), and Bosnian appeared as a new census language in 2002 and was chosen by 1.6% of speakers.

If the ethnic affiliation data are taken into account, it is evident that, although according to the 1991 census the number of those with Slovene as their mother tongue almost matched the number of those who declared themselves Slovene by ethnic affiliation, in 2002 nearly 100,000 more individuals declared Slovene to be their mother tongue than declared their ethnic affiliation to be Slovene. Interpretative caution notwithstanding, this suggests that 'the Slovenian language has been denationalised to some degree' in the last two decades, and the data present 'an image that speaks of the vitality of the Slovenian language, and indirectly also of its prestigious status in the Republic of Slovenia' (Stabej, 2006: 686–687).

In Slovenia as an independent country, a new type of temporary emigration due to work opportunities in diplomacy and in the European Union institutions among others has increased to a moderate degree, as well as immigration, and statistical data also show indirectly that the country has become more linguistically diverse than it was before 1991[9] (Stabej, 2006: 687–688).

The languages that most markedly colour the linguistic map of the territory of the Republic of Slovenia are the Slavic languages of the former Yugoslavia (in the 2002 national census, the total percentage of those whose mother tongue was one of these languages was 8%[10]), Hungarian (0.4% of the population declared Hungarian to be their mother tongue), Italian (0.2%), Romani (0.2%) and German (0.1%).[11]

As far as the language(s) of communication are concerned, 91.1% of the population in 2002 stated that they used Slovene only as the language of communication at home, 3.3% said Slovene and 'Serbo-Croatian', 1% 'Serbo-Croatian' only, 0.2% Hungarian, 0.2% Slovene and Italian, 0.2% Slovene and Hungarian, 0.1% Italian, 0.1% Romani, 0.1% Albanian, 0.7% Slovene and other languages, 2.9% other languages, combinations of other languages or unknown (Šircelj, 2003: 106).[12]

A considerable difference can be observed between the proportion of speakers of Croatian, 'Serbo-Croatian', Serbian, Bosnian or Macedonian as their first language (8%), who have no special status and legal protection in Slovenia, and the proportion of the members of both official national minorities with Hungarian or Italian as their mother tongue (0.6%). Furthermore, as might be expected in view of the status of languages, the proportion of those who use the Slavic languages of former Yugoslavia (also in combination with Slovene) at home is much lower than the proportion of those who declared these languages to be their mother tongues (4.3% compared to 8%), whereas with the speakers of Italian or Hungarian, the proportions almost match (0.7% compared to 0.6%).

When speaking about Slovene, one should be aware of the high internal diversity of the language.[13] What is especially noticeable is the high degree of dialectal (geographical) variability, at least when compared to other Slavic languages. This is clear from the phonetic and lexical maps of the Slavic linguistic atlas. The Slovene language features seven dialectal groups and more than 40 distinct dialects that have different levels of mutual intelligibility and prestige. The speech of different cities should also be mentioned: for example, the speech of Ljubljana, including elements of slang, is increasingly present in the mass media, provoking a range of responses.

The supposedly low 'language culture' of speakers of Slovene in written as well as oral discourse, especially in public, is often seen as one of the most pressing (socio)linguistic problems within the Republic of Slovenia. The term refers particularly to the gap between standard Slovene and (elements of) vernacular varieties, the use of which is perceived by some as problematic in public discourse (cf. Toporišič, 1997: 12; Vidovič Muha, 2009: 623). There is still a firmly rooted belief that 'pure and beautiful' Slovene is the best and only genuinely correct form of the language, although it is very rare and is mastered only by a few (cf. Stabej, 2004: 21). This can be explained by the fact that the supposedly questionable quality of Slovene was used as an argument by the German-speaking community against the introduction and use of Slovene in the public sphere before the 20th century.

Today, the Slovene language has a secure position in the mass media and press of the Republic of Slovenia. There are 98 radio and 81 television programmes, including local programmes (the national radio/television broadcasts seven radio programmes and six television programmes). All are in

Slovene except the national radio and television programmes for Italian and Hungarian national minorities and Radio Slovenia International, a national programme broadcasting in three languages (Slovene, English and German), primarily intended for foreigners and tourists in Slovenia.[14] Foreign films and soap operas are subtitled, but cartoons for children are dubbed. There is a great deal of popular modern music in different varieties of Slovene, and the Media Act[15] determines in Article 86 that at least 40% of music transmitted daily on national television and radio programmes, 25% on television and radio programmes of special importance[16] and 20% on any other television or radio programme must be Slovene music or music produced by Slovene musicians. The press in Slovenia is conducted virtually exclusively in Slovene[17] and the most read publications (according to the national reading study[18]) are all in the Slovene language. The most watched television programmes are all in Slovene, although foreign television channels are available through cable and satellite television, some with Slovene subtitles.

Language Policy

In the first years following independence, few activities were recorded in the field of language policy.[19] The main issues were the public use of Slovene and the search for a framework for institutionalized activity on language policy. In 1994, a permanent working body for language policy and language planning was established in the parliamentary committee for culture, education and sport, with the task of presenting suggestions for language policy and language planning to parliament and to the wider public.[20] Also in 1994, a group of authors, mostly writers and scientists, wrote an open letter to the National Assembly, warning about supposedly problematic questions concerning the public use of Slovene and suggesting that these matters be regulated by a special law (Stabej, 2000: 241–244; Nećak Lük, 2001: 12–13). In terms of language policy, the new millennium was most noticeably marked by debate concerning the law on Slovene. The discussion regarding the drafts[21] was long and controversial, with critics primarily concerned with the fact that the authors had in mind an ideological construct of the pure Slovene language as a value in itself, and that they were trying, from a position of institutionalized power, to maintain the idealized image of 'pure and correct' Slovene as a goal of language and corpus planning (cf. Gorjanc, 2009: 14–15). Finally, in July 2004, the Public Use of the Slovene Language Act,[22] a text that differed considerably from the first draft, was adopted by the Slovene National Assembly.

The Sector for the Slovene Language at the Ministry of Culture[23] was assigned by the government the task of writing a national programme for language policy, legally anticipated in the abovementioned Act. The Resolution on the National Programme for Language Policy 2007–2011[24] was passed by the National Assembly in 2007, and was the first integral legal document about language policy in the history of the Slovene language community (Stabej, 2007b). It sets strategic guidelines in different domains of language policy activities and consists of 12 main goals and 113 items. Great emphasis is placed on the importance and role of Slovene as a national language, developing language competence and raising language awareness (cf. Dular, 2008: 79). Although in some segments (e.g. in the 'Vision' section) the document seems to be a coherent text of a national programme, numerous weaknesses have been pointed out, such as the lack of a thorough analysis of the situation based on empirical research; the lack of a clear concept, and, as a result, a failure to provide a proper hierarchy of the topics and to address the main issues of the current situation; and some arbitrary and absurd solutions as far as the distribution of financial resources is concerned[25] (Gorjanc, 2009; Stabej, 2007b; Vidovič Muha, 2009).

Another problem is the lack of a systematic analysis and evaluation of the practical implementation and social and political effects of the Public Use of the Slovene Language Act and the Resolution on the National Programme for Language Policy 2007–2011.[26] It seems that the Sector for the Slovene Language that is also responsible for this task could be more efficient, and its administration could be better organized.[27]

For the future writing of new fundamental political documents regarding the Slovene language, such as a new resolution for the years 2012–2017, it seems to be particularly important that they be based on empirical research and expert evaluation of the current issues, and that discussion of the documents be open and democratic, allowing for the constructive cooperation of both political and (socio)linguistic experts. Only by paying heed to the nature of linguistic phenomena and by adapting to the changes in the language situation will it be possible to plan and implement constructive language policy acts that address the main challenges facing the Slovene language.

The Infrastructure of Slovene

Another important issue in the current sociolinguistic situation of Slovene seems to be the planning of its infrastructure, especially in view of its current shortcomings. Slovene orthography and grammar are sanctioned by the Orthographic Commission and the Fran Ramovš Institute of the Slovene Language, which are both closely linked to the Slovene Academy of Sciences and Arts. The existing reference books include *Slovene Orthography*

(2001), *The Dictionary of Standard Slovene*, 1–5 (1970–1991, single volume 1994, also available online at http://bos.zrc-sazu.si/sskj.html) and *Slovene Grammar* by Jože Toporišič (1976, 1984, 1991, 2000), all of which are written on the basis of classical methods and are not corpora-based.[28]

Language corpora of Slovene have been built since the 1990s, the biggest include FidaPLUS (http://www.fidaplus.net/), with approximately 620 million words,[29] Nova beseda (http://bos.zrc-sazu.si/s_beseda.html), with approximately 318 million words,[30] and two recent corpora, both built within the Communication in Slovene project (www.slovenscina.eu):[31] the 1.18-billion-word Gigafida (demoversion: http://demo.gigafida.net), and the million-word GOS corpus of spoken Slovene (http://www.korpus-gos.net). Unique is a new corpus of student texts, anotated with teacher corrections, compiled within the same project to serve as the basis for corpus-based pedagogic grammar (cf. Kosem *et al.*, 2011).

The biggest Slovene multilingual corpus is the *Evrokorpus* (http://evrokorpus.gov.si/), which consists of parallel bilingual corpora including approximately 222 million words[32] and containing texts in English, French, German, Italian, Slovene and Spanish. As for automatic translations, the Google automatic translator (http://translate.google.com) includes Slovene as one of its 51 languages, and a Slovene English–Slovene translator Presis is available online (http://presis.amebis.si/prevajanje/index.asp?jezik=sl).

Regarding the shortage of contemporary, user-friendly reference books, two points need to be made. The first is the tradition of language revision/proofreading. It is currently held that practically every text written for publication should be proofread by a professional language reviser (cf. Dermol-Hvala, 2002). In practice this (still) actually occurs, at least at the main publishing and media houses. Language revisers can change the text considerably, not only according to the normative rules as defined in reference books (which are themselves in many respects arbitrary and largely inelastic) but also in terms of style, supposedly upholding the purity and beauty of the language, fighting against the violation of the aesthetic ideal, based on their individual perceptions, tendencies, professional experience and taste (cf. Vitez, 2009). With such interventions in texts, the responsibility of the author diminishes and he/she may consequently feel less self-confident and independent about writing.

The other tradition is that of language consultancies, traditionally in the form of newspaper columns (cf. Kalin Golob, 1996). Recently, several online language consultancies have been set up, and the national broadcaster also carries a radio and television broadcast. Although some language experts still take a traditional point of view and advise language users in terms of what is right or wrong, some take a broader perspective, making people aware of the distinctions between structural linguistic rules and social norms in a language, thereby stressing the general equality of different varieties of language and diminishing language-based intolerance and discrimination (cf. Žaucer & Marušič, 2009).

In order to rectify the shortcomings of the infrastructure, certain investment is needed in researching and reorganizing Slovene linguistics. Modern reference corpora and other language sources raise hope for more reference books that are user-friendly, written in a contemporary style and for specific target groups. What also seems important for the support that users of Slovene need are democratic language consultancies and proof-reading, that take into account the reality of the language and its diversity.

Foreign Languages in Slovenia

In Slovenia, competence in foreign languages is seen as an asset. In the educational sphere foreign languages are generally popular because of economic interests, the size of the country and the presence of Hungarian and Italian minorities (cf. Skela, 2008: 187). However, the (public) use of foreign languages is often perceived as problematic, partly due to historical memories of the times when Slovene was not used publicly in the territory of Slovenia.

According to Eurobarometer (2005), 89% of the Slovene population stated that they could speak at least one language other than their mother tongue at the level of being able to undertake a conversation, which places Slovenia sixth among the countries of the EU. 'Serbo-Croatian' (61%) is the most widely known language besides Slovene, followed by English (56%) and German (45%) (European Commission, 2005: 3–4). As far as the actual use of foreign languages in Slovenia is concerned, a research project (Požgaj-Hadži *et al.*, 2009, $N = 700$) showed that in the private sphere 32.3% of the respondents use no foreign languages, 34.4% use the languages of former Yugoslavia, 32.6% use English, 24.6% German and 11% Italian, However, in business communication the percentage of those who use no foreign languages is 65.6%, with the most frequently used foreign language being English (25.4%), followed by German (15.3%), with the languages of the former Yugoslavia in third place (12.6%).

In the context of Slovenia's EU entry, and in the more general context of globalization, the need for foreign language competence has increased significantly. The greater extent of foreign language teaching and learning has also been influenced by strong support for the promotion of foreign languages and multilingualism from the European Council and the European Commission. In the primary school system this is reflected in a greater number of foreign language lessons, the earlier introduction of the first foreign language (mostly

English) and the introduction of a second foreign language as a compulsory subject in the last three grades (Skela, 2008: 188).

There is a clear need for an all-embracing, transparent language strategy for foreign language learning that incorporates a greater number of qualified foreign language teachers (cf. Skela, 2008). The efficient planning of foreign language teaching and its effective implementation are essential for speakers of Slovene to be able to participate actively in the international framework. On the other hand, the question remains, '[i]n what way will the new Slovene multilingualism [...] shape the Slovene public language sphere and to what extent will Slovenia be able to operate as a monolingual public sphere?' (Stabej, 2006: 688).

Minorities, Immigrants and their Language(s)

The ethnic minorities in the territory of the Republic of Slovenia can be classified into two categories: the classical (territorial) minorities and the newly emerged ethnic communities. The latter (which in total number 119,440, or 6.07% according to the 2002 national census[33]) predominantly comprise members of the nations of the former Yugoslavia who migrated to Slovenia mainly for economic reasons between the mid-1960s and the beginning of the 1980s (Komac, 2004: 39). The category of historical ethnic minorities consists of Italian (2258 or 0.11% of the Slovene population according to the 2002 national census[34]), Hungarian (6243 or 0.32%) and Romani (3246 or 0.17%, although it is estimated that between 7000 and 10,000 Roma live in Slovenia; cf. Komac, 2000: 44).

Italian and Hungarian minorities enjoy relatively complete legal protection,[35] and according to Article 11 of the Constitution of the Republic of Slovenia,[36] Italian and Hungarian have the status of regional official languages in municipalities where the autochthonous Italian and Hungarian national communities live. In accordance with legislation, the two national communities and their members have the right to education in their own languages. Two different models have developed, largely as a result of historical differences. For the members of the Italian ethnic community in the bilingual coastal area there are Slovene and Italian schools where the other language is taught as a compulsory subject, whereas in the ethnically mixed area of Prekmurje pupils attend bilingual schools with Slovene and Hungarian as the languages of instruction and communication, and also learn about the history and geography of Hungary.

However, despite satisfaction with the legislation and the frequently expressed conviction that the system of minority protection in Slovenia is exemplary (cf. Tollefson 1997), there are problems with the implementation of the linguistic rights of ethnic minorities in everyday life. A number of studies have confirmed the perception that in ethnically mixed territories functional bilingualism is formally guaranteed but not practised, and that there is a situation of diglossia in which the minority language is used mainly in private, mostly informal communication among members of the national minority (cf. Nećak Lük, 1996; Novak-Lukanovič, 2003).

Members of the Romani community, with the status of a special ethnic community and newly formed minority, have considerably less protection and fewer rights compared to the two national minorities.[37]

Romani children with Romani as their mother tongue are mostly integrated into Slovene schools and it is presumably also because of the language problems that the majority of these children do not complete elementary school (cf. Komac, 2000: 44). In the Romani Education Strategy in the Republic of Slovenia, implemented in 2004, representatives of the Romani community called for a special optional subject of Romani language and culture (cf. Vižintin, 2009: 81).

Following independence, the sociolinguistic position of immigrants from the former Yugoslavia changed considerably (cf. Introduction and Stabej, 2007a). The main challenges relating to immigrant children concern the right to learn their mother tongue and access to systematic instruction in Slovene. Although classes in the mother tongue and culture must be organized for immigrant children in accordance with Article 10 of the 1996 Elementary School Act[38] and in accordance with international agreements, this is rarely fulfilled,[39] and there seems to be no clear vision as to how to compensate for this shortage of opportunities. According to a paragraph added to Article 10 of the Elementary School Act in 2007, assistance with learning Slovene as a second/foreign language is supposed to be offered at the child's entry to school if needed.[40] However, for now, immigrant children can obtain additional expert help in the form of a maximum of 35 lessons in the first year of their education in Slovenia. For any further assistance, schools have to find other ways and means of financing. The question of competent teachers also remains open (cf. Knez, 2009). Various activities and projects have been organized to improve the integration of immigrant children, one of them at the Centre for Slovene as a Second/Foreign Language at the Faculty of Arts of the University of Ljubljana.[41]

In particular as far as Romani and new minorities are concerned, it seems that more should be done in practice in order to improve their children's communicative competence in Slovene and thus to ensure smoother integration into the Slovene school system, better results, and more opportunities for further education and employment.

Slovene Minorities in Neighbouring Countries

Three autochthonous Slovene speech communities exist in the linguistically mixed border regions of contemporary Italy (between 70,000 and 80,000 members[42] in the Trieste, Gorizia and Udine provinces), Austria (between 20,000 and 30,000 Slovenes in Carinthia and around 1500 in Styria) and Hungary (approximately 3000 Slovenes in Porabje). As a result of their development in different historical, sociopolitical and socioeconomic circumstances, these communities present major differences in areas such as legal status, the opportunities for the use of Slovene and the organization of minority education,[43] ranging from a situation in which the diglossia is total, where Slovene functions only as a dialect in the life of the larger community and in private conversation within families, friends and colleagues, to partial diglossia, where Slovene is also used in a number of formal situations, although it is limited to communication within Slovene minority institutions (cf. Nećak Lük & Nećak, 1990: 176–179).

In most of these minority communities the Slovene share of the population is decreasing. Their members are concerned with day-to-day efforts to maintain Slovene, but with the lack of public domains in which their mother tongue can be used, the majority languages are being used increasingly for communication amongst family members, thus endangering intergenerational language continuity. A knowledge of Slovene is very rare amongst the majority community, because in schools where the majority language is the language of instruction, Slovene is generally not taught. This is one of the signs that the status and position of Slovenes in these countries is worse than the position of Hungarian and Italian national minorities in Slovenia, although bilateral agreements are in place for both situations (cf. Bogatec, 2004; Busch, 1997; Kaučič-Baša, 2004; Nećak Lük & Nećak, 1990; Nećak Lük, 1994–1995).

On the other hand, with the fall of the Iron Curtain on the Slovenian–Hungarian frontier and the opening up of Slovenia's borders due to its integration into the EU, there have been more opportunities for closer communication between Slovenia and the minority communities abroad. Furthermore, the statistics show that recently, despite the negative demographic trend (and, for example, the progressive shrinking of the network of public schools with Slovene as the language of instruction in Italy due to the falling number of children from Slovene families), interest in Slovene language instruction and enrolment in bilingual schools (in Špeter in Italy and Št. Peter in Austria) is on the increase, particularly because of an increasing number of children from non-Slovene families (cf. Bogatec, 2004; Kern,

2009). The reason for this trend seems to be primarily economic, connected with Slovenia's accession to the EU and the consequently greater prestige of Slovene as one of its official languages. However, it can also be interpreted in terms of making use of the opportunity for the revitalization of the (previously abandoned) language/national identity. In a way, the two interpretations can be seen as two sides of the same coin.

Taking these encouraging signs into account, the Slovene language community and the minorities should try to meet the new needs by ensuring a suitable quality of instruction in schools where Slovene is taught (increasingly as a second/foreign language) and by giving serious thought to providing specific assistance to parents from mixed marriages and parents with the majority language as their mother tongue, in order 'to convey to them the basic information on the linguistic education of children in a multilingual family environment and to raise their awareness of and interest in these issues' (Bogatec, 2004: 32). Thus, nationally mixed families, and even non-Slovene families, can be considered as potential vehicles of the Slovene language and culture.

Slovene in Higher Education and Science

One of the controversial language policy questions in the Slovene language situation is concerned with language in higher education and science. A clash between a functional and a symbolic view of language can be observed in the discussions on this topic. Stabej (2006: 698) summarizes the issue as follows:

> Internationalisation seems to be absolutely indispensable to growth in quality and competitiveness of Slovene higher education. Many see this process as being thwarted precisely by Slovene as the prescribed obligatory language of the educational process, since it supposedly represents an insurmountable obstacle to a greater extent of both teacher and student mobility. To those seeing it this way, the judgment of Solomon usually appears to be to abolish the obligatory use of Slovene and liberalise the language side of higher education. But de facto this most probably means a significant increase in the use of English as the language of instruction.

A discrepancy can be observed between legal provisions at the highest level, with the Constitution ensuring Slovene as the language of instruction, with the Higher Education Act[44] allowing for some exceptions to this rule, and with strategies of individual universities. The rectors' conference suggested in the draft of the new University Act of 18 November 2008[45] that the decision about the language of instruction be left to universities, which would probably lead to the increasing use of foreign languages, primarily English. Thus the question arises as to the level at which certain guidelines should be provided.

The Higher Education Act (Article 8) protects Slovene as the language of instruction in higher education. However, the same article states that the following may be provided in a foreign language: study programmes in foreign languages, parts of study programmes if visiting teachers participate in the provision thereof or if significant numbers of foreign students are enrolled therein, and study programmes if they are also provided in Slovene. At this point some dilemmas may arise, as the meaning of the term 'significant numbers' is open to interpretation. The Strategy of the University of Ljubljana,[46] taking into account the Bologna Declaration and the Framework of Economic and Social Reforms for Greater Prosperity in Slovenia,[47] aims to have at least 10% of foreigners among its students and 10% of programmes carried out by foreign professors and programmes or subjects in a foreign language.

With the arrival of ever greater numbers of foreign students,[48] and also to prepare Slovene students for international careers, English has been increasingly used in certain classes in particular study programmes.[49] The faculties offer different options for exchange students, but generally there is not enough financial support for parallel programmes in Slovene and English.[50]

Regarding the languages of scientific publications, it seems that in Slovenia there is no consensus about, and no conception of what the ideal relationship between Slovene and the global English and other foreign languages should be. However, in order to ensure the development of Slovene terminology and the popularization of science amongst the Slovene public, the Slovene Research Agency, which finances most research, has established a normative principle that every research programme financed by the state budget has to publish one expert article and one popular article in Slovene at least once a year (Demšar & Sorčan, 2007: 95). However, there are deficiencies with regard to Slovene textbooks and scientific journals, especially in the field of natural sciences, and consequently also deficiencies in Slovene terminology.[51]

Another problematic issue at the University of Ljubljana is the fact that, according to the proposal of the document entitled Criteria for the Appointment of University Teachers, Scientific Workers and other University Staff, Slovene scientific achievements only gain half of all of the available points (the 'national' sciences being exceptions to this), thus encouraging writing and publishing in English and neglecting publishing in Slovene. In public discussions of this suggestion, university teachers and scientists, mostly from the field of humanities and social sciences, have expressed dissatisfaction with it (cf. Kalin Golob & Stabej, 2007; Zupan Sosič, 2009), but at the time of writing this chapter, its fate is still unknown.

On the other hand, although no reliable quantitative data are available, it can be said that a lack of ability in English for some undergraduates represents an obstacle to their studies, and that not mastering English proficiently may leave those who are expected to work in the international sphere somewhat stalled in terms of their career (cf. Stabej, 2006: 699). Because Slovenes are generally relatively good at foreign languages (cf. Eurobarometer data, Foreign Languages in Slovenia, in Chapter 5), this can also be seen as a lack of self-confidence in using a certain (foreign) language, possibly connected with the ideology of the supposedly low 'language culture' and an image of pure and correct Slovene, mastered only by a few (cf. The Sociolinguistic Situation in Slovenia).

The retreat of Slovene from higher education and science would mean a retreat from a highly representative domain of public use and could indirectly cause a decrease in the (efficient) use of Slovene in other public domains with definite corpus language dimensions. Moreover, to access higher education, Slovenes would first have to learn another language thoroughly – in the long run also causing adjustment of primary and secondary school curricula – which would represent a severe regression in the Slovene historical memory (Stabej, 2006: 699). In order for this to be averted, and at the same time for Slovene students and experts to gain adequate competence in English and other foreign languages, thus enabling them to participate actively in the international sphere, the search for an appropriate balance between the local and the global in the language(s) of higher education and science is a key concern.

Conclusion

In the new circumstances that Slovenia and the Slovene language have faced since achieving independence, one of the main challenges seems to be in relation to questions of the vitality of the Slovene language community and of ensuring the dominance of Slovene as a fully functional, public, official and national language in the territory of the Republic of Slovenia, both as a prerequisite for the further development of its corpus and for the maintenance or increase of the number of speakers. At the same time, public communication should be accessible to residents of Slovenia whose first language is not Slovene, and here the key role is played by the efficient planning of the possibilities for learning Slovene. Furthermore, Slovenes should achieve adequate foreign language proficiency (especially English as the modern lingua franca) in order to be able to communicate efficiently in the global world. Another of the fundamental questions is how to establish and maintain a sensitive, constructive balance between Slovene and English in certain domains where English is used with increasing frequency, for example in science and higher education.

A step forward in language policy and language planning would be a more systematic and transparent organization of language policy bodies (such as the Sector for Slovene) and a reduction (or at least marginalization) of defensive discourses and ideologies that, among other things, in the name of purist attention to language and the fostering of language actually impede its development, hinder broad accessibility to language and public communication for both native and foreign speakers, consider problematic foreign languages as a potential threat to the national language, and view language as a cultural value and much less as something functional (cf. Stabej, 2008: 64). It is crucial that, besides the status and corpus of Slovene in the Republic of Slovenia, language policy and language planning become concerned more systematically with the description and codification of the Slovene language, its status as one of the official languages of the EU and the complex specific chapters of the Slovene language: Slovene as a second/foreign language, its immigrants' first languages, foreign languages and Slovene language communities outside Slovenia.

Language planning in Slovenia has to some extent taken into account the needs of the increasing number of people who need or want to obtain active linguistic competence in Slovene as a foreign language, and has offered some efficient solutions in the acquisition and assessment of Slovene linguistic competence. Among the positive signs is the increasingly wide range of facilities on offer for learning Slovene as a second/foreign language, and also the increasing number of learners, with the primary role being played by the Centre for Slovene as a Second/Foreign Language at the Department of Slovene Studies at the Faculty of Arts of the University of Ljubljana. What remains a challenge in the field of Slovene as a second/foreign language is the question of the offer of Slovene language instruction for immigrant children and the availability of courses, especially for those from disadvantaged social backgrounds and for foreign students at Slovene universities[52] (cf. Kobos & Pirih Svetina, 2009).

In the light of EU membership, a challenge seems to be how to make Slovene and other medium-sized languages more accessible and attractive to a wider international public (cf. Stabej, 2008: 64).[53] The data regarding Slovene at foreign universities are encouraging,[54] and it has been proposed that within the framework of the EU, common support be given to endeavours for the offer of the study of the official languages of the Union in each of the Member States, at least at one university (not necessarily every year) (Nidorfer Šiškovič, 2008).

What raises hope for Slovenes abroad is an increased interest in learning Slovene and in bilingual schools, especially among children who have not learned Slovene at home; this can be seen as a precious opportunity for the revitalization of the (previously abandoned) language/national identity of Slovene communities. In addition, it can be stated that among Slovene emigrants in Europe and overseas, despite the general language shift towards the majority language (cf. Šabec, 1997), the younger generations also feel connected with Slovenia and wish to preserve Slovene. Their integration in a foreign environment does not thus exclude the feeling of Slovene identity, and they can be important ambassadors for Slovenia abroad and a precious bridge between Slovenia and their country of residence (cf. Ban & Špelko, 2006; Bitenc, 2006).

Hopefully, with the help of effective language policy and language planning, the following prophecy will be realized in the future: Slovene will remain capable of, and primed for, any communicative task, and its speakers will use it self-confidently and proudly as the most functional and prestigious language in Slovenia. Speakers of other languages who reside in Slovenia for a longer period of time, and who wish to, or have to, speak Slovene, will have adequate opportunities for learning the language and will consequently be able to communicate actively in Slovene society. At the same time, foreigners living in Slovenia will be able to preserve their mother tongues and will thus represent a valuable connection between their own culture/country and Slovenia, just as the Slovene people living abroad will link Slovenia with their country of residence. Through the efficient learning of other languages, Slovenes will also be able to communicate in the international sphere. In conclusion, Slovene will remain on the cultural map, where it carved out its space soon after the birth of its standard form, continuing the story of the successful establishment of a national language.

Notes

(1) The author would like to thank Prof. Dr Marko Stabej for assistance with drafting this chapter and for valuable comments regarding the text.
(2) There are Slovenes living in European countries (Germany, France, Sweden and Switzerland), in the countries of ex-Yugoslavia (Croatia, Bosnia and Herzegovina, Serbia, Montenegro and Macedonia) as well as overseas (USA, Canada, Argentina and Australia).
(3) The oldest preserved Slovene text, *The Freising Manuscripts*, was written around AD 1000 and the first Slovene books, *The Catechism* and *The Spelling Book* (Primož Trubar, 1550) as well as the first Slovene translation of the Bible (Jurij Dalmatin,

1584) and the first Slovene Grammar (Adam Bohorič, 1584) were printed in the period of the Reformation.
(4) A proven knowledge of Slovene also became an obligatory requirement (after a transition period) for the acquisition of Slovene citizenship and employment in Slovenia.
(5) Data are taken from the website of the Statistical Office of the Republic of Slovenia (http://www.stat.si/Popis2002/gradivo/si-92.pdf).
(6) According to Eurobarometer research (Europeans Commission, 2005: 2), the proportion of the respondents who declared Slovene to be their mother tongue was 95% ($N = 1045$).
(7) The number of people with Slovene as their mother tongue is increasing, but slower than the total population. Therefore, the percentage of people with Slovene as their mother tongue has been decreasing since 1953 (Šircelj, 2003: 88).
(8) The concept of a common language was replaced in the former Serbo-Croatian language area by the emphatic separation of languages; therefore, today we speak of the Serbian, Croatian, Bosnian and Montenegrin languages (cf. Stabej, 2007a: 21–22).
(9) The 2002 census registered Arabic, Chinese, Spanish, Bosnian and Montenegrin as new mother tongues (the last two relate to the new definition of languages, cf. footnote 8). The number of declared speakers (although mostly negligible in terms of percentage) increased for 11 foreign languages and decreased for 6.
(10) Croatian 2.8%, Serbo-Croatian 1.8%, Serbian 1.6%, Bosnian 1.6%, Macedonian 0.2%.
(11) 0.1% declared other languages, 2.7% fall into the category 'unknown'.
(12) In public (at work, in shops, at the doctor's and so on – the question was only asked in the 1991 census). People said that they used Slovene only (94.4% of the population), Slovene and 'Serbo-Croatian' (1.1%), 'Serbo-Croatian' (0.9%), Slovene and Italian (0.3%) and Slovene and Hungarian (0.2%), other (combinations of) languages 0.9% and unknown 2.3% (Šircelj, 2003: 111).
(13) The Slovene theory of language varieties (cf. Toporišič, 2000: 13–27) presents social variability in terms of the division between standard (literary) varieties (standard formal language versus standard colloquial language) and non-standard (non-literary) varieties (local dialects; regional colloquial varieties; slang, jargon, cant). There has been a great deal of reflection on the theory (cf. Kržišnik, 2004), among other things expressing doubt as to how far it actually reflects the real linguistic situation and raising concerns that such a conception of linguistic diversity can, instead of flexible language competence, cause a schematized image of language and fail to prepare children for effective communication in life in the process of schooling (cf. Stabej, 2004: 21).
(14) See http://www.apek.si (Post and Electronic Communications Agency of the Republic of Slovenia) and http://www.rtvslo.si (Radio-television Slovenia).
(15) See http://zakonodaja.gov.si/rpsi/r08/predpis_ZAKO1608.html.
(16) Local/regional, student or non-profitable radio and television programmes with a defined minimal proportion of relevant contents of their own production and with defined minimal broadcasting time (for the exact criteria regarding this status, cf. rules on programmes of special importance, see http://zakonodaja.gov.si/rpsi/r07/predpis_PRAV4357.html).
(17) Two exceptions to my knowledge are *The Slovenia Times*, a Slovene newspaper issued every two weeks in English and intended for business and diplomatic foreign public,

and the *New York Times*, a weekly supplement that accompanies *Delo*, the third most read daily newspaper in Slovenia (footnote 18), including the most important articles from daily editions of the *New York Times*, which is intended, as the publisher puts it, for more demanding readers and for foreigners in Slovenia.

(18) See http://www.nrb.info/
(19) Especially if compared to the activities in the 1970s and 1980s, which were predominantly concerned with the status and public use of Slovene in multinational and multilingual Yugoslavia (cf. Pogorelec, 1983).
(20) The working group was dissolved after the constitution of the new parliament subsequent to the 2004 elections (Stabej, 2006: 690).
(21) The text had different titles in its various versions. The first draft was prepared in 1997 by the then Minister of Culture, Dr Janez Dular, and the text first entered parliamentary procedure in 2000 (cf. Nećak Lük, 2001: 13; Stabej, 2006: 685).
(22) See http://zakonodaja.gov.si/rpsi/r04/predpis_ZAKO3924.html
(23) See http://www.mk.gov.si/si/delovna_podrocja/kulturni_razvoj_in_mednarodne_zadeve/slovenski_jezik/ The body was established as the Office for Slovene Language of the Government of Slovenia by a governmental decree in 2000, but was reorganized and renamed the Sector for the Slovene Language at the Ministry of Culture after the acceptance of the Public Use of the Slovene Language Act in 2004. An explanation for these changes is beyond the scope of the present article.
(24) See http://zakonodaja.gov.si/rpsi/r00/predpis_RESO50.html
(25) For example, there was a great deal of public disapproval regarding the fact that €250,375 was designated for tests with the synchronization of films (the public is generally satisfied with subtitled films), but only €104,323 was devoted to general and specialized reference books for Slovene, for example (cf. Stabej, 2007b).
(26) Regarding the Public Use of the Slovene Language Act, Stabej comments that 'anecdotal cases do show, however, that some legal stipulations are only enforced with grave difficulty – because they interfere with the wishes/needs of members of the Slovenian language community that the norm concerns (e.g. obligatory names of firms in the Slovenian language, obligatory use of Slovenian in the media, etc).' This confirms the fact that 'adopting a legal norm in opposition to the ideas of the majority of members of the language community' is nonsensical, something that was repeatedly pointed out during the procedures of drafting and adopting the law (Stabej, 2006: 700). Meden and Zadnikar (2009) examine the adequacy of legislative objectives, evaluate the appropriateness of legislative solutions and analyse factors that hinder the implementation of individual provisions.
(27) According to Stabej (2006: 690), '[t]he only publicly visible form of its operation is the yearly "public tender for the funding of projects intended for the assertion, promotion, and development of the Slovenian language." The public is not informed about the results of the tender, nor are the yearly reports of the sector's activities at its disposal.' Cf. also Stabej (2007b).
(28) For example, the extensive materials for the Dictionary of Standard Slovene can be considered of historical value, as the compilation of materials commenced 40 years ago and was completed 20 years ago. The dictionary part of the Slovene Orthography is based on the same materials (cf. Vidovič Muha, 2009: 623).
(29) The institutions that carried out the project were the Faculty of Arts and the Faculty of Social Sciences of the University of Ljubljana, and the Jožef Stefan Institute.
(30) Compiled at Fran Ramovš Institute of Slovenian Language at the Research Centre of the Slovene Academy of Sciences and Arts.

(31) In addition to the corpora, the project's activities include a corpus interface for pedagogical purposes, a training corpus, a lexicon of inflected forms, a Slovene lexical database, a new didactics of Slovene language teaching, a pedagogical corpus-based grammar and a manual of style.
(32) The Translation Unit of the Slovene Government Office for European Affairs and the Secretariat-General of the Government of the Republic of Slovenia have contributed most to its compilation.
(33) 38,964 or 1.98% Serbians, 35,642 or 1.81% Croatians, 21,542 or 1.10% 'Bosniacs' (one of the three constitutive nations of Bosnia and Herzegovina) 10,467 or 0.53% Muslims, 6186 or 0.31% Albanians, 3972 or 0.20% Macedonians, 2667 or 0.14% Montenegrins.
(34) See http://www.stat.si/Popis2002/gradivo/si-92.pdf
(35) Legal provisions comprise constitutional regulations, approximately 80 laws and provisions covering different areas of the life of minorities, multilateral documents and bilateral agreements. Article 64 of the Constitution guarantees these communities and their members special rights.
(36) See http://www.dz-rs.si/index.php?id=351&docid=25&showdoc=1
(37) Article 65 of the Constitution envisages a special law regulating the status and special rights of the Romani community, which was passed in 2007. The only legal provisions the new national minorities can rely on for preserving their ethnic particularities can be found in Article 61 (the expression of national affiliation) and Article 62 (the right to use one's own language and script) of the Constitution.
(38) See http://zakonodaja.gov.si/rpsi/r08/predpis_ZAKO448.html
(39) In the 2008/2009 school year, this occurred at only eight Slovene schools. Classes in the following languages were organized: Albanian (three schools), Macedonian (four schools), German, Russian, Finnish and Croatian (one school each) (Vižintin, 2009: 85).
(40) In 2007, the document Strategija vključevanja otrok, učencev in dijakov migrantov v sistem vzgoje in izobraževanja v Republiki Sloveniji (Strategy for the Inclusion of Children and Pupils – Immigrants in the Education System of the Republic of Slovenia; available at http://www.mss.gov.si/si/delovna_podrocja/razvoj_solstva/projekti/enake_moznosti/) was also written, pointing out the problems and aims in this field.
(41) See http://www.centerslo.net/l1.asp?L1_ID=8&LANG=slo
(42) Estimates of the numbers of members of Slovene minorities are taken from the website of the Government's Office for Slovenians Abroad (http://www.uszs.gov.si).
(43) For an overview of the current models of education and the position of Slovene as a language of instruction and as a subject in minority education, see Kern (2009). An extensive report on Slovene language in education in Italy is available in Bogatec (2004), and on Slovene language in education in Austria in Busch (1997).
(44) See http://zakonodaja.gov.si/rpsi/r02/predpis_ZAKO172.html
(45) See http://www.uni-mb.si/dokument.aspx?id=13628, cf. pp. 4 and 12
(46) See http://www.uni-lj.si/files/ULJ/userfiles/ulj/o_univerzi_v_lj/strategija_ul/5.4%20StrategijaUL2006_2009.pdf. The University of Ljubljana, established in 1919, is the oldest of the four Slovene universities, and also the largest, with more than 63,000 graduate and postgraduate students (cf. http://www.uni-lj.si/).
(47) See http://www.vlada.si/fileadmin/dokumenti/si/projekti/projekti_do_2009/Okvir_gosp-soc-reform-2005-Vlada.pdf
(48) The number of foreign students at higher education institutions in Slovenia rose from 1511 in 2006/2007, to 1674 in 2007/08, 1969 in 2008/2009 and 2185 in

2009/2010 (information from the Statistical Yearbooks of the Statistical Office of the Republic of Slovenia: http://www.stat.si).
(49) The proportion of subjects in foreign languages at the University of Ljubljana was 3.15% in 2008/2009 and 4.33% in 2009/2010 (see http://www.uni-lj.si/files/ULJ/userfiles/ulj/o_univerzi_v_lj/letno_porocilo/PoslovnoPorociloUL2009.pdf, p. 89).
(50) Some faculties offer certain subjects in English that can also be chosen by Slovene students as optional subjects. Teachers at other faculties write English handouts and give a short English explanation at the end of each (Slovene) lecture, as well as offering individual consultations in English. There are examples of study programmes where only English is used, such as the 'English track' at the Faculty of Economics, which can also be chosen by Slovene students, and an international programme of postgraduate studies at the Jožef Stefan Institute. Goal 10 of the Resolution on the National Programme for Language Policy 2007–2011 is the consolidation of Slovene in higher education and science, highlighting (amongst other things) parallel study programmes in English and Slovene. However, no financial support has been assigned to achieving this aim.
(51) The Slovene Research Agency partly financed 115 Slovene scientific periodic publications in 2009 (the majority of them published in Slovene): 28 in the humanities, 27 in the social sciences, 13 in natural sciences and mathematics, 11 in technical sciences, 5 in fields of medical and biotechnical sciences, and 16 in interdisciplinary journals (http://www.arrs.gov.si/sl/infra/period/rezultati/08/inc/period-publikacije-09.pdf). This agency's list of Slovene journals in international databases is available at http://home.izum.si/COBISS/bibliografije/seznami_za_mednarodne_baze/slo/SVNPUBL.ASP.
(52) Currently, the only courses available free of charge are those for Socrates/Erasmus students (which are financed by the EU). Students have to pay for the Slovene exam that is a condition for progressing to the next year of their studies (cf. Kobos & Pirih Svetina, 2009: 208). Ensuring the availability of the capacities needed for foreign students at all high school institutions is among the aims of the Resolution on the National Programme for Language Policy 2007–2011; however, this should have been implemented by 2007.
(53) One of the problems is a lack of qualified teachers of these languages (cf. Skela, 2008; Stabej, 2008). English, French, German, Spanish and Russian represent 95% of the foreign languages that pupils learn (Skela, 2008: 184).
(54) In the 2010/2011 academic year, Slovene lectureships (for language, literature and culture) are available at 58 universities around the world. Slovene study programmes are offered at many European universities, and in Japan, China, Argentina and the USA. At 22 foreign universities in Europe, students can obtain a degree in Slovene and can continue their study of Slovene at postgraduate level. More than 2000 students study Slovene at various levels at foreign universities (http://www.centerslo.net/).

References

Ban, J. and Špelko, T. (2006) Slovenska jezikovna skupnost v Argentini. *Jezik in slovstvo* 54 (3/4), 71–84.
Bitenc, M. (2006) Slovenščina in njeno poučevanje pri slovenskih zdomcih: raziskava med učenci dopolnilnega pouka slovenskega jezika in kulture v Baden–Württembergu. *Jezik in slovstvo* 54 (3/4), 55–69.

Bogatec, N. (ed.) (2004) *Slovene: The Slovene Language in Education in Italy*, 2nd edn. Ljouwert/Leeuwarden: Mercator-Education.
Busch, B. (1997) *Slovenian: The Slovenian Language in Education in Austria*. Ljouwert/Leeuwarden: Mercator-Education.
Demšar, F. and Sorčan, S. (2007) Znanstvene objave v slovenskem in tujem jeziku. *Jezik in slovstvo* 52 (5), 94–103.
Dermol-Hvala, H. (2002) Lektorjeva skrb za jezik. In *Nacionalno, Regionalno, Provincialno* (Zbornik Slavističnega društva Slovenije 13) (pp. 155–156). Ljubljana: Slavistično društvo Slovenije.
Dular, J. (2008) Usmeritve nacionalnega jezikovnopolitičnega programa na področju vzgoje in izobraževanja. In M. Ivšek (ed.) *Jeziki v izobraževanju* (pp. 61–69). Ljubljana: Zavod RS za šolstvo.
European Commission (2005) *Europeans and Languages: Eurobarometer*. Online document: http://ec.europa.eu/public_opinion/archives/ebs/ebs_237.en.pdf
Gorjanc, V. (2009) Slovenska jezikovna politika pred izzivi Evropske unije. In V. Požgaj-Hadži, T. Balažic Bulc and V. Gorjanc (eds) *Med politiko in stvarnostjo* (pp. 13–25). Ljubljana: Znanstvena založba Filozofske fakultete.
Kalin Golob, M. (1996) *Jezikovna kultura in jezikovni kotički*. Ljubljana: Jutro.
Kalin Golob, M. and Stabej, M. (2007) Sporazumevanje v znanosti in na univerzi: Uboga slovenščina ali uboga jezikovna politika? / Strategija univerze ter slovenščina kot znanstveni in učni jezik. *Jezik in slovstvo* 52 (5), 87–90.
Kaučič-Baša, M. (2004) Ohranjanje slovenščine pri Slovencih na Tržaškem in Goriškem: Nekaj elementov za tezo o vzrokih opuščanja manjšinskih jezikov. *Slovenščina v šoli* 9 (3), 12–29.
Kern, D. (2009) Slovenski jezik v vzgojno-izobraževalnih ustanovah v manjšinskem prostoru. In M. Stabej (ed.) *Infrastruktura slovenščine in slovenistike* (Obdobja 28) (pp. 191–196). Ljubljana: Znanstvena založba Filozofske fakultete.
Knez, M. (2009) Jezikovno vključevanje (in izključevanje) otrok priseljencev. In M. Stabej (ed.) *Infrastruktura slovenščine in slovenistike* (Obdobja 28) (pp. 197–202). Ljubljana: Znanstvena založba Filozofske fakultete.
Kobos, Z.K. and Pirih Svetina, N. (2009) Učenje in poučevanje slovenščine kot neprvega jezika v Sloveniji. In M. Stabej (ed.) *Infrastruktura slovenščine in slovenistike* (Obdobja 28) (pp. 203–209). Ljubljana: Znanstvena založba Filozofske fakultete.
Komac, M. (2000) Ethnic minorities in Slovenia. In *Papers Delivered at EBLUL Council Meeting* (pp. 35–44). Brusseles: EBLUL.
Komac, M. (2004) The protection of ethnic minorities in the Republic of Slovenia and the European charter for regional or minority languages. *Revista de llengua i dret* 41, 39–104.
Kosem, I., Rozman, T. and Stritar, M. (2011) *How do Slovenian primary and secondary students write and what their teachers correct: A corpus of student writing*. Paper at The Corpus Linguistics 2011 conference. Available at: http://www.birmingham.ac.uk/documents/college-artslaw/corpus/conference-archives/2011/Paper-198.pdf
Kržišnik, E (ed.) (2004) *Aktualizacija jezikovnozvrstne teorije na Slovenskem: členitev jezikovne resničnosti* (Obdobja 22). Ljubljana: Center za slovenščino kot drugi/tuji jezik pri Oddelku za slovenistiko Filozofske fakultete.
Meden, A. and Zadnikar, G. (2009) Analiza zakona o javni rabi slovenščine in njegovega uresničevanja. In M. Stabej (ed.) *Infrastruktura slovenščine in slovenistike* (Obdobja 28) (pp. 463–470). Ljubljana: Znanstvena založba Filozofske fakultete.
Nečak Lük, A. and Nećak, D. (1990) Slovene as a minority language: Historical background and sociolinguistic prospects. *Slovene Studies* 12 (2), 169–181.

Nećak Lük, A. (1994–1995) Jezik in etnična pripadnost v Porabju. *Razprave in gradivo* 29/30, 5–23.
Nećak Lük, A. (1996) Jezik kot kazalec stanja medetničnih odnosov. *Razprave in gradivo* 31, 11–24.
Nećak Lük, A. (2001) European plurilingualism from a national language perspective. *Razprave in gradivo* 38/39, 6–25.
Nidorfer Šiškovič, M. (2008) Program Slovenščina na tujih univerzah in slovenistike v Evropski uniji. In M. Ivšek (ed.) *Jeziki v izobraževanju* (pp. 151–154). Ljubljana: Zavod RS za šolstvo.
Novak-Lukanovič, S. (1995) Jezikovne značilnosti mikrookolja učencev. *Uporabno jezikoslovje* 3 (4), 132–141.
Novak-Lukanovič, S. (2003) Multicultural settings and school–parent relations. In K. Broekhof (ed.) *Ethnic and Cultural Minorities in Education* (pp. 100–111). Utrecht: Sardes Educational Services.
Pogorelec, B. (ed.) (1983) *Slovenščina v javnosti: gradivo in sporočila*. Ljubljana: Slavistično društvo Slovenije.
Požgaj-Hadži, V., Balažic Bulc, T. and Miheljak, V. (2009) Srbohrvaščina v Sloveniji: nekoč in danes. In V. Požgaj-Hadži, T. Balažic Bulc and V. Gorjanc (eds) *Med politiko in stvarnostjo* (pp. 27–40,288). Ljubljana: Znanstvena založba Filozofske fakultete.
Šabec, N. (1997) Slovene–English language contact in the USA. *International Journal of the Sociology of Language* 124, 129–183.
Šircelj, M. (2003) *Verska, jezikovna in narodna sestava prebivalstva Slovenije: Popisi 1921–2002*. Ljubljana: Statistični urad Republike Slovenije.
Skela, J. (2008) Nazaj v prihodnost: Teorija, praksa in politika poučevanja tujih jezikov v Sloveniji. In M. Ivšek (ed.) *Jeziki v izobraževanju* (pp. 175–195). Ljubljana: Zavod RS za šolstvo.
Stabej, M. (2000) Nekatera vprašanja formalnopravnega urejanja statusa slovenskega jezika v Republiki Sloveniji. In I. Štrukelj (ed.) *Kultura, identiteta in jezik v procesih evropske integracije*, Vol. 1 (pp. 234–245). Ljubljana: Društvo za uporabno jezikoslovje Slovenije.
Stabej, M. (2004) Kaj je to, slovenščina? Slovenščina v narodni in mednarodni razsežnosti. In *Poučevanje materinščine – načrtovanje pouka ter preverjanje in ocenjevanje znanja* (pp. 14–22). Ljubljana: Zavod Republike Slovenije za šolstvo.
Stabej, M. (2006) Obrisi slovenske jezikovne politike; The outlines of Slovenian language policy. *Slavistična revija* 54 (special issue), 309–325, 685–702.
Stabej, M. (2007a) Size isn't everything: The relation between Slovenian and Serbo-Croatian in Slovenia. *International Journal of the Sociology of Language* 183, 13–30.
Stabej, M. (2007b) Samopašne ovce: Pomisleki ob Resoluciji o nacionalnem programu za jezikovno politiko 2007–2011. *Mladina* 19, 30–31.
Stabej, M. (2008) Večjezičnost: Vojna, tekma, sožitje? In M. Ivšek (ed.) *Jeziki v izobraževanju* (pp. 61–69). Ljubljana: Zavod RS za šolstvo.
Tollefson, J.W. (1997) Language policy in independent Slovenia. *International Journal of the Sociology of Language* 124, 29–49.
Toporišič, J. (1997) Slovene as the language of an independent state. *International Journal of the Sociology of Language* 124, 5–28.
Toporišič, J. (2000) *Slovenska slovnica: Četrta, prenovljena in razširjena izdaja*. Maribor: Založba Obzorja.
Vidovič Muha, A. (2009) Jezikovnopolitični vidik sodobne javne besede: (Ob nacionalnem programu jezikovne politike). *Slavistična revija* 57 (4), 617–626.

Vitez, P. (2009) Lektoriranje in odgovornost. In M. Stabej (ed.) *Infrastruktura slovenščine in slovenistike* (Obdobja 28) (pp. 393–400). Ljubljana: Znanstvena založba Filozofske fakultete.

Vižintin, M.A. (2009) Pravica do maternega jezika pri manjšinah in priseljencih v Sloveniji. In *Slovenski mikrokozmosi – medetnični in medkulturni odnosi* (Zbornik Slavističnega društva Slovenije 20) (pp. 79–91). Ljubljana: Zveza društev Slavistično društvo Slovenije.

Žaucer, R. and Marušič, F. (2009) Jezikovno svetovanje, praksa in ideali. In M. Stabej (ed.) *Infrastruktura slovenščine in slovenistike* (Obdobja 28) (pp. 449–456). Ljubljana: Znanstvena založba Filozofske fakultete.

Zupan Sosič, A. (2009) In English we trust: Slovenska univerza ali univerza na Slovenskem. *Delo* 51 (108), 21.

5 Challenges Faced by a Medium-Sized Language Community in the 21st Century: The Case of Hebrew

Anat Stavans

Introduction

Alhough language communities are usually an established fact in societies, countries, nations and states, they are all part of a historical past. Therefore, the challenges faced by medium-sized language communities (MSLCs) in Europe can be laid out along a continuum, for there is no one language that embodies the same historical and current phenomena as another; nor do languages enjoy the same status or undergo the same historical processes. For a serious exploration of the challenges that MSLCs face and will face in the coming decades, some basic historical background is required. The situation of Modern Hebrew in Israel is a case in point. In what follows, I will first explain some basic historical and current facts about the linguistic ecology of Modern Hebrew in Israel, presenting a brief history of the language, the revival of Hebrew, the contextualization of Hebrew in and outside Israel today in relation to the ideas of homeland, transnationalism, the diaspora and heritage language, and some facts about Modern Hebrew in Israel. In the second part I will discuss Hebrew in Israel in terms of overt and covert language policy. The third part includes a description of Israel's educational language policy. I will conclude with an overview of the challenges that MSLCs face, the ways in which Israel deals with these challenges, and whether these are realistic goals to meet.

Language Ecology from Past to Present: The Case of Modern Hebrew in Israel

The history of the Hebrew language is usually divided into four major periods: Biblical or Classical Hebrew, which was used until about the third century BC and is the language in which most of the Old Testament was written; Mishnaic or Rabbinic Hebrew, which was the language of the Mishna (a collection of Jewish traditions) that were written about 200 AD (this form of Hebrew was never used as a spoken language); Medieval Hebrew, used from about the 6th to the 13th century AD, when many words were borrowed from Greek, Spanish, Arabic and other languages; and Modern Hebrew, the language of Israel in modern times.

Hebrew is one of the world's oldest languages. It is spoken and written today in much the same way as it was over 2000 years ago. After ceasing to exist as a spoken language in around 250 BC, it was reborn as a modern language in the 19th century, and is now the main language of the State of Israel. For over three millennia, Hebrew has been the religious, and often the literary and secular, language of the Jewish people. In the post-biblical period, Hebrew gradually gave way to Aramaic as the spoken language, but served as the language of ritual and prayer. The renaissance or revival of Hebrew as a spoken language in the 19th century was propelled by Eliezer Ben Yehuda, who devoted his life to this cause, and at the same time adapted Hebrew for modern use through the introduction of thousands of modern terms. Hebrew gradually came into use among the Jewish settlers in Palestine and became the official language of the State of Israel at its creation in 1948 (Rabin, 1973).

Modern Israel has been multilingual since its foundation. When the British took over the Mandate for Palestine in 1920 after the collapse of the Ottoman Empire, Hebrew, Arabic and English were declared the official languages of the nation state. English was dropped when the British mandate ended and the State of Israel was declared. Although Hebrew was used by the Jewish population in the region from the late 19th century onwards, it was left to the different communities to determine their education and language policies. Eventually, many language policies aimed to replace immigrant and heritage languages (such as Yiddish, Ladino and others) with Hebrew, presumably in the belief that this would promote the building of the nation. Today, Israel does not have a written Israeli constitution or a law that lays down language policy. The situation is somewhat unclear, as it leaves 'a confusion of possibilities' (Spolsky & Shohamy, 1999: 26). Stavans and Narkiss (2003) discuss Israeli language policy in relation to the language policies outlined by Lambert (1994), in which three main categories are established from a national rather than a minority group perspective: the 'homogeneous' category comprises states that have a main, majority language (for instance the USA); the 'dyadic' category characterizes countries with two or three main linguistic groups (e.g. Canada); and the 'mosaic' category includes countries that have various ethnic groups linguistically catered for by the language policy. Israel does not fall into any of these categories, as it is a mixture of all three: there is Hebrew hegemony although both Arabic and Hebrew have official status; English enjoys *de facto* recognition in the public sphere; and the education system makes allowances for immigrant languages.

The revival of Hebrew was a gradual process that came at a price. Shohamy (2008) argues that attempts to revive and preserve languages have high costs for individuals due to the regulations that might conflict with their own practices and personal beliefs or those of a given group. Moreover, the need to revive a language is the ideologically driven agenda of a specific group, which may continue even after the revival has been achieved. The revival of Hebrew involved such costs, as shown in the three major ideological and factual stages of the process. In the beginning, there was a diglossic situation in which written Hebrew was known by all the Jewry in the diaspora and spoken Hebrew was only known to some. When the Jewish nation state was established, there was a divide: written Hebrew was a unifying force for the entire Jewish world, and spoken Hebrew was a divisive force. Hence, there was a need for a common language for all the people in the new homeland. In 1881 and 1882, this language was promoted in the diaspora (Europe) by Ben Yehuda, with the 'Hebrew in Hebrew' movement to educate people under the ideological credo that 'Hebrew-man speaks Hebrew'. In 1889, the first Hebrew-only school was established. Since then, Hebrew has slowly penetrated all levels of education from kindergarten to graduation. From 1900 to 1910, the generation that had been educated in Hebrew and had grown up speaking the language was getting married and forming families. This led to the first generation of monolingual Hebrew homes.

Modern Hebrew is based on the biblical language, but includes innovations to meet contemporary needs. Colloquial speech is related to the written language. The overriding pronunciation is closer to that of Sephardic (Hispano-Portuguese) Jews rather than Ashkenazi (East European) Jews. The syntax is taken from the Mishna or Rabbinic Hebrew. The lexicon and morphology come from a system in which a root form consisting of three-consonant patterns can be used to generate a broad lexicon, mainly through inflection. For example, the root [k.t.v] yields kotev (*writes*) and ktiva (*writing*). Hebrew is written from right to left in a Semitic script of 22 consonants. The vowels are represented by a system of signs that underscore these letters.

Hebrew is regarded as a successful case of language revival, although its status as an endangered language is questionable. Some argue that the revival of Hebrew was the result of people gathering and needing a common language of communication, while others argue that Hebrew is not a case of revival but rather of re-vernacularization (Ben-Rafael, 1994). Hebrew went from being a vernacular language to a liturgical language. It remained liturgical until the 19th century, when the *Haskala* movement in Europe set out to expand traditional Judaism to the secular populace, to promote national ideologies (Ben Rafael, 1994; Shohamy, 2008). The revival process was completed by 1920, when Hebrew was declared the language of instruction. In the late 1930s, measures were introduced to encourage immigrants to learn Hebrew, even at the expense of their language of origin. This policy was quickly embraced and applied to educational programmes that have been in place since then. Consequently, the idea was introduced that maintaining, fostering and, worst of all, using another language was detrimental to educational achievement. Most importantly, this policy was exported by proxy to Jewish communities in the diaspora to facilitate Jewish immigration and settlement in Israel. In fact, for a long time, Hebrew curricula and materials were drawn up in Israel, where teacher training also took place. This led to the creation of school practices that catered for the inclusion of members into the local Jewish community.

Today, Hebrew in Jewish communities outside Israel is undergoing major and radical changes, not in its implementation in the educational system, but in its significance and centrality in the lives of those in the diaspora. The branch of the Hebrew language community that is outside Israel is undergoing a process of community transnationalization, in which the role of Hebrew is changing. As part of this process, the Hebrew language is deterritorialized, and thus stripped of its economic, social, cultural and political power to define relations between the diaspora and homeland. The place of Hebrew in new interpretations of past conditions and experiences of migratory flows in diaspora communities changes the nature of the new social/communal formations. Transnationalism characterizes world Jewry for the following reasons: Jews commonly have a birth place that is different from their place of residence/nationality as a result of migratory flows; they re-made and shaped their communal life in the new place; they built their associational and institutional profile and their collective consciousness as part of a broader feeling of people yearning for the homeland (Israel); and they developed a sense of belonging in the new land that expressed itself through global interactions. In what follows, we move from the early stages to the modern era of Hebrew in Israel today.

Hebrew in Israel today

Hebrew in Israel and in the diaspora is undergoing major changes as a result of the effects of globalization (Nevo & Olshtain, 2007). Some (particularly those with a purist perspective) would argue that modern, colloquial Hebrew is drastically impoverished by globalization, as it is losing its authenticity, pure form and properness. Others argue that Hebrew is a dynamic communication system and therefore must change in response to globalization (Zuckermann, 2008). As Hebrew is a revived language, it is not yet endangered in Israel, but its popularity is declining sharply in the transnational Jewish community. It is not threatened by extinction, but its practicality is diminished in an increasingly globalized and material world. Hebrew falls into the category of medium-sized language communities, with around 7 million Hebrew speakers in Israel (the nation state) and over 13 million users of the language in the rest of the world. Figure 5.1 presents the distribution of Hebrew users.

The language policy of Israel is defined in two official statements that establish that there are two official languages, Hebrew and Arabic, a mandatory requirement of one foreign language (usually English) and optional languages (mainly heritage languages). The language policy of the region prior to the creation of Israel stated:

> All ordinances, official notices and official forms of the Government and all official notices of local authorities and municipalities in areas to be prescribed by order of the High Commissioner shall be published in

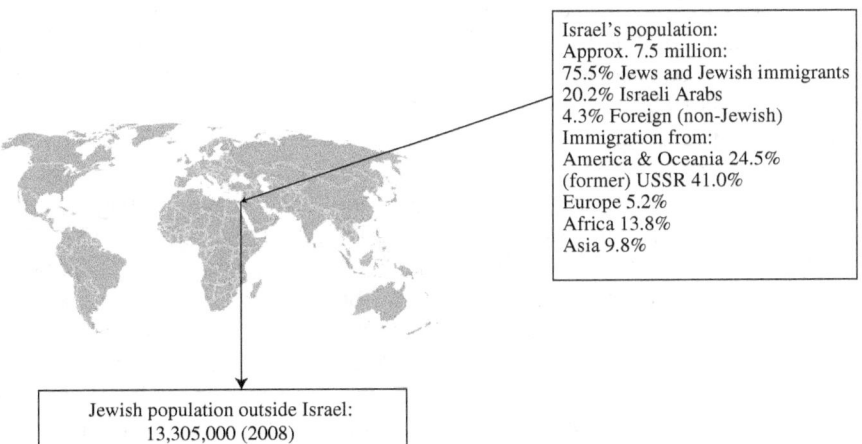

Figure 5.1 Jewish population and Hebrew around the world (April 2010)

English, Arabic and Hebrew. (The 82nd paragraph of the Palestine Order in Council issued on 14 August 1922 for the British Mandate of Palestine)

After the establishment of the State of Israel in 1948, the following statement was made:

Any order in the law which requires the use of the English language is hereby abolished. (Adopted and amended by the State of Israel, 19 May 1948)

Essentially, Israel's covert language policy considers some of the languages of Israel today. Hebrew is regarded as the main official language and is spoken by most of its citizens. Arabic is the second official language, the medium of instruction in the Arabic sector of public schools and the heritage language of Jews from Arabic countries. English is the main foreign language. Yiddish, Ladino, Judeo-Arabic, Juhuri and Judeo-Berber are endangered Jewish languages brought by the first waves of immigration. Russian, Polish, Hungarian, Spanish, French, Amharic and Tigrinya are some of the community languages of later immigrants. French, German and Japanese are some of the foreign languages taught in high schools and universities. Finally, Armenian, Assyrian (Aramaic) and Circassian are some of the community languages of non-Jewish Israelis.

The status, propriety and longevity of Hebrew are currently being contested. Purists and Hebraists argue that the language is being distorted, degenerated and anglicized. Others would argue that Hebrew is dynamic and evolving, as it is influenced and affected by trends, just like many other languages. These perspectives are driven by issues such as the intergenerational transmission of Hebrew and the use of Hebrew for interpersonal communication with immigrants who speak minority languages, rather than the use of a foreign lingua franca.

In essence, new generations usually adopt the Hebrew language quickly, depending on their cultural heritage, their language and cultural prejudices, their reason for immigration, their socioeconomic level and their educational and occupational experiences. The generation of adult immigrants, particularly Russians, maintain and bring their children up in a Russian-speaking environment, whereas Ethiopian immigrants forgo their heritage language faster to bridge the gap between the older and younger generations. This gap leads to two intra-familial problems. First, the older generation becomes highly dependent on the younger for survival and management of daily life within the larger Hebrew-speaking community. Second, there is an enormous cultural and language rift between older and younger generations, which leads to communication problems and a loss of cultural heritage, a lack of identity and a struggle to adopt the local majority's identity. Within immigrant communities, the language of origin is used for identification and group membership, for establishing intimacy and solidarity and for maintaining ties with the 'old world' from which they came. Immigration is both the physical and spiritual transfer of the individual. However, the physical self immigrates much faster than the mental and emotional one.

In Israel, Hebrew is an evolving language that is influenced by foreign languages, geopolitical context, demographics, technology and progress. The Hebrew Language Academy is fast at work inventing Hebrew alternatives for Latinized words, some of which are adopted and some rejected. For example, alternatives for 'telephone' (sax raxok) or for 'pyjamas' (namnemet) were rejected. However, new words for medical, economic and technological terms have and are being invented. Some of these are used frequently, such as 'interface' (mimshak), 'jetlag' (xamarmoret) and 'mouse' (axbar).

Arabic has full status as one of the official languages of Israel. It is found on the currency, stamps and official inscriptions, can be used in the Israeli parliament and on official documents, and is the language of instruction in Arabic schools. Arabic is thus used in the public, semi-private and private domains, that is, in the community, on radio and television broadcasts, as a vehicle for a vibrant literary output and in the family. Nevertheless, in spite of this official equality, Hebrew is the preferred language in Israel. Knowledge of Hebrew is a requirement for Israeli citizenship. Arabic is a compulsory subject in Hebrew schools, as is Hebrew in Arab schools. The issue of any change to the formal status quo remains extremely sensitive (Koplewitz, 1992).

The Declaration of Independence defines Israeli Arabs as citizens of a democratic country and equal to Jews. However, Ben-Rafael (1994) describes issues of language, identity and social cleavages in Israel, which characterize Israeli pluralism as allowing non-Jewish communities to retain their cultural, social and political identity within an Israeli setting, as long as they maintain the position of being a minority, which is inevitably an alienating reality. The urge to be equal yet different is also explicit in the minorities themselves. This is further supported by the findings of Stavans and Narkiss (2004), who showed that, among Arab teachers of language and other subjects, the perception of linguistic and cultural pluralism is 'equal but separate'.

Arabs in Israel are a native minority whose trilingualism may be seen as a matter of necessity rather than choice. Their language skills do not guarantee the same degree of success as those of the Jewish majority and are not accompanied by the same positive attitudes to multilingualism is in other places in the world. Perhaps the geopolitical situation in Israel inevitably generates a type of multilingualism that is not optional but essential for existence.

Until the mid-1940s, the Jewish population of Israel was ethnically fairly homogeneous, as the vast majority came from European and Eastern European backgrounds. However, since then, the population has become ethnically much more mixed, with immigrants from Northern Africa, America, Asia and the Middle East. Another major demographic change was brought about by a disproportionately large influx of Russian immigrants, who arrived in two waves of immigration in the 1970s and 1990s, and are the second largest minority group after the Arabs.

As suggested by Spolsky and Shohamy (1999), there is increasing 'recognition of the possibility of plurilingualism and multilingualism,' which has 'shaken the status quo' in terms of Hebraic hegemony and the realization that the country needs to become more pluralistic. Stavans and Narkiss (2004) make a similar point in their discussion of teachers' attitudes to linguistic and cultural pluralism. Whereas teachers in both the Arab and Jewish sector recognize the need, or unavoidable emergence, of multilingualism, they have different ideas about how this should be introduced. The Arab sector favours the 'equal but separate' approach, whereas the Jewish sector wants it to be Hebrew/Jewish/Israeli-shaped.

The pressure and drive for pluralism on the one hand and sectorialism on the other also seem to be encoded in public spaces. For instance, the street signs in Tel Aviv shown in Figure 5.2 combine the public and private sectors' indications of a current street name, and are also a historical record of the first street signs in Tel Aviv. The street name sign is located in a downtown business and shopping area of central Tel Aviv that is mostly frequented by

Figure 5.2 Street signs in Tel Aviv

veteran Israelis, tourists and some foreign workers. It is on the façade of a private business building. The sign on the left is modern and lights up at night, and is therefore visible at all times. This sign is in Hebrew only. The sign on the right is a historical sign that was put up long ago when the Arab population from Yaffo frequented this area of south Tel Aviv. It has remained as a historical record, so to speak. The street name is first written in Hebrew, then in the Latin alphabet and finally in Arabic. The sign is also a historical document because the street was named after Baron Sir Moses Haim Montefiore, who was one of the most famous British Jews (a financier, banker, philanthropist and the Sheriff of London) in the 19th century.

Public spaces also show the changing linguistic landscape in other areas of Israel where there are heterogeneous populations of different groups of immigrants. One such example is the city of Rehovot, which is located southeast of Tel Aviv in central Israel. The sign in Figure 5.3 is posted at the entrance to the local branch of the Ministry of Immigrant Absorption.

The fairly recent sign on this government office is written in Hebrew, English, Russian, Amharic, French and Spanish, but not in Arabic (there is no real audience for Arabic in this city, apart from a few families who have immigrated recently from Yemen). The office is in a central street in the business area of Rehovot, close to the central bus station. This area is frequented by veteran Israelis and immigrants from different countries who are served by the office. In contrast, the sign on the Ministry of Housing is written in Hebrew and English only.

Across the street from the office of the Ministry of Immigrant Absorption there are two businesses fairly close to one another. The first is a store with a sign for Russian dairy produce (Figure 5.4); this is in Hebrew (quite predominantly) and in Russian, as the shop is mainly for Russian clientele.

Figure 5.3 The local branch of the Ministry of Immigrant Absorption in Rehovot

90 Survival and Development of Language Communities

Figure 5.4 Hebrew–Russian bilingual store sign in Rehovot

A few metres away there is a small restaurant that caters for the Ethiopian population. This locale has no business sign but is known to exist and is frequented by Ethiopian men. On the door of this restaurant is a poster announcing a cultural event: a concert by a great singer. This sign is written in Hebrew and Amharic, in almost equal proportions (Figure 5.5).

English is a dominant language in the professional, economic and political arenas, especially as it is the link with the world outside Israel. In fact, for a small country enclave with most of the Arab-speaking population in

Figure 5.5 Poster announcing a concert in Amharic and Hebrew in Rehovot

conflict, the only bridge to the outer world is through English and cyberspace, much of which functions in English. However, Hebrew is the predominant language for the internal management of Israel. Its position in the mass media, the new digital media, cultural industries and entertainment varies according to the status that is attributed to the various languages for different uses and for geographical or social reasons.

There are approximately 10 Hebrew television channels. Cable television channels are produced in different countries, so the languages vary. Some radio and television channels are in Russian and Amharic and there is a daily newscast in English (in the early afternoon) on the main, public national television channel. Newspapers are available in nearly 20 languages, some of which are locally printed and some of which are flown in. There are bookstores and video stores that specialize in Russian books, videos and toys. Grocery stores can be found that are predominantly for Russian clientele, and these are frequently non-kosher (i.e. they do not adhere to Jewish dietary laws). Local grocery stores in particular neighbourhoods may stock items that are specific to the population in that neighbourhood. For example, there are dairy stores for Russians in cities and neighbourhoods that have a high concentration of Russian immigrants, just as there are spices in specific stores in Ramleh, where there are high numbers of Indian immigrants. Stores selling Asian groceries can be found in south Tel Aviv for the Asian population of foreign workers. Specialized Russian restaurants and entertainment facilities can be found in cities such as Ashdod that have a high concentration of Russian immigrants, and there are certain areas within cities such as Rehovot in which shows are aimed at the Ethiopian public.

Organizations such as the Association of Latin American Immigrants (OLEI) organize gatherings, provide material for informal libraries, and put on cultural events in Spanish. Most of these institutions are community or private enterprises rather than government initiatives, much like some after-school programmes in the Russian community. Generally, Hebrew is not jeopardized in public spaces and in the media. However, the fact that Russian immigrants predominate in service jobs, in particular, creates linguistic enclaves that may be resented. Hospitals, banks and stores are places in which patients and clients may find that employees discuss their cases in Russian, even when this is not a language that they speak. In this situation, veteran Hebrew-speaking Israelis will frequently turn to the employee and ask them to speak in Hebrew.

The status of English is uncontested in the area of 'imported' entertainment or commerce. Television is not dubbed into any language and subtitles are mainly provided in Hebrew, and sometimes in Arabic. In emergencies or wartime, all public announcements are made in 10 or 15 languages. Public companies for services such as electricity and telephone have a call routing system that starts by allowing people to choose the language they want to use. The list usually includes English, Arabic and Russian and, less frequently, Amharic, Spanish and French. It invariably starts with Hebrew, but the order of the other languages varies. The main newscasts of the day (the longest one at 20.00 on national television) have a sign language interpreter.

In Israel today, the general patterns of pop culture and leisure activities, including the media and other resources, are very similar to those found throughout the Western world. Israelis may stay at home and watch CNN, Sky, the BBC or one of 50 other channels on cable television. Or they may choose to go out and see the latest Hollywood blockbuster at the cinema, attend a live concert featuring a famous European or American pop group, eat a hamburger at McDonald's or drink Coca-Cola. Yet, within these global trends, there is a distinctive Israeli culture, which reflects both the country's modern reality and its Jewish traditions, including the Hebrew language, Israeli music, dance, literary traditions and cuisine.

Most television viewers prefer to watch channels that broadcast in Hebrew (there are three main channels, one national and the other two privately and semi-privately owned). These channels broadcast original documentaries and drama in Hebrew that deal with Israeli topics as well as issues of universal interest. Several dozen local movies are produced each year, and local pop groups have excelled in the creation of uniquely Israeli music. Hamburgers, hot dogs, pizzas and schnitzels are rivalled in popularity by falafel and shawarma (grilled meat eaten in pita bread). With a diet of game shows, fast-moving soap operas and imported serials, commercial television has consistently out-rated the national broadcasting channels. However, homegrown series such as Ramat Aviv Gimmel and Lethal Money, which have also been sold overseas, show that Israelis, like other television viewers worldwide, are interested in the everyday, mundane problems of personal relationships, particularly when they unfold in Hebrew and involve the rich and beautiful, as well as the broader issues of war and peace.

Although Hebrew, the biblical language of the Jews, has been resurrected for modern use and is the contemporary linguistic vehicle of Jewish culture, another distinctive aspect of Israeli life is its multilingualism. As you sit in an outdoor cafe, the people at the neighbouring table may be speaking Arabic or Russian, Yiddish or Amharic, English or French, Spanish or Hungarian. Israelis switch languages with consummate ease. Cable television reflects this polyglot culture, with material broadcast regularly in most of the above languages, as well as others. Moreover, Israelis will go to the cinema to see an eclectic selection of the latest movies from around the world. In the past, fewer resources were available and the cinema was extremely popular. However, fewer Israelis indulged in other luxury leisure activities like dinner dances or going to restaurants, cafes or bars. Consequently, Israelis spent much more time in each other's apartments, visiting friends and family. In the pre-television era, conversation, games and songs were the main socializing patterns. The mass media – the radio and the press – were also popular. The government-run Voice of Israel (*Kol Israel*) broadcast on four wavelengths and there was a proliferation of newspapers, including around 25 in Hebrew alone, half a dozen Arabic daily newspapers and many foreign language publications, such as the *Jerusalem Post* in English. Within a few years, the afternoon newspapers *Maariv* and *Yediot Ahronot* emerged as the leading dailies, together with the more highbrow *Ha'aretz* and the Histadrut's *Davar*. Venues for entertainment and leisure were modest and people would socialize by strolling down the main street or going to the nearby beach, parks and nature resorts, as transportation was primarily public.

In shaping the local and new national culture, Israelis took pride in their cultural institutions. The country has one of the world's highest theatre-going rates and the 'Habimah Theatre' has become Israel's national theatre. Together with the 'Cameri' and the Haifa Municipal Theatre, this theatre puts on original productions in Hebrew and translations of English language hits. Initially, there was also a Yiddish theatre. However, its popularity waned while the Hebrew theatre grew in leaps and bounds, producing many original works, some of which have been performed abroad. In more recent years, Russian immigrants set up the world-class Gesher Theatre Company, with performances in Hebrew as well as a number of Russian productions. Amateur English-language theatrical productions can also be found.

Israelis remain avid readers, despite the popularity of television. A Gallup Poll (2002) showed that although watching television is the preferred leisure activity of 31% of Israelis, 21% would rather read a book. Israelis bought 14 million books a decade ago. After the introduction of cable and commercial television, book sales in 1996 totalled only 11 million. Still, this figure means that book consumption per capita is on a par with that of the world's greatest book consumers – Scandinavia and Iceland. Four thousand new books are published in Israel each year, mainly in Hebrew but also in Arabic, Russian and English. This is the world's second highest output of new titles per capita, after the People's Republic of China. A large percentage of these books are sold during Hebrew Book Week, when nearly 45% of Israelis visit the book fairs.

For Israel, in a geopolitical conflict with minority status, the new world order meant that the country had to move into the rapidly changing fields of technology and science, given that know-how and expertise in agriculture and the humanities were no longer lucrative exports. This resulted in a need for close contact with the rest of the world and to move to the forefront of science and technology internationally. An increasing number of Israelis use computers in their everyday life. Nearly all Israeli schools have computer centres and most kindergartens have computers. Most offices and many homes are equipped with computers, and surfing the internet is becoming a popular pastime, especially among people under 30 years of age. In fact, Israel has one of the highest rates of internet users in the world and one of the highest per capita rates of website production. Communication by email is rapidly becoming the norm for commercial purposes and for personal correspondence among younger Israelis. The Prime Minister's Office has launched a campaign called 'A Computer for Every Home' to provide computers for disadvantaged children.

Tourists in Israel need alternatives to the Hebrew that is found in public spaces. In addition, as many Israelis travel for enjoyment, they are exposed to other languages, particularly English. Responses to these factors can clearly be seen in normal popular landscapes, cyberspace and other public spaces. Street signs and road signs are usually written in Hebrew and accompanied by a version in the Latin alphabet, which usually represents the Hebrew pronunciation of the place name, even though some Arab villages or cities have a different name or different pronunciation in Arabic. The various languages in Israel have different levels of prestige and prejudice. Clearly, English has an overall high status among the population as a prestigious and important language, one that provides opportunities in the world and guarantees a prosperous future. Other than that, Hebrew is the most dominant language in the public space, although this dominance has been jeopardized over the past 15 years, with an increasing number of 'Hebrew-ists' (purists) protesting against the deterioration of not only the quality but the presence, use and dominance of Hebrew in people's lives and in the public space.

For example, many stores now advertize their seasonal sales with the sign 'SALE' rather than *'sof ona'* ('end of season sale' in Hebrew). Moreover, many businesses that wish to add an exotic touch will put up a sign in Latin letters or in English. Some companies are given foreign names, such as *Intima, Cotton, Comme il faut, Lambada, Tapas* or *El Gaucho*. Figure 5.6 shows a shopping bag labelled with two alphabets and one that is written only in the Latin alphabet.

Purist scholars, mainly in academia and universities, have begun to resent this trend, and have made public protests in popular newspapers and on television series, as well as some serious contentions, especially in the Ministry of Education. The issue is discussed widely in public by lay people and academics of both sexes from different age groups, ethnic origins and sectors. The dispute is likely to continue.

Figure 5.6 Shopping bags from Israel labelled with two alphabets

Internal diversity has been managed and perceived either as a threat, a nuisance or an asset by the various linguistic minorities and the veteran Israeli majority. Diversity is not only linguistic, but also ethnic, ideological and political, all of which influence the identity and power individuals have in relation to themselves and others. There are several ways in which diversity has been managed and has managed itself, and three different perspectives can be found in this area in the ways a minority perceives and manages itself in relation to the majority, in relation to other minorities, and in response to the majority's perception and management. If we take as an example two of the large waves of immigration to Israel in the 1990s, those of Russians and Ethiopians, it becomes clear that we cannot speak of a single internal diversity perceived by the majority towards the minority. Likewise, it is difficult to define the very diverse management and perception of each migratory group towards itself, the majority or other minorities. For instance, although Russian immigrants make up a heterogeneous group, the veteran Israeli majority regards them as homogeneous. Spanish speakers in Israel are always labelled Argentinian, even if they are Mexican. Alternatively, they are called South Americans (Mexicans take this as a personal insult, as Mexico is part of North America). In turn, the Russian immigrant group tends to segregate and even devalue the majority group (but not all the minorities, and it is more tolerant of the Arab and Anglo minorities). Ethiopian immigrants, who come mainly from two regions of Ethiopia (Tigrinya and Gundar), tend to relate much more closely to one another, although there are differences and segregation based on religious authenticity rather than educational or regional background. This group, unlike the Russian immigrants, tends to see itself as inferior to the majority and to most of the minorities. These findings were reported in Stavans and Goldzweig (2008) and are illustrated in Table 5.1.

Table 5.1 Comparison of ethnolinguistic vitality between the study groups: Russian and Ethiopian immigrants of the early 1990s

		Ethiopians		Russians		ANOVA	
		Mean	Std	Mean	Std	$F(1,109)$	p
Hebrew	Language	8.68	0.09	8.38	0.09	4.14	< 0.0442*
	Community	9.69	0.17	9.02	0.16	6.47	< 0.0124*
L1	Language	2.91	0.19	5.50	0.19	71.27	< 0.0001**
	Community	3.63	0.21	6.90	0.20	97.26	< 0.0001**
Arabic	Language	6.92	0.25	4.67	0.24	32.00	< 0.0001**
	Community	5.42	0.25	4.30	0.24	8.06	< 0.0054**
English	Language	8.05	0.15	8.37	0.15	1.80	< 0.1826
	Community	6.66	0.25	7.51	0.24	4.82	< 0.0303*

*$p < 0.05$; **$p < 0.01$

The results show that Russian and Ethiopian immigrants have different opinions of the majority and the other minorities, in terms of language and the status of their community. The Ethiopians hold the majority language and community in higher esteem than the Russians. The Ethiopians consider that their language and community is inferior to others, while the Russians regard their language and community as superior. The Ethiopians have a higher regard than the Russians for both the language and community of the Arabs in Israel (the largest minority group). Ethiopians and Russians both have a high regard for the English language, but the Russians hold the Anglo-Saxon community in higher esteem than the Ethiopians. These differences may take generations to overcome. In the absence of constitutional stipulations, it falls on the educational system to bridge these gaps. Important changes in education policy were initiated by the 1995–1996 statement of Policy for Language Education.

The Education Language Policy of Israel

The policy for Language Education in Israel was explained by the Ministry of Education in a Director-General's Circular on 1 June 1995. It was revised on 15 April 1996 and implemented by schools and teachers from September 1996 (Ministry of Education, 1995, 1996). The circular addressed language education policy in terms of *mother tongue* teaching and *second and foreign language* education.

Mother tongue was defined as one of the two official languages of Israel (Hebrew or Arabic) to be taught as a first language (not the first language of the pupil or the mother tongue of each pupil). The Policy established literacy goals in Hebrew and in Arabic (the official languages of the nation state) as the mother tongues for the two main sectors of the population: Jewish and Arab. For children whose mother tongue is neither Hebrew nor Arabic, further provisions are made for language maintenance in their languages, with special reference to Russian in particular, and Amharic to a lesser extent. Moreover, a long-established policy enables immigrant students and students who have been overseas for long periods to take the school-leaving examination in a language of their choice. However, few pupils select this option, as they feel less able to deal with contents in languages other than Hebrew.

Second language educational policy refers to Hebrew or Arabic for non-speakers of these languages. In this case, several scenarios should be considered. First, the policy stresses that Hebrew should be taught to immigrants for whom it is a second language. The course should continue for one year after arrival, in order to gain literacy. A second scenario is Hebrew as a second language for the Arab sector. The policy states that Hebrew should be taught to this group optionally in the first grade and compulsorily from the second grade until the 12th grade (the end of secondary education). The third scenario is that of teaching Arabic as a second language. The policy establishes that the study of Arabic should be compulsory for Hebrew speakers from 7th to 10th grades (the fourth year has just been added to this new policy), and optional for the two previous years (5th and 6th grades) and subsequent years (11th and 12th grades). It is up to individual schools to choose whether to offer French instead of Arabic in these optional grades. New immigrants are exempt from this requirement. Although the policy for second language education seems rather egalitarian for the Jewish and the Arab sector, in fact Hebrew is compulsory as a second language for the Arab sector, whereas Arabic is optional as a second language for the Jewish sector. Inevitably, the number of years of Hebrew as a second language in the Arab sector is greater than the number of years of Arabic for the Jewish sector, and the curricular plan and the external (out-of-class) language support and language needs are substantially different for both sectors.

In terms of *foreign language* education, English is considered the first foreign language and is optional in 3rd and 4th grades and compulsory from the 5th grade onwards. In an increasing number of schools in the Jewish sector and especially in affluent areas in Israel, English is introduced in the 1st and 2nd grades within the regular school schedule. Sometimes, parents must make an additional payment for these classes, even though schooling in Israel is free. Although the policy mentions French as an option, popular sentiment, globalization and exposure to media and cyber-communication as well as university entrance requirements mean that French is rarely preferred over English. Although, French is recognized as important because of cultural, political and economic ties and is the community language of a sizable body of immigrants, it is offered as optional (or as a required subject instead of Arabic) from 5th to 12th grades. Russian is also an optional language for new immigrants (as an alternative to Arabic or French). In the past 10 years, with the introduction of Spanish-language soap operas, schoolchildren have shown great interest in learning Spanish instead of French and Arabic. Muchnik (2010) concluded that, among teenage schoolchildren, 'the conditions that assure success in the learning of the language are the positive and appreciative attitude towards [Spanish], previous knowledge, and the use of it', although not necessarily exposure to it through pop culture. Yet, provisions for Spanish courses are not part of the policy, as this interest arose after the policy had been established, and no revisions have been made in the past 13 years. The policy encourages students to study another foreign language, but this is not mandatory. There are Yiddish courses (which is also used as the language of instruction and taught in independent ultra-orthodox schools), Ladino, Spanish and German, and recently we have seen the presence (again in affluent areas and through parent initiatives and support) of others languages such as Japanese, Chinese and Israeli Sign Language. The new policy also encourages the development of special language schools, but these have not been introduced to date.

Over a decade after the policy was launched, it has not been rigorously implemented and many of the recommendations have been interpreted in a free, lax way. This is perhaps because it was not turned into a law, but remained merely in the form of recommendations published by the Ministry of Education in a circular. Fishman (1994) states that policies, whether overt or covert, are worthless unless they are implemented. The question is therefore where and how this policy has been introduced. The 1996 policy set general goals, and some funding was allocated initially for teaching languages in schools. Israel's Ministry of Education shares responsibilities with the Chief Inspectors for the various languages/disciplines (under the authority of the Pedagogical Secretariat), the directors of the various levels of education, the curricular division, and the local supervision and management by the districts. Nevertheless, the final policy decisions are made at individual school level. As a result, there is a great deal of variability, which is best characterized by the way in which language education is organized in schools, the curriculum and materials used, evaluation, and teachers' profiles and training (Shohamy, 1994; Spolsky, 1996, 2004).

In terms of *school organization*, all schools in the Arab sector use Arabic as their language of instruction, teach Hebrew as a second language, and offer English as a foreign language. In Jewish state schools, Hebrew is the language of instruction, and all pupils learn English (many schools start English classes before the official 3rd grade). Nearly 50% of pupils learn Arabic for the required four years and a significant number of students opt to learn French, Russian and, more recently, Spanish and Chinese. A curriculum is drawn up by the chief inspector for each language, with the advice of a national professional committee. Curricula must be approved by the Ministry and are driven by the requirements for the school-leaving examinations. Although the Ministry states the optional and required teaching hours for each language, hours may be supplemented by local educational districts and by schools through their own resources (often in extracurricular programmes financed by parents, philanthropic organizations and aid in less affluent areas). At elementary and secondary school level, English is a mandatory language studied by all students. All students must continue with English at high school, and a large proportion also studies Arabic (about 50%), French (about 10%) or Russian (2–3%). The mandatory language subjects in school-leaving examinations are Hebrew and English for all students from all sectors of the population.

The curriculum and material for Hebrew are structured in a standard way and include Hebrew grammar, language, and cultural and ideological aspects of both Hebrew and world literatures. Hebrew is often separated into language and grammar courses and literature courses. The disciplines are well established in university departments and formal examinations. In the past 7 to 10 years there has been an increased interest in teaching literacy, especially in the last year of kindergarten and mainly in elementary schools, with provisions made by teacher training colleges to train specialized teachers. The teaching of Arabic in the Jewish sector is hampered by the difficulty of dealing with diglossia and the Palestinian local variety of spoken Arabic, which is highly influenced by dialects from neighbouring Arab-speaking countries and Hebrew. While some programmes focus on the spoken variety, most classes are taught in Hebrew and concentrate on the grammar and literature of the Modern Standard (Literary) language (Ministry of Education, 1996). Much of the instructional material for Arabic as a native language comes from abroad, especially from the big book fair that takes place annually in Cairo. One could argue that there is good reason to focus on the 'standard' Arabic that is found mostly in written language, as this is the Arabic that unites the entire Arab-speaking world and thus provides a more 'global' variety for the Jewish sector. However, the issue underlying this argument is that such Arabic is not learned for communication within Israel – between the Jewish and Arab population – but for the purposes of wider communication and particularly for written communication with the Arab world (Hallel & Spolsky, 1993).

The centrality of English in the school curriculum is a result of globalization and the needs established by high-tech and scientific developments in Israel. Inevitably, there has been a change in emphasis in English teaching. In the period before the 1960s, the focus was on literature, grammar and culture, rather than on English as an international language of communication. Waves of immigration of English speakers from the UK and USA provided a corpus of native speakers, who contributed greatly to teaching English, particularly in high schools. As most of the teachers were native English speakers and few had been trained to teach, there was great emphasis on oral language until two years after the language policy was launched. In re-thinking the language policy and the new needs of pupils, a curriculum was created to parallel that of Hebrew teaching, which involves literacy in early childhood and new world trends, communication, reading and writing. This has had an impact on teaching materials, the structure of school-leaving examinations, and university admission and graduation requirements. There is a large industry in English textbooks and computer-assisted language material, which is highly sensitive to changes in the curriculum and examinations. Competition in this sector has led to relatively high-quality materials, some of which are exported to other countries.

A new French curriculum has been expected for some time to emphasize the cultural value of the language. The Russian curriculum aims to include the grammatical and literary goals of the native-language curricula in the former Soviet Union. A new syllabus has been developed to teach Russian as a foreign language to speakers of Hebrew or to other immigrant children who did not attend high school in Russia. As for Spanish, soap operas have created a demand for the language, especially among young teenagers and young adults. A curriculum is still being developed.

The driving force behind the implementation and success of the language education policy is *evaluation.* At the end of high school, the *Bagrut* (school-leaving) examination serves both for graduation and university entrance purposes, and sets the guidelines for the curriculum, materials and teaching in the schools. The examinations are fairly traditional and the marking is objective. However, the diploma mark from the Bagrut and a school mark provide a final grade that is not uniformly reliable. Consequently, higher-education institutions such as colleges and universities also require a psychometric examination, which includes sections on verbal and analytic ability as well as proficiency in mainly English reading comprehension. Other assessments during the school years are carried out at local or district levels. From time to time, there are national proficiency assessments, especially in Arabic and

English, and there are literacy assessments at national level in the 2nd grade for Hebrew and in the 4th grade for Hebrew and English. Israel has also taken part in the international PISA and TIMM exams, all of which have an English language component.

Officially, *teacher training* colleges have a mandate to train kindergarten, elementary, middle school and special education teachers (for kindergarten to 10th grade), while high school teachers (10th to 12th grades) are trained at universities. Although this is stipulated by the Ministry of Education, the scarcity of teachers, especially in the field of languages, means that teachers who were trained at teacher training colleges also teach at high school level. Unlike in universities, college teacher training involves disciplinary, pedagogical and pre-service training for four years. In universities, degrees (BA and BSc, among others) are completed in three years, and there is an additional teacher training year. The supply of trained teachers varies by subject.

As the teaching profession has been devalued worldwide in the past three decades, fewer people opt to train as teachers. They see teaching as a vocation rather than a profession. There is a shortage of English teachers, so, in addition to existing programmes, the Ministry is conducting a programme to recruit native English speakers with university degrees and offer them training in Hebrew and in the methodology of teaching English as a Foreign Language. As a result of the recent financial crisis, new accelerated programmes with advantageous benefits were launched for English and mathematics teachers. The training of Arabic teachers for Hebrew speakers is also supported by the Israeli Defence Force, which conducts joint programmes with teachers colleges for elementary and middle school teachers and with the universities for high school teachers. As most Arabic teachers in the Hebrew sector only work part-time, there is ample opportunity to expand these programmes. However, few of the qualified teachers are fluent enough to teach in Arabic. Often, if not always, they are not from the Arab sector. A good number of French teachers were trained in French-speaking countries or in Romania before they immigrated to Israel. Others are graduates of Israeli university courses. There are many Russian teachers with university qualifications.

Language teachers are supported by the Ministry of Education and by local education inspectors and advisers. Each language has its own support and in-service training. For example, there is a support unit especially for the teaching of Arabic to Hebrew speakers. The cultural institutes and attachés of the various countries also provide different types of support. In addition, there are associations such as the English Teachers' Association (ETNI) and academic organizations such as the Language and Literacy Association (SCRIPT) or the Israeli Applied Linguistic Association (ILASH), and smaller and newer teachers' groups for other languages.

Challenges, Trends and Sustainable Goals for Language Policy in MSLCs in the 21st Century

There is no doubt that there are challenges from within and outside MSLCs in an increasingly globalized world. However, it would be unrealistic and impossible to predict what the needs and outlook of these communities will be 10, 30, 50 or 100 years from now. However, if we consider the history of the communities and the present situation, we may be able to at least make some educated inferences. It is clear that language policies are needed in geopolitical regions, but the question is what for and for whom. When it comes to language policy, things are not always as they seem, and we must look beyond explicit policy to understand how it works in practice.

In doing so, we must recognize that language policy is embedded in culture and is the main vehicle for the construction, replication, perpetuation and transmission of culture itself. As language is a cultural construct, it cannot be deconstructed, changed or radically altered by the application of particular theoretical frameworks or political scrutiny of one sort or another. Language(s) are different things to different people. Therefore mainstreaming, standardizing and policy formulation are usually difficult, unsuitable and misinterpreted. Israel is a good example of this. It has no explicit language policy, but there is a linguistic culture that predominantly supports the use of Hebrew and makes a semi-legitimate space for other languages such as Arabic.

Although a language policy is necessary, there appears to be a need to establish a linguistic culture to accompany it. A language policy cannot be the sum of language issues driven by the economy, history, attitudes, beliefs and ideologies. Such policy ends up being undifferentiated, oversimplified and simplistic, as in a one-size-fits-all approach. Therefore, one of the biggest challenges for MSLCs, including Israel, is to establish that they are essential and legitimate as the cultural vehicles of their speakers. This of course must be a top-down and bottom-up initiative by individuals and nations alike. Perhaps the challenges of the 21st century will be a change from globalization, namely the mainstreaming of world economy and power, to individualization, that is, finding cultural heritage an asset. Israel's language education policy, which was introduced in 1996, aimed to gradually move from the traditional monolingual (Hebrew) plus English programme and philosophy to more open acceptance of linguistic and ethnic pluralism, embedded in multilingualism and language maintenance. Of course, we cannot foresee future challenges and it is naïve to speculate. However, we may be able to better prepare our future generations if we strengthen education, and in particular language education, at least for one decade if not throughout the 21st century. Thus, we can use the acronym MSLC to say that **M**edium **S**ize **L**anguage **C**ommunities have **M**any **S**teps **L**eading to the 21st **C**entury.

Some questions can be answered within today's reality, but we are left with just as many unanswered questions. New world orders are formed every day – some man-made and some nature-driven. Our predictions are constrained but our learning is not. The challenges of MSLCs involve a battle for power that is not necessarily language-driven today. However, perhaps more value will be given to this issue in the future. I am not sure that challenges such as English ultimately threatening MSLCs (such as Hebrew) are realistic, especially given the history of Hebrew. However, the language status will be contested and much more acceptance will be required for the new forms that will evolve. The challenges of minority languages within a majority MSLC are much more serious, as they help to maintain the heritage of people and also contribute to the evolution of the MSLC (for example, Arabic has filtered into Modern Hebrew and Hebrew has filtered into the Palestinian dialect; immigrant languages borrow from other languages and lend features of their language of origin). Whether minorities will maintain their languages or the majority will learn the minorities' languages depends on many factors. Some of these factors can and should be enhanced through the educational system by making realistic provisions, while others must emerge from within the community. The big question that will accompany the linguistic reality of Israel (both in the homeland and the diaspora) will be whether the educational system will make linguistic allowances and accept other minority languages as legitimate heritage languages. This will only be possible when the 'organic' multilingualism of Israel outlives the 'synthetic' need to mainstream its people both linguistically and culturally. A first step in this process would be to value and cherish the linguistic and cultural capital of the diverse immigrant population of Israel.

References

Ben-Rafael, E. (1994) *Language, Identity and Social Division: The Case of Israel*. Oxford, New York: Clarendon Press/Oxford University Press.
Fishman, J.A. (1994) Critiques of language planning: A minority languages perspective. *Journal of Multilingual and Multicultural Development* 15, 91–99.
Hallel, M. and Spolsky, B. (1993) The teaching of additional languages in Israel. *Annual Review of Applied Linguistics* 13, 37–49.
Koplewitz, I. (1992) Arabic in Israel: The sociolinguistic situation on Israel's linguistic minority. *International Journal of the Sociology of Language* 98, 29–66.
Lambert, R.D. (ed.) (1994) *Annals of the American Academy of Political and Social Science: Vol. 532. Foreign Language Policy: An Agenda for Change*. Newbury Park, CA: Sage.

Ministry of Education, Culture and Sport (1995) *Policy for Language Education in Israel* (in Hebrew). Jerusalem, Israel: Office of the Director General.

Ministry of Education, Culture and Sport (1996) *Policy for Language Education in Israel* (in Hebrew). Jerusalem, Israel: Office of the Director-General.

Muchnik, M. (2010) Is it just the *telenovelas*? Learning Spanish in Israeli schools. *Sociolinguistic Studies* 4 (1), 45–62.

Nevo, N. and Olshtain, E. (eds) (2007) *Hebrew Language in the Era of Globalization* (in Hebrew). Jerusalem: Magnes.

Rabin, Ch. (1973) *A Short History of the Jewish Language*. Jerusalem: The Jewish Agency.

Shohamy, E. (1994) Issues in language planning in Israel: Language and ideology. In R.D. Lambert (ed.) *Language Planning Around the World: Contexts and Systematic Change* (pp. 131–142). Washington, DC: National Foreign Language Center.

Shohamy, E. (2008) At what cost? Methods of language revival and protection: Examples from Hebrew. In K. King, N. Schilling-Estes, L. Fogle, J. Lou Jia and B. Soukup (eds) *Sustaining Linguistic Diversity: Endangered and Minority Languages and Language Varieties* (pp. 205–218). Washington, DC: Georgetown University Press.

Spolsky, B. (1996) Prologomena to an Israeli language policy. In T. Hickey and J. Williams (eds) *Language, Education and Society in a Changing World* (pp. 46–53). Clevedon: Multilingual Matters.

Spolsky, B. (2004) *Language Policy*. Cambridge: Cambridge University Press.

Spolsky, B. and Shohamy, E. (1999) *The Languages of Israel: Policy, Ideology and Practice*. Clevedon: Multilingual Matters.

Stavans, A. and Narkiss, D. (2004) Creating and implementing a language policy in the Israeli educational system: The producers, the product, the consumers, and the market. In C. Hoffman and D. Yetsma (eds) *Trilingualism in Family, School and Community* (pp. 139–165). Clevedon: Multilingual Matters.

Stavans, A. and Goldzweig, G. (2008) Learning Hebrew as a second language by Ethiopian and Russian immigrants in Israel: 'Must' or 'have'. *Israel Studies in Language and Society* 1 (2), 59–85.

Zuckermann, G. (2008) 'Realistic prescriptivism': The Academy of the Hebrew Language, its campaign of 'good grammar' and *Lexpionage*, and the native Israeli speakers. *Israel Studies in Language and Society* 1 (1), 135–154.

6 Challenges for the Estonian Language: A Poststructuralist Perspective

Delaney Michael Skerrett

Introduction

This chapter examines the specific challenges faced as part of the process of promoting Estonian as the language of wider societal, interethnic use in Estonia. These challenges are largely a result of the Soviet occupation and the ensuing ethnolinguistic divide and tensions that came about following independence. Although these social and historical contingencies have led to diverging perspectives on the status of Soviet-era Russian-speaking immigrants and their need to speak Estonian, as we will see, there is certainly evidence of a growing rapprochement between the two major ethnolinguistic groups, opening the way towards a more integrated and open society based on a new common language – Estonian. I assess the Estonian case from a poststructuralist perspective, arguing that there are sound ethical reasons to continue Estonian-based integration efforts but that more attention needs to be paid to the specific circumstances that have led to and maintain social inequalities among many of the country's non-ethnic Estonian inhabitants.

Estonia, Estonian, and the Present Sociolinguistic Situation from a Sociohistorical Perspective

Although this chapter deals with challenges for the future of the Estonian language, it is useful to begin with an overview from the sociohistorical perspective (see also Skerrett, 2011c). Indeed, as will become clear, within the kind of poststructuralist framework that I employ, it is essential. Let us begin, however, with an introduction to Estonia and Estonian in order to contextualize this field of research and orientate the reader at this preliminary stage. Estonia is one of the three countries known as the Baltic states, located on the northeastern shore of the Baltic Sea. Latvia and Lithuania, the other two Baltic states, lie to the south of Estonia; to its north is Finland across the Gulf of Finland, to its west Sweden across the Baltic Sea, and directly bordering it to the east, Russia. Estonia is relatively small in terms of population and land area: the estimated number of inhabitants for July 2009 is just short of 1.3 million and the total land area is 43,211 square kilometres, which is slightly larger than either Denmark or the Netherlands (Central Intelligence Agency, 2009a, 2009b, 2009c). Estonia has been an independent country since 1918; however, it was occupied in 1939, and annexed in 1940, by the Soviet Union. The breakup of the Soviet Union in 1991 allowed Estonia to return to sovereignty. The post-Soviet period has seen Estonia forge ever closer ties with the West, including joining both the EU and NATO in 2004 and the Eurozone in 2011.

Estonian, the national language of Estonia, has approximately 1.1 million native speakers, 950,000 of these living in Estonia itself and the remainder elsewhere (Sutrop, 2004). Outside Estonia, the language is spoken by significant populations of ethnic Estonians in Australia, the USA, Canada and Sweden (by exiles from the Soviet occupation and their descendents), as well as Russia (by descendents of economic immigrants from the end of the 19th century) (Viitso, 1998). Estonian is a member of the Finno-Ugric branch of the Uralic family of languages, closely related to Finnish and more distantly to Hungarian (Abondolo, 1998). Although several other Finno-Ugric languages are spoken in Europe, such as Saami in Norway, Sweden, Finland and Russia, Võro in Estonia, and (the now moribund) Livonian in Latvia, Estonian, Finnish, and Hungarian are the only members of the Finno-Ugric branch – indeed, the entire Uralic family – to constitute national languages. Estonian and its Uralic cousins are genetically unrelated to Russian, Latvian, Swedish, English or any of the other Indo-European languages, the largest linguistic grouping in Europe and the world.

The present sociolinguistic environment in Estonia – that is, attitudes towards and use of language across different social groups – has been comprehensively shaped by the events that occurred during the Soviet occupation (Skerrett, 2011c). The inequalities imposed through language in Soviet Estonia are well documented (for a review see Skerrett 2007a, 2007b, 2010b). A major factor influencing language use was the demographic change that occurred during World War II annexation and the ensuing years of occupation.

Misiunas and Taagepera (1993) estimate that in total Estonia lost 25% of its pre-War population through deportations, murder and exile. State-controlled in-migration (industrial workers, functionaries, Soviet military personnel as well as ex-convicts under the so-called 101 km rule, according to which released prisoners could not settle under 100 km from a major city, Leningrad being 101 km from Estonia), combined with (later) personal spontaneous migration to Estonia, resulted in a massive fall in the autochthonous proportion of the population: the native Estonian population fell from 88.2% in 1938 to 74.6% in 1959 and approximately 60% at independence in 1991 (Lieven, 1994). The city of Narva in northeast Estonia re-emerged after the War as exclusively Russian-speaking, due to a combination of migrant-staffed industrialization and other immigration, and the fact that pre-War Estonian inhabitants were prohibited from returning to the area (Kallas, 2004).

The population changes were compounded by the fact that Russian was allowed to co-exist in Estonia and the other non-Russian republics alongside local languages (Skerrett, 2011c). Thus, Russian speakers (or other Slavs such as Ukrainians or Belarusians whose language was not provided outside their home Republic and thus became 'Russian-speaking') had no imperative to learn Estonian. Russian was indeed the lingua franca (language of communication between speakers of different languages) of the Soviet Union. By the 1950s, Communist Party Secretary Khrushchev had already introduced the notion of 'iazyk mezhnatsional'nogo obshcheniia' (language of international communication), and Russian emerged as 'one of [the regime's] strongest hallmarks' (Clachar, 1998: 108). In fact, as Sussex and Cubberley (2006: 575) suggest, Russian was promoted as 'more of a second native language than a *lingua franca*'. Estonian lost many basic functions and a definite hierarchy emerged: 'in many everyday situations, the Balts [sic] were forced to speak Russian [....] The result was [...] the superior position of the Russian language' (Nørgaard *et al.*, 1996: 178). As Adrey (2005: 458) states,

> Russian was the exclusive dominant language in official spheres, i.e. state government, transport, industry, military, and in highly qualified employments and higher education, while Estonian [...] essentially channelled informal social communication.

There was a prevailing mindset in many Russian speakers, furthermore, that they had 'a human right to be monolingual no matter where they live[d] and work[ed] [in the Soviet Union]' (Karklins, 1994: 158). According to the census of 1989, only 14.9% of non-Estonians could speak Estonian fluently (Kolstø, 1996).

Estonia was declared the official language of the Estonian Soviet Socialist Republic in 1989, before independence in 1991 (Galbreath, 2005). This initial language law allowed for parallel use of Russian in public administration and made no reference to usage in private spheres (Adrey, 2005; Galbreath, 2005; Järve, 2002). Post-independence, the law was modified to require employees in both public and private sectors to speak Estonian, although pressure from the Organisation for Security and Cooperation in Europe (OSCE) and the EU saw that most requirements for Estonian proficiency in the private sector were dropped (Kelley, 2004; Ozolins, 2003). This resulted in Estonian language planners producing a list of occupations for which it was considered that knowledge of Estonian was of 'legitimate public interest' (Ozolins, 2003: 223) and there are public health and safety-related proficiency requirements for those dealing with the public, but there is no *general* requirement for private sector service staff (Kelley, 2004). Indeed, in majority Russian-speaking areas in parts of Tallinn and the Ida-Virumaa county in the northeast, it may be impossible to get by only in Estonian. There is also variation by employment sector; industry, for example, is often still heavily Russified, whereas agriculture tends to function solely in Estonian (Hogan-Brun *et al.*, 2007). Public servants are required to know Estonian, but those that were employed prior to the switchover were given a period to gain proficiency. Again, however, it is possible to come across public employees (tram drivers, for example) with very limited command of the language and certain public institutions, such as the corrections system, function primarily in Russian (Hogan-Brun *et al.*, 2007). Estonian is the only language of the parliament (Ozolins, 2003).

There were plans to transfer all Russia medium secondary schools to Estonian by 2003, which was later reduced to 60% of subjects taught and postponed initially to 2007 (Adrey, 2005; Asser *et al.*, 2002) and later to 2011 (Skerrett, 2011c). Estonia can be contrasted in this sense to Latvia, which implemented similar plans at the outset, amid much controversy. Nevertheless, the proportion of students studying in Estonian-medium schools has been increasing gradually (from 72% in 1999 to 78% in 2006, which compares with 28% and 20%, respectively, in Russia medium schools), driven by the overall decline in the number of Russian speakers (see below) and the increase in preference for Estonian-medium education among non-ethnic Estonians. Presently, approximately one-sixth of Russian-speaking students are studying in Estonian-medium schools (Lauristin *et al.*, 2008). State-sponsored higher education degrees are available only in Estonian. However, students from Russia medium secondary schools are able to attend a transitional language course to prepare them for university studies (Hogan-Brun *et al.*, 2007). Without doubt, the most far-reaching change to language policy in the post-Soviet period is the requirement for Soviet-era immigrants to naturalize in order to obtain citizenship, one of the requirements of the process being a basic knowledge of Estonian (Skerrett, 2011b, 2011c). According to the 2000 census (Statistics Estonia, n.d.), the proportion of Russian speakers that were able to speak Estonian was 38.9%. Although this represents a 159% increase since independence, so Estonianization had therefore been reasonably successful, language policy had not brought about a full switchover to an Estonian-speaking society (Skerrett, 2011b, 2011c).

Language Policy and Planning in the Poststructuralist Paradigm

Before beginning a discussion of the challenges facing the Estonian language, let us first turn to the theoretical framework and specific model that will inform the discussion: poststructuralism and the historical-structural approach (Tollefson, 1991) respectively. (For a more comprehensive account of critical language policy and the case of Estonia, see Skerrett, 2011c.) A poststructuralist perspective can be characterized by the need to question taken-for-granted categories in order to deconstruct naturalized discourses, or culturally contingent ways of seeing the world that have become regularized or normalized over time. As Mills (2004: 43,45) explains, 'discourses are highly regulated groupings of utterances or statements with internal rules which are specific to discourse itself'; that is, 'statements do not exist in isolation since there is a set of structures which makes those statements make sense and gives them force'. These structures or 'rules delimit the sayable' (Henriques as cited in Mills, 2004: 43), and the Cartesian notion of the fixed and unitary self, capable of fully independent thought or behaviour, is rejected (Francis, 1999; Mills, 2004). The self is, rather, positioned within and constituted by discourse: 'what we think we might want to express is constrained by systems and rules which are in some sense beyond human control', or at least immediate individual control, in that '[t]hese systems are ones which we are not always necessarily aware of' (Mills, 2004: 67,68). If we consider ourselves to be a 'woman', or 'gay' or 'Estonian', it is because discursive structures (in other words available cultural categories) allow us to, not because these are essential characteristics springing from within. As Nietzsche (1968: 17) argues, we need to cease looking 'for the origin [of social phenomena] *behind* the world'.

Foucault (1984: 72,73), a highly influential author in poststructuralist thought, explains 'Truth is a thing of this world: it is *produced* only by virtue of multiple forms of constraint. And it induces regular effects of power. Each society has its regime of truth, its "general politics" of truth: that is, the types of discourse which it accepts and *makes function as true'* (emphasis added). Elsewhere he notes, 'there is no power relation without the correlative constitution of a field of knowledge, nor any knowledge that does not presuppose and constitute at the same time power relations' (Foucault, 1991: 27). Specifically, then, in terms of applied linguistic research, a poststructuralist approach means resisting the temptation to 'decontextualize' linguistic contexts under analysis, that is, taking up the challenge to find 'ways of mapping micro and macro relations' (Pennycook, 2006: 5; Skerrett, 2010a): individual linguistic behaviour (the micro, cf. Tollefson's 'neoclassical approach', below) occurs within and is constituted by the sociohistorical environment (the macro, cf. Tollefson's 'historical-structural' approach, below).

Turning, then, to the specific model for analysing language planning and policy challenges in Estonia, the general analytical framework I employ is that of Tollefson (1991). Broadly poststructuralist (although as a neo-Marxist, not fully so), Tollefson (1991) makes the distinction between, on the one hand, the study of language and its use centred on the individual – in other words, an essentialist approach, in that it diverts attention away from the social, what he refers to as the 'neoclassical' approach – and on the other hand, the sort of analysis that sees the individual as always operating within a network of social and historical relations, what he terms the 'historical-structural' approach (see also Skerrett, 2010a). In the mid-1990s, Ricento and Hornberger (1996) noted that this had been the dominant general framework of analysis in language policy and planning for some 20 years already, having emerged with more socially critically aware trends of postmodernist thought of the period.

There are, however, weaknesses with the model, and Tollefson is not without his critics. Ricento and Hornberger (1996) note that much of the research that Tollefson criticizes for its neoclassical approach in his text, which specifically deals with language policy and planning, does not in fact deal with this field. Nevertheless, what matters is that Tollefson aims to remain immanent (non-positivistic) in his approach to the analysis of linguistic behaviour and, for the most part, succeeds in doing so. In other words, he explains social phenomena through analysis of what is occurring and has occurred *within* the realms of the social, rather than searching for extra-social or extra-cultural (transcendental) explanations. Ricento and Hornberger (1996) also note that the focus on the social in this approach can become 'deterministic, or even circular, leaving little room for human creativity, innovation, or choice' (Ricento & Hornberger, 1996: 407). That is, while it is important to recognize that individual choices cannot ever be seen as completely 'free' (the micro can never occur *outside* the macro), there is nevertheless room for creativity and macro structures do indeed change over time, not least because of individual movement within these structures to prolong, resist or restructure existing ways of interacting with the world. As Shohamy (2006) notes, '[l]anguage policy manifests itself not only through such items as policy documents and test materials but also through the language used [by individuals] in the public space' (p. 133). In this analysis of language practices and planning in Estonia, then, we need to remain mindful of the historical and structural contingencies constraining *and producing* individual behaviour (Foucault, 1978, 1980) as people circulate through the discursive framework, the network of compelling notions, about which language(s) to speak and when. To quote Pennycook (1994: 33), '[t]his is not, therefore, an attempt to find a relationship between the individual or language and society, but rather to suggest that they are inseparably intertwined'.

Challenges for the Estonian Language

Without doubt, the most significant challenging facing the Estonian language is its (non-) usage among the large Russian-speaking population: chiefly, as noted, the Russian, Ukrainians and Belarusians that settled in Estonia during the Soviet period, and their descendents. According to recent figures, ethnic Estonians now constitute 68% of the total population and Russian speakers make up 29% (ethnic Russians 26%) (Asari, 2009). The proportion of non-ethnic Estonians in the population, furthermore, continues to decline, with ethnic Estonians now constituting over 77% of school-aged children (7–16 years of age) (Lauristin *et al.*, 2008). The proportion of non-citizens in the population in 2007 was 16.3%, around half of these individuals (8.5% of the total) being stateless and the majority of the remainder citizens of the Russian Federation having permanent resident status in Estonia (Lauristin *et al.*, 2008). Although non-citizens enjoy most of the social and legal rights enjoyed by citizens, they cannot vote or stand for election, and, as we will see, many suffer from social exclusion due to geographic and linguistic isolation from the rest of the country (Lauristin *et al.*, 2008). Also, despite the fact that procedures have been simplified since independence, approximately 4000 children born in independent Estonia are stateless (Lauristin *et al.*, 2008).

According to Statistics Estonia (Asari, 2009), the immigrant population (foreign-born individuals and Estonian-born individuals with at least one foreign-born parent) in the majority of the country's regions constitutes less than 15% of the total, with the exception of Harjumaa, where Tallinn is located (33% immigrant population), and Ida-Virumaa, bordering Russia in the northeast (63% immigrant population). Taking a look at the regional specificities of Estonian language competence among immigrants, we can see an inverse relationship with the relative concentration of their population: 38% of immigrants in Ida-Virumaa and 69% in Harjumaa can speak Estonian, whereas elsewhere the proportion is 79% or more (Asari, 2009). We can therefore speak of the presence of minorities and related language concerns as regionally specific phenomena in Estonia.

There are identifiable patterns related to the linguistic repertoire of the Estonian population due to post-independence language policy. On the one hand, Russian proficiency among ethnic Estonians has remained reasonably stable. Overall, the proportion of those with at least passive knowledge has increased slightly from 88% in 1987 to 91% in 2007. However, the proportion that are fluent has dropped from 23% to 22%, and, in the youngest age groups, more than half (56%) are not even able to understand Russian (Lauristin et al., 2008). On the other hand, Russian speakers with at least a passive knowledge of Estonian have jumped from 42% in 1987 to 83% in 2007, with the highest level of proficiency among the youngest age cohorts (Lauristin et al., 2008). Proficiency in English has increased in both ethnolinguistic groups during the same period (1987–2007), from 39% to 73% and 20% to 53% for ethnic Estonians and Russian speakers, respectively (at least passive knowledge).

Given that the younger generation of ethnic Estonians cannot get by in Russian, does this mean that it is possible to live daily life with knowledge of Estonian alone? As we have already seen, in Ida-Virumaa, the answer is clearly no, although the relatively low proportion of ethnic Estonians living in the region and therefore also the lesser degree of interethnic contact reduces the potential for communicative difficulties in that particular case. For the country in general, however, we can see evidence at this point in time of pragmatic mixing strategies: 48% of ethnic Estonians and 63% of other ethnicities claim to switch between languages (Lauristin et al., 2008). However, more Russian speakers claim to use only Russian (40% overall and 54% for the oldest age group) compared to ethnic Estonians using only Estonian (30%); 49% of Russian speakers state that it is possible to get by with just Russian (Lauristin et al., 2008). That is, overall, Russian still functions more as a lingua franca than Estonian. The highest proportion of ethnic Estonians who report only using Russian with Russian speakers does not exceed 8% for any age group (it is a mere 1% for the youngest cohort) (Lauristin et al., 2008), however, indicating a definite if somewhat gradual shift to Estonian. Similarly, 45% of youths claim that they only ever use Estonian in interethnic communication (Lauristin et al., 2008).

In particular domains, from 1997 to 2003, we can see an increase in Estonian usage in more informal areas (the following figures indicate having used Estonian in the previous month): with friends and acquaintances 20% to 34% overall and 22% to 47% for Tallinn; with strangers in public places 23% to 38% overall and 29% to 53% for Tallinn; with colleagues or classmates 15% to 22% overall and 13% to 31% for Tallinn; and in night clubs and bars 7% to 22% overall and 12% to 28% for Tallinn (Vihalemm et al., 2004). Thus we can again see that a 'slow but steady' shift towards Estonian in interethnic communication is taking place.

Results from a qualitative study of Russian speakers living in Tallinn (Skerrett, 2011b) suggest a tendency to use Estonian as a default language in public places such as shops and restaurants, at least for bilinguals. However, one interviewee did assert the right to use Russian, even though she knew Estonian: 'sometimes I want to be served in Russian [....] If I go to a place where I know it's a very... you know, high quality' (Skerrett, 2007a: 83). There is also evidence from the study that bilingual Russian speakers see knowledge of Estonian as having clear integrative value: 'I know what is happening around me. Others, they live like in their own small communities, like a small environment. They don't know the language, they don't care about the country [...] But they live poor lives, they have miserable lives' (p. 85). Furthermore, there is a belief in the national language paradigm – that is, that Estonian has a place as the language of Estonia. As one informant noted, '[i]f we go to live in another country we definitely learn the language [...] I think [Estonians] are right. I mean, if some Russian people in Estonia or wherever go to France [...] how would they live without French?' (p. 86). Another stated, '[b]ecause it's very funny, you try to go to Russia [and say] you know now I think that Arabic is better, let's [make] this the state language. What [would] Russians say? You know?' (p. 86).

Lauristin and colleagues (2008) have found that, overall, there is a growing belief among both ethnolinguistic groups that the increasing competence in Estonian among Russian speakers will solve interethnic problems. In 2005, 77% of ethnic Estonians and 64% of Russian speakers agreed with the statement 'If a person knows the Estonian language, there is no difference whether they are ethnically Estonian or not (it is not important whether they belong to another ethnic group)' (Lauristin et al., 2008: 66). Nevertheless, over half (53%) of Russian speakers believe it is possible to get a good job if the individual is 'a capable specialist or [has] good contacts [...] without knowing Estonian' (p. 66). Ethnic Estonians are also aware of this (Lauristin et al., 2008). Thus knowledge of Estonian is useful in employment, but not essential.

Another crucial domain is the media. While one-fifth of Estonia's Russian speakers regularly follow Estonian language media, the lack of high-quality locally produced Russian-language media has constituted a major challenge for integration and thus also Estonian language promotion (Lauristin et al., 2008). Local Russian-language press and radio are popular, but until very recently there have been hardly any Estonian television broadcasts in Russian. Apart from a Latvian-based Baltic version of a Russian national station that broadcasts 20 minutes of Estonian news per day, Estonia's Russian speakers have had to rely on programming from Russia, which comes with its own particular worldview, often contrasting sharply with that of both Estonians and Estonian Russian speakers: 60% of Estonian Russian speakers trust Estonian-produced media and but only 38% trust Moscow-produced media (Lauristin et al., 2008). However, the propensity of Russian media to produce and maintain anti-integrative tendencies among local Russian speakers should not be discounted. A positive recent development has been the establishment of a second state-funded digital television channel (ETV2), which features a greater proportion of Russian-language programming.

The Russian language itself, as it is used in Estonia, is undergoing a set of changes indicative of integration. Specific lexical and morphosyntactic shifts in the direction of Estonian and unique to Estonia have been observed (Verschik, 2004a, 2004b, 2005, 2006, 2007). In the example *stavit' v golovu* from *pähe panema* (*put to the head*, i.e. *put on* [a hat]), Verschik (2007: 91) observes that the construction would be 'impossible in monolingual Russian' and '[f]or a monolingual speaker of Standard Russian [...] the meaning [...] remains opaque'.

Given the increased competence in English for both ethnolinguistic groups and the only partial knowledge of Estonian among Russian speakers (and vice versa), how large is the threat suggested by some theorists (see for example Laitin, 1998) that English will become an interethnic lingua franca? Russian speakers under the age of 30 generally speak both Estonian and English (in addition to Russian), whereas ethnic Estonians speak only English (as well as Estonian); the future lingua franca may thus indeed be either English or Estonian. Overall, 10% of ethnic Estonians and 5% of Russian speakers already claim to use a third language in interethnic communication and 43% of Russian speakers agree that it is 'normal' to use English with ethnic Estonians (Lauristin et al., 2008). Nevertheless, Estonian retains a certain advantage over English, as we saw with the (growing) legitimacy it enjoys as the national language. In the 2000 census, even in Ida-Virumaa, there was not a single city in which competence in English was higher than competence in Estonian; the highest was in Sillamäe, but, even there, the number of people speaking Estonian outnumbered those speaking English by almost two to one (Statistics Estonia, n.d.). An ethnic Estonian informant in an online study (Skerrett, 2011a) recently reported having had to resort to English when dealing by telephone with Narva Hospital, however, and it is clear that particular attention needs to be paid to the language situation in Ida-Virumaa, an issue I revisit below.

One domain in which English is particularly prominent is information technology. Although Estonian-language IT products are available, they are not necessarily used. Amongst ethnic Estonians, 69% report using an English-language operating system; this figure is 62% among Russian speakers (Vihalemm et al., 2004). Ethnic Estonians are more bothered by having to use English-based products (because they are cheaper, for example) than Russian speakers, but the tendency is for younger members of both groups to be more accepting of English-language IT environments (Vihalemm et al., 2004). Nevertheless, Estonian usage is high in the access of online services (75% for ethnic Estonians and 52% for Russian speakers) and in online communication (73% and 29%, respectively) (Vihalemm et al., 2004). In the latter case, however, usage of Russian (64%) and English (35%) is higher among Russian speakers (Vihalemm et al., 2004).

As we have seen, post-independence legislative changes have attempted to integrate Soviet-era immigrants and their descendants to a large extent by increasing their need to know Estonian and hopefully thus to improve their competence in this language. But how successful have integration attempts been, overall? Naturalization rates have slowed since the immediate post-independence period, with a moderate increase following EU accession in 2004, only to be tempered by Estonia's entry into the Schengen Zone, which offered all permanent residents the right to travel visa-free throughout most of Europe, regardless of citizenship status. Thus, the composition of the population according to citizenship is now quite stable, and although most stateless individuals report that they would like to naturalize, few (20%) feel they have the required language skills to take the exam (Lauristin et al., 2008). Given this divide in the population, how do non-ethnic Estonians see themselves? Almost 90% consider themselves to be 'Russian', but the same proportion see themselves as members of the 'Russian-speaking population of Estonia' (Asser et al., 2002: 26). That is, in Estonia, the term 'Russian' does not necessarily mean that the individual identifies with the Russian nationality or the country Russia; the identification may be with the language. Indeed, over one-half of the immigrant population in 2008 stated that their homeland is Estonia, with less than one-quarter naming both Estonia and Russia as their homelands and less than 20% stating Russia alone (Asser et al., 2002). Among the second generation of immigrants, this phenomenon is even more pronounced with almost 80% fully agreeing that Estonia is their homeland (Asser *et al.*, 2002). Asked whether they consider themselves to be part of the 'Estonian nation', 80% of those non-ethnic Estonians with citizenship agreed, as did more than half of stateless individuals (59%) as well as those with citizenship of another country (54%) (Lauristin *et al.*, 2008). Clearly, people can feel that they belong to the nation socially, even if legally they do not. Although the social and linguistic divisions in Estonian society are still quite pronounced, the potential for a more integrated future is high. Over half of the immigrant population 'feels proud of [the] achievements of Estonia' and three-quarters 'part of [...] Estonian society' (Asari, 2009: 28).

It should be recognized, nonetheless, that as integration also requires an effort from ethnic Estonians, negative attitudes towards immigrants hinder its progress, thereby, paradoxically, intensifying challenges for the language. According to a 2007 survey, more ethnic Estonians thought that 'the wider participation of non-Estonians in Estonian politics and economic life' would be negative (34%) than positive (28%) (Lauristin *et al.* 2008: 58). In 2000, less than half of ethnic Estonians thought that non-ethnic Estonians were loyal 'to the Estonian state', with the proportion even decreasing in 2008 (Asari, 2009); the (slight) decrease is probably due to negative reactions to the April 2007 Tallinn street riots by large numbers of Russian-speaking youths protesting the relocation of the Soviet 'unknown soldier' war memorial away from the city centre. Indeed, most integrative indexes have shown negative trends in the aftermath of the riots. Of course, we also need to take into account factors such as Russia's compatriot policy, according to which 'all people with a Russian ethnic background – even the ones who are citizens of other countries – still belong to the sphere of interest of the Russian Federation' (Lauristin *et al.*, 2008: 58). As Lauristin and colleagues (2008) rightly argue, this particular Russian foreign policy does 'Estonian Russians a disservice' (p. 58) by strengthening the divide with ethnic Estonians; it revives painful memories of the Soviet occupation and heighten fears of a recurrence on the part of the Soviet regime's successor. Nevertheless, over half of the immigrant population felt welcome in Estonia in 2008, with just over 20% feeling unwelcome (the remainder being neutral) (Asari, 2009). A 2007 poll found that 29.5% of non-ethnic Estonians regularly experience discrimination, although 25.2% rarely do and 19.9% never do (Lauristin *et al.*, 2008). Any discrimination against minorities is unacceptable but again, and I stress, the potential for a more harmonious and integrated Estonian society is high.

Voting trends in elections are also encouraging. One party in particular, Keskerakond (the Centre Party), has found strong support among those who feel disenfranchised by many of the post-independence (market economy) reforms in Estonia, among ethnic and non-ethnic Estonians alike (Lauristin *et al.*, 2008). Although this party is not popular among many ethnic

Estonians, it has facilitated the greater representation of Russian speakers in local government, where, for example, in 2005, 24 of 63 elected members in Tallinn were Russian-speaking (Lauristin et al., 2008). What is perhaps most reassuring is that the party also helps to bridge the ethnolinguistic divide in the country. As Lauristin and colleagues (2008: 62) observe, the 'desire [of Russian speakers] to distance themselves from ethnic party politics gives us reason to believe that the potential for the development of multiethnic worldview-based parties and a corresponding electorate in Estonia is high [which] is clearly more beneficial to [...] separation along ethnic lines'.

One further and final challenge stemming from the inflexible attitudes of some ethnic Estonians is the purist discourse circulating in policy and planning and other linguistic elite groups. In an interview with the national broadsheet *Postimees* on the annual Estonian 'Mother Tongue Day' in 2008, Urmas Sutrop, Director of the Estonian Language Institute, had this to say in response to the question, 'is the Estonian language viable?':

> Meil räägivad siin näiteks venelased, ukrainlased eesti keelt nii, nagu nad räägivad. Vead hakkavad levima ja võimenduvad. Meie riigi integratsioonipoliitika tulemusena muutub keel tundmatuseni. Keelekaitse seisukohalt on kõige parem, kui integratsiooni ei toimuks—venelased räägiksid oma keelt ja eestlased omavahel eesti keelt, ilma et nad kokku saaks.
> *Translation*: Here we've got, for example, Russians, Ukrainians who speak Estonian their own way. The mistakes will spread and get stronger. As result of our country's integration policy, the language will become unrecognizable. From a language protection perspective, the best thing would be not to have integration – Russians would speak their own language and Estonians would speak Estonian amongst themselves, without dealing with each other. (Filippov, 2008: no page, para 3–4)

It remains unclear how Sutrop envisages ethnic Estonians and Russian speakers avoiding all contact with each other in their daily lives. Propositions such as these only serve to create obstacles for integration and the maintenance and further promotion of Estonian as a language of wider usage; the alternative, as we have seen, is English. Recent proposals for amendments to the language law have also smacked of purism and anti-integrative tendencies. They have included fines for journalists for incorrect use of language in the media (Kruuse, 2009). This particular change is unlikely to come into effect, however, and the proposals have received a substantial amount of criticism (Sulbi, 2009). As Director of the Institute of Estonian Language and Culture at Tallinn University, Mart Rannut observes, '[k]õige nurgakivi on eesti keele staatus, sellega aga uues eelnõus rahul olla ei saa' ('[t]he cornerstone of everything is the status of the Estonian language, that's why I can't be satisfied with the new draft policy') (as cited in Kruuse, 2009: no page, para 5).

Understanding and Confronting the Challenges

With these challenges in mind, how can we conceptualize the case of Estonia within the poststructuralist and historical-structuralist approaches? What, with this critical perspective in mind, can be done to bring about the desired outcomes? And do 'desired outcomes' necessarily mean the continued promotion of the Estonian language? Let us begin with the challenges for the Estonian language within a poststructuralist context.

Why would a proportion of Russian speakers 'choose' to remain unintegrated and not learn – or at least not speak – Estonian, when the language has clear instrumental, economic value in post-Soviet Estonia? The answer lies in how language fits into the sociohistorical structure of the country, and the diverging ways of viewing life among different groups of the population that have emerged from it (Skerrett, 2011c). While, on the whole, Estonians never stopped seeing incorporation into the Soviet Union as an *occupation* and never accepted *Soviet* as a term to denote their nationality (Kõresaar, 2004a, 2004b), Russian speakers tended to see themselves as having (been) moved domestically within the same state and so did not consider themselves immigrants in the traditional sense, and largely accepted the myth of a singular Soviet nation (Fournier, 2002; Kymlicka, 2000). Many did not even know that an independent Estonia had existed (Kõresaar, 2004a; Lauristin, 2004). And for many – especially older– Russian speakers, this framework continues to maintain a certain currency (Sztompka, 2004). The downfall of the Soviet Union brought about a rewriting of history 'showing terror and extermination rather than a workers' paradise' (Sztompka, 2004: 164), a trauma that, according to Sztompka, has had broad repercussions among Russian speakers throughout the post-Soviet space. This is especially true for non-Russian Russian speakers, who were more easily socialized into the Soviet national mentality and whose homeland (the Soviet Union) has now ceased to exist. Thus, for many, the shift to an officially Estonian-only society is discrimination, as it has taken away their right to use their mother tongue in what is to them their home territory. Opportunities for social advancement, as they see it, are denied to them as their language is no longer useful on its own in higher-paying jobs or in the higher education system. This also explains why the seemingly reasonable move by Estonian authorities to relocate a Soviet war monument, mentioned above, resulted in the largest and most violent demonstrations the country has seen since its renewed independence. Even many young Russian speakers saw the move as an insult; despite the fact that they certainly do not have a Soviet identity, Soviet symbols remain part of the discursive environment that they inhabit. They are not Russian, but nor are they (yet) fully admitted into the Estonian national identity construct. They are Estonian-born descendants of Soviet-identified people, and their worldview, understandably, comprises symbols, values and beliefs from the repertoires of both Estonian and Soviet – and, to a lesser extent, present-day Russian – identity constructs. Rather than seeing non-users of Estonian as lazy or unmotivated, we therefore need to understand the particular social and historical contingencies that have brought about the current situation.

Before looking at specific recommendations to address the challenges faced by the Estonian language, let us turn to the question of whether the continued promotion and maintenance of Estonian constitute desired future outcomes. That is, what basis do we have for justifying Estonian language policy and planning activities? From the poststructuralist perspective, we need to be careful not to uncritically accept these efforts as being worthwhile in and of themselves. There are several interrelated reasons for this. First, as Tollefson (1991: 183) maintains, '[l]anguage itself leads neither to equality nor inequality, but instead is a tool to further them'. That is, we need to be alert to inequalities and ways of doing things in and through languages that lead to different forms of domination. From a critical stance, we need to remember that concern and compassion for others should be central in our work (Pennycook, 2006). Second, although as Pennycook (2001, 2006) suggests there is indeed a pronounced humanistic element in a great deal of work in contemporary applied linguistics, including that of Tollefson, from a poststructuralist perspective, we need a more nuanced approach. Much recent work in language policy, including Tollefson's and also, notably, that of Phillipson and Skutnabb-Kangas (Phillipson, 1992; Skutnabb-Kangas, 1998, 2000), takes a rights-based approach to solving social inequalities maintained through linguistic regimes. As Pennycook (2001: 64) contends, however, 'the dichotomizing between the haves and have-nots [of linguistic rights] can obscure social realities far more than they reveal them [...] [T]here is a related tendency to then suggest that those that have rights have full access to all aspects of language, while those without such rights do not.'

As we have seen, in the case of Estonia, the social reality is by no means a simple projection of policy producing a set of haves and have-nots (Pennycook, 2001). There is no clear division between 'A-team, the élites [...] and the B-team, the dominated, ordinary people' (Skutnabb-Kangas, 1998: 16; see also Pennycook, 2001: 64), not only because of the complexities of the power dynamics at play in the country, but also because it is not entirely clear who speaks what 'language' (Verschik, 2004a, 2004b, 2005, 2006, 2007; Zabrodskaja, 2006) (see the discussion, above, of changes to the use of Russian in Estonia and the mixing strategies used in interethnic communication). The concept of an inalienable right belonging to particular groups in perpetuity (generally, what is meant by 'human rights'), furthermore, cannot stand up to critical, poststructuralist analysis. It is speculative to claim that a form of social organization that reduces inequalities under current (social) conditions will also do so under the unpredictable conditions of the future. Furthermore, language rights are based on the premise that there is some underlying, essential characteristic that 'belongs' to a particular internally homogeneous group. The notion of a group, moreover, relies on the existence of shared identities:

> [an] *imagined sameness* [...] *at all times and in all circumstances*; [through the illusion of the group] being, and being able to continue to be, itself and not [...] something else. [Group] identity may be regarded as a fiction, intended to put an orderly pattern and narrative on the actual complexity and multitudinous nature of both psychological and social worlds. (Robbins, 2005: 172)

This is problematic for any study of language in its social context. As Coulmas (2005) contends, traditionally:

> social factors to which linguistic variation was tied—social class, sex, age and ethnicity—were seen as fixed categories that remained stable [...] Variation in language was interpreted as being conditioned by these factors, understood as permanent properties of speakers, and varieties were seen as encoding speaker identities based on social membership. (Coulmas, 2005:178)

What is more, the native speaker – the proof, as it were, of the existence of languages – does not exist as something stable, clear or well defined (Coulmas, 2005). The native speaker, in other words, 'has no real-world referent' (Coulmas, 2005: 172). Language (use) is in a continual state of flux and cannot be claimed to reflect anything constant or essential about its speakers: it is 'a multifunctional variable instrument whose identity is perpetually reconstructed by its users rather than being categorically given' (Coulmas, 2005: 178).

Language, too, just like identity groups, relies on an imagined homogeneity where there is in fact great diversity. It is believed that members of a group speak the same discrete language. Yet, discrete languages are, like groups, problematic simplifications, and thus positivistic constructs. The way language has come to be perceived needs to be understood within a particular social and historical context: that is, there is not necessarily anything inevitable or natural about the way we perceive language. As Williams (1999: 169) suggests, the many presently defined Indo-European languages in Europe have no linguistic basis, suggesting that 'they could well have been limited to three' (presumably, Slavic, Germanic and Romance, with varieties or 'dialects' between and within). The current linguistic divide emerged with the present political map, where '[t]he naming performatively [of nations] called the languages into being' (Makoni & Pennycook, 2007: 10). This discourse of 'national language', where each nation has its own language (usually just one although in some cases more) that 'belongs' to it, has become a dogma of the contemporary world.

The official designation of the separate national languages of Serbian, Montenegrin, Croatian and Bosnian out of what was formerly considered – with some ethnic and cultural qualifications – to be a single language (Serbo-Croatian) in the respective independent states that have emerged from the breakup of Yugoslavia (Sussex & Cubberley, 2006; Wardhaugh, 2006), is a good example of the discursive mechanism of the national language at work. Governments in these states have made deliberate attempts to intensify differences between the varieties (Wardhaugh, 2006). The relationship between Hindi and Urdu in India and Pakistan, respectively, is a similar case (Sussex & Cubberley, 2006). A further example is that of Soviet Moldova. The Cyrillic script was introduced in Moldova after the Soviet takeover in order to affiliate the Romanian (a Romance language) spoken there with Russian and thereby distinguishing the region from Romania itself, which, although communist, was not part of the Soviet Union (Munteanu, 2002; Skvortsova, 2002). In all these cases, language has been *constructed*, through intentional reification and manipulation, to support a nationalistic framework.

Fortunately, all this does not leave us, as linguists, without a field of study, even if we accept 'the conclusion that modern linguistics has been based upon a myth' (Harris, 1990: 45; see also Makoni & Pennycook, 2007: 19) (the myth being the reification of individually definable objects called languages). We still have *language* to research; it is the epistemology that requires refocus, as does that of any discipline reorienting itself towards a poststructuralist awareness. But can there be an argument for maintaining linguistic diversity for its own sake, as many contemporary policy theorists (Harrison, 2007; Martí *et al.*, 2005; Mühlhäusler, 2001; Nettle & Romaine, 2000; Skutnabb-Kangas, 1998, 2000) contend? While there may well be, it should now be clear that I am not advocating a rights-based approach, given that it relies on notions (such as ethnic groups, nations, languages) that can be shown to be fictitious, and is thus, ultimately, inadequate. The same is often true with the ecological approach (Pennycook, 2004; Skerrett, 2010a). I agree with Pennycook (2004: 229) that those that advocate an ecological approach do so with an aim to maintain diversity and the parallel they draw between diminishing biological diversity on the one hand and linguistic diversity on the other, and the threat this trend poses to our existence, is 'seductive'. Nevertheless, as he reminds us, languages are cultural artefacts, not living creatures; if we talk about 'natural' language we exclude the social (and therefore the political) – to pretend that language use exists or could exist in an extra-discursive environment (Bourne, 1988; Pennycook, 2004). Pennycook (2004) locates this danger within the general and continuing positivist tendency in the sciences, hard and soft alike, for modernist essentializing:

> At the same time that a particular social, economic, cultural and political world order is emerging, so too are attempts to biologize the world to match that order, to find biological explanations (either in hard science through DNA modelling or the softer sciences such as evolutionary psychology) for gender relations, sexual orientation, states of mind, ways of being. Language ecology, whether seen as a metaphor or as a relationship between languages and the natural environment, is inevitably tied to this cultural climate to negate the social, cultural and political. (Pennycook, 2004: 220)

As with all grand narratives, the danger is that attention is diverted away from what is actually going on, socially speaking: '[T]he sad irony for language ecology is that while singing the song of diversity and the environment, it unwittingly reproduces the discourses of the natural that have long served dominant articulations of the world'; the approach, thus, 'is ultimately anathema to critical theory' (Pennycook, 2004: 222) and therefore also to poststructuralism.

Returning to the issue of maintaining linguistic diversity, then, if we can only know what our discourses allow us to know, is there an argument that we, with our western (European) knowledge – bound up in western (European) languages – can do without the collected knowledge of other languages and other discourses from around the world? I would contend that we cannot, given the inequality and environmental destruction taking place in the western industrialized world. As Nettle and Romaine (2000), Harrison (2007) and Mühlhäusler (2001) all maintain, many non-western societies were much more adept at living harmoniously with their respective environments, and the knowledge required to maintain such an existence has been transmitted through local varieties of language. Thus, it can be argued that, as linguists, we have a moral imperative to help maintain and promote global linguistic diversity (Skerrett, 2010a, 2011c). That is why I treat linguistics as a social discipline (Hudson, 2001). To try to divorce linguistics from its social milieu is counter-productive and even potentially dangerous (Skerrett, 2010a).

What are some of the specific things that can be done in order to address the challenges facing the Estonian language? And what, importantly, are the alternatives for a more equitable and ethical future in Estonia? Above all, the construct of Estonianness needs to be more flexible and admit more diversity (Skerrett, 2011c). Even the tiny autochthonous Võro language, spoken in the country's southeast, is presently excluded from notions of a genuinely Estonian identity, as this identity is not perceived to be robust enough to support more than one language of its own (K.D. Brown, 2005; Siiner, 2006). As Brown (2005: 84) states, 'the vitality of the nation is expressed through the vitality of the national language. In this ideology there is little room for the study of regional languages'. In this sense, we could say that we need to *queer* what it means to be Estonian (Skerrett, 2011c): although queer theory has its origins in the deconstruction of genders and sexualities, it has useful applications in its ability to deconstruct any identity category (Jagose, 1996). Indeed queer is quintessentially poststructuralist: the queer project denaturalizes the naturalized by locating the discourses that frame human social behaviour. It questions, analyses and critiques the taken-for-granted. Estonianness, like any identity category, and specifically, any nationality or ethnicity, is a social construction. The Estonian identity needs to be inclusive of people of all backgrounds living in the country. More attention (by way of government campaigns, for example) needs to be given to the *reconstruction* of Estonianness through the promotion of solidarity between all residents of Estonia, regardless of ethnicity, by emphasizing the commonalities they share in inhabiting the same physical and, in many ways, social space. At the same time, respect for diversity, promoted through continued minority language maintenance in the case of 'Estonian Russian' and by strengthening revivals efforts of Võro, would, it is hoped, see a queerer, more equitable sense of what it means to be Estonian.

Maintaining global linguistic diversity, in order to maintain a diversity of knowledge systems, does entail some form of language policy in favour of Estonian in Estonia (Skerrett, 2011c). The playing field between Russian and local languages in the constituent republics at the end of the Soviet Union was not equal (N.A. Brown, 2005; Druviete, 1997). Had the occupation not ended when it did, given the prestige and usefulness of Russian under the

Soviet system, linguistic Russification in Estonia might well have prevailed (Lieven, 1994). As has been the case in other postcolonial environments (for a discussion of Estonia as postcolonial, see Račevskis, 2002), promoting the local language has been seen as a tool for preserving local interests in a way that the colonial language cannot (Tollefson, 1991). This promotes Estonia's equality on an international level. Nevertheless, integration and a greater willingness on the part of Russian speakers to speak Estonian can only occur when societal conditions are conducive to these efforts. What is still needed is a more carefully targeted approach to access to public and private services for Russian speakers. In Ida-Virumaa, for example, quality Estonian language education needs to be intensified if the people are to enjoy mobility throughout the whole country. The Estonian Language Development Plan 2011–2017, currently being formulated, will be addressing this issue, but it remains to be seen whether the initiatives will be bold enough. While many services are still widely available in both languages, they may generally be available only in Estonian in the near future, given the eventual mortality of the bilingual ethnic Estonians schooled in the Soviet period. Furthermore, in order to prevent a shift to English as lingua franca, language planners need to create and maintain a discursive environment in which Estonian operates *and is available* as the language of access to social resources throughout the country.

As well as more language learning opportunities for adults in Russian-speaking areas, other ways of strengthening social cohesion include the integration of Estonian- and Russia medium schools; if current trends continue, this may well take place gradually. Additionally, if language acquisition strategies prove unsuccessful, further opportunities to naturalize should be provided for those who can no longer be reasonably expected to learn the language. And finally, greater localized recognition of Russian in some official capacity in Ida-Virumaa would almost certainly improve the sense of belonging and societal trust of Russian speakers living in that region. Although it could be argued that it would be counterproductive, in that it would discourage those people from learning Estonian, I am not advocating any lessening of efforts to increase their competence in Estonian, but rather a decided attempt to strengthen it.

Conclusion

To conclude, I would like to reiterate that I am optimistic about the potential for greater societal integration on the basis of the Estonian language. First, the growing relative proportion of ethnic Estonians in the population will, it is hoped, offset the postcolonial fears and defensive attitudes that many hold (Lauristin et al., 2008). This should also increase the usefulness of the language in the wider Estonian society, further strengthening its status. Improved efforts to teach the language and a growing tendency among younger Russian speakers to see Estonian as the legitimate language of the nation also help to increase the significance of the language.

Second, as we have seen, the foundations for creating a more inclusive Estonia are solid: the majority of Russian speakers feel at home in Estonia and there is great potential for political integration. Nevertheless, further removal of barriers to social and economic advancement, especially in Ida-Virumaa, would help foster a discourse of greater mutual trust and respect. Realistically, however, given the high concentration of Russian speakers, especially in Narva, much of the region will remain functionally monolingual for some time to come; closer attention needs to be paid to the specific needs of the area in order to promote Estonian acquisition, while showing compassion and understanding towards the people involved. The potential for positive outcomes for all residents of Estonia through the Estonian language is high, but we simply cannot ignore the problems of social exclusion and isolation that many people face. That, after all, would do nothing to help overcome the challenges faced by the Estonian people or the language.

References

Abondolo, D. (1998) Introduction. In D. Abondolo (ed.) *The Uralic Languages* (pp. 1–42). London: Routledge.
Adrey, J-B. (2005) Minority language rights before and after the 2004 EU enlargement: The Copenhagen Criteria in the Baltic states. *Journal of Multilingualism and Multicultural Development* 26 (5), 453–468.
Asari, E-M. (2009). Attitudes towards integration in Estonia. In K. Põder (ed.) *Immigrant Population in Estonia* (pp. 12–34). Tallinn: Statistics Estonia.
Asser, H., Pedastsaar, T., Trasberg, K. and Vassilchenko, L. (2002) From monolingual to bilingual Russian schools in Estonia 1993–2000: Problems and perspectives. In M. Lauristin and M. Heidmets (eds) *The Challenge of the Russian Minority: Emerging Multicultural Democracy in Estonia* (pp. 237–254). Tartu: Tartu University Press.
Bourne, J. (1988) 'Natural acquisition' and a 'masked pedagogy'. *Applied Linguistics* 9, 83–99.
Brown, K.D. (2005) Estonian schoolscapes and the marginalization of regional identity in education. *European Education* 37 (3), 78–89.
Brown, N.A. (2005) Language and identity in Belarus. *Language Policy* 4, 311–332.
Central Intelligence Agency (2009a) Denmark, accessed 15 April 2009. https://www.cia.gov/library/publications/the-world-factbook/geos/en.html
Central Intelligence Agency (2009b) Estonia, accessed 15 April 2009. https://www.cia.gov/library/publications/the-world-factbook/geos/en.html
Central Intelligence Agency (2009c) Netherlands, accessed 15 April 2009. https://www.cia.gov/library/publications/the-world-factbook/geos/en.html

Clachar, A. (1998) Differential effects of linguistic imperialism on second language learning: Americanisation in Puerto Rico versus Russification in Estonia. *International Journal of Bilingual Education and Bilingualism* 1 (2), 100–118.

Coulmas, F. (2005) *Sociolinguistics: The Study of Speakers' Choices*. Cambridge: Cambridge University Press.

Druviete, I. (1997) Linguistic human rights in the Baltic states. *International Journal of Sociology of Language* 127, 161–185.

Filippov, M. (2008) Urmas Sutrop: Eesti keele suurim vaenlane on integratsioon (Urmas Sutrop: Integration is the Estonian language's biggest enemy). *Postimees*, http://www.postimees.ee/140308/esileht/siseuudised/317528.php

Foucault, M. (1978) *The History of Sexuality: Volume 1. An Introduction* (R. Hurley, trans.). London: Penguin.

Foucault, M. (1980) *Power/Knowledge: Selected Interviews and Other Writings 1972–1977*. New York: Pantheon.

Foucault, M. (1984) Truth and power. In P. Rabinow (ed.) *The Foucault Reader* (pp. 67–75). Harmondsworth: Penguin.

Foucault, M. (1991) *Discipline and Punish*. London: Penguin.

Fournier, A. (2002) Mapping identities: Russian resistance to linguistic Ukrainisation in Central and Eastern Ukraine. *Europe–Asia Studies* 54 (3), 415–433.

Francis, B. (1999) Modernist reductionism or post-structuralist relativism: Can we move on? An evaluation of the arguments in relation to feminist educational research. *Gender and Education* 11 (4), 381–393.

Galbreath, D.J. (2005) *Nation-Building and Minority Politics in Post-Socialist States: Interests, Influences and Identities in Estonia and Latvia*. Stuttgart: ibidem-Verlag.

Harris, R. (1990) On redefining linguistics. In H. Davis and T. Taylor (eds) *Redefining Linguistics* (pp. 18–52). London: Routledge.

Harrison, K.D. (2007) *When Languages Die: The Extinction of the World's Languages and the Erosion of Human Knowledge*. New York: Oxford University Press.

Hogan-Brun, G., Ozolins, U., Ramonienė, M. and Rannut, M. (2007) Language politics and practices in the Baltic states. *Current Issues in Language Planning* 8, 469–631.

Hudson, R.A. (2001) *Sociolinguistics* (2nd edn). Cambridge: Cambridge University Press.

Jagose, A. (1996) *Queer Theory*. Carlton South, Australia: Melbourne University Press.

Järve, P. (2002) Two waves of language laws in the Baltic states. *Journal of Baltic Studies* 33 (1), 78–110.

Kallas, K. (2004) The formation of interethnic relations in Soviet Estonia: Host-immigrant relationships. Unpublished MA thesis. Central European University, Budapest.

Karklins, R. (1994) *Ethnopolitics and Transition to Democracy: The Collapse of the USSR and Latvia*. Washington, DC: Woodrow Wilson Center Press.

Kelley, J.G. (2004) *Ethnic Politics in Europe: The Power of Norms and Incentives*. Princeton: Princeton University Press.

Kolstø, P. (1996) The new Russian diaspora – an identity on its own? Possible identity trajectories for Russians in the Former Soviet Republic. *Ethnic and Racial Studies* 19 (3), 610–639.

Kõresaar, E. (2004a) Memory, time, experience, and the gaze of a life stories researcher. In T. Kirss, E. Kõresaar and M. Lauristin (eds) *She Who Remembers Survives: Interpreting Estonian Women's Post-Soviet Life Stories* (pp. 35–61). Tartu, Estonia: Tartu University Press.

Kõresaar, E. (2004b) The notion of rupture in Estonian narrative memory: On the construction of meaning in autobiographical texts on the Stalinist experience. *Ab Imperio* 4, 313–339.

Kruuse, M. (2009) Uus keeleseadus soovib keelekasutust rangemaks muuta (New language law seeks to make language use stricter). *Eesti Päevaleht*, http://www.epl.ee/artikkel/474238
Kymlicka, W. (2000) Estonia's integration policies in a comparative perspective. In A. Laius, I. Proos and I. Pettai (eds) *Estonia's Integration Landscape: From Apathy to Harmony* (pp. 29–57). Tallinn: Jaan Tõnisson Instituut.
Laitin, D.D. (1998) *Identity in Formation: The Russian-Speaking Populations in the Near Abroad*. Ithaca: Cornell University Press.
Lauristin, M. (2004) Lives and ideologies: A sociologist's view on the life stories of two female tractor-drivers. In T. Kirss, E. Kõresaar and M. Lauristin (eds) *She Who Remembers Survives: Interpreting Estonian Women's Post-Soviet Life Stories* (pp. 178–202). Tartu, Estonia: Tartu University Press.
Lauristin, M., Kasearu, K., Trumm, A., Kallas, K., Vihalemm, T., Kalmus, V., Korts, K. and Vihalemm, P. (2008) Non-Estonians as part of Estonian society. In M. Heidmets (ed.) *Estonian Human Development Report 2007* (pp. 46–87). Tallinn: Eesti Koostöö Kogu.
Lieven, A. (1994) *The Baltic Revolution: Estonia, Latvia, Lithuania and the Path to Independence* (2nd edn). New Haven: Yale University Press.
Makoni, S. and Pennycook, A. (2007) Disinventing and reconstituting languages. In S. Makoni and A. Pennycook (eds) *Disinventing and Reconstituting Languages* (pp. 1–41). Clevedon: Multilingual Matters.
Martí, F., Ortega, P., Idiazabal, I., Barreña, A., Juaristi, P., Junyent, C., Uranga, B. and Amorrortu, E. (2005) *Worlds and Worlds: World Languages Review*. Clevedon: Multilingual Matters.
Mills, S. (2004) *Discourse* (2nd edn). London: Routledge.
Misiunas, R.J. and Taagepera, R. (1993) *The Baltic States: Years of Dependence 1940–1990*. Berkeley: University of California Press.
Mühlhäusler, P. (2001) Babel revisited. In P. Mühlhäusler and A. Fill (eds) *The Ecolinguistics Reader: Language, Ecology and Environment* (pp. 159–164). London: Continuum.
Munteanu, I. (2002) Social multipolarity and political violence. In P. Kolstø (ed.) *National Integration and Violent Conflict in Post-Soviet Societies: The Cases of Estonia and Moldova* (pp. 197–231). New York: Rowman & Littlefield.
Nettle, D. and Romaine, S. (2000) *Vanishing Voices: The Extinction of the World's Languages*. Oxford: Oxford University Press.
Nietzsche, F. (1968) *Twilight of the Idols and the Anti-Christ*. Harmondsworth: Penguin.
Nørgaard, O., Hindsgaul, D., Johannsen, L. and Willumsen, H. (1996) *The Baltic States after Independence*. Cheltenham: Edward Elgar.
Ozolins, U. (2003) The impact of European Union accession upon language policy in the Baltic states. *Language Policy* 2, 217–238.
Pennycook, A. (1994) *The Cultural Politics of English as an International Language*. Harlow: Longman.
Pennycook, A. (2001) *Critical Applied Linguistics: A Critical Introduction*. Mahwah, NJ: Lawrence Erlbaum Associates.
Pennycook, A. (2004) Language policy and the ecological turn. *Language Policy* 3, 213–239.
Pennycook, A. (2006) Critical applied linguistics. In A. Davies and C. Elder (eds) *The Handbook of Applied Linguistics* (pp. 784–807). Malden, MA: Blackwell.
Phillipson, R. (1992) *Linguistic Imperialism*. Oxford: Oxford University Press.
Račevskis, K. (2002) Towards a postcolonial perspective on the Baltic states. *Journal of Baltic Studies* 33 (1), 37–56.

Ricento, T. and Hornberger, N.H. (1996) Unpeeling the onion: Language planning and policy and the ELT professional. *TESOL Quarterly* 30 (3), 401–427.

Robbins, K. (2005) Identity. In T. Bennett, L. Grossberg and M. Morris (eds) *New Keywords: A Revised Vocabulary of Culture and Society* (pp. 172–175). Malden, MA: Blackwell.

Shohamy, E. (2006) *Language Policy: Hidden Agendas and New Approaches*. Milton Park: Routledge.

Siiner, M. (2006) Planning language practice: A sociolinguistic analysis of language policy in post-communist Estonia. *Language Policy* 5, 161–186.

Skerrett, D.M. (2007a) *From Nationalism to Normalisation: A Sociolinguistic Analysis of the History of Language Policy in Estonia*. Master's thesis, University of Tartu.

Skerrett, D.M. (2007b) La represión de lenguas nacionales bajo el autoritarismo en el siglo XX: Los casos de Estonia y Cataluña (The repression of languages under authoritarianism in the 20th century: The cases of Estonia and Catalonia). *Revista de Llengua i Dret (Journal of Language and Law)* 48, 251–311.

Skerrett, D.M. (2010a) Can the Sapir–Whorf Hypothesis save the planet? Lessons from cross-cultural psychology for critical language policy. *Current Issues in Language Planning* 11, 331–340.

Skerrett, D.M. (2010b) Language and authoritarianism in the 20th century: The cases of Estonia and Catalonia. *Eesti Rakenduslingvistika Ühingu Aastaraamat (Estonian Papers in Applied Linguistics)* 6, 261–276.

Skerrett, D.M. (2011a) Suhtlemine Eestis eesti keeles (Communicating in Estonian in Estonia). http://keelepoliitika.blogspot.com/

Skerrett, D.M. (2011b) How normal is normalization? The discourses shaping Finnish- and Russian-speakers' attitudes towards Estonian language policy. *Journal of Baltic Studies* 43 (3), 1–26.

Skerrett, D.M. (2011c) Languages and lives through a critical eye: The case of Estonia. *Critical Inquiry in Language Studies* 8 (3), 236–260.

Skutnabb-Kangas, T. (1998) Human rights and language wrongs: A future for diversity? *Language Sciences* 20 (1), 5–27.

Skutnabb-Kangas, T. (2000) *Linguistic Genocide in Education: Or Worldwide Diversity and Human Rights?* Mahwah, NJ: Lawrence Erlbaum Associates.

Skvortsova, A. (2002) The cultural and social makeup of Moldova: A bipolar or dispersed society? In P. Kolstø (ed.) *National Integration and Violent Conflict in Post-Soviet Societies: The Cases of Estonia and Moldova* (pp. 159–196). New York: Rowman & Littlefield.

Statistics Estonia (n.d.) Statistical database. http://stat.ee/

Sulbi, R. (2009) Uus keeleseadus ajakirjanduskeelt reguleerima ei hakka (New language law will not regulate language in the press). *Postimees*, http://www.postimees.ee/?id = 169100

Sussex, R. and Cubberley, P. (2006) *The Slavic Languages*. Cambridge: Cambridge University Press.

Sutrop, U. (2004) *Estonian Language*. Tallinn: The Estonian Institute.

Sztompka, P. (2004) The trauma of social change: A case of postcommunist societies. In J.C. Alexander, R. Eyerman, B. Giesen, N.J. Smelser and P. Sztompka (eds) *Cultural Trauma and Collective Identity* (pp. 155–195). Berkeley: University of California Press.

Tollefson, J.W. (1991) *Planning Language, Planning Inequality: Language Policy in the Community*. Harlow: Longman.

Verschik, A. (2004a) Aspects of Russian–Estonian codeswitching: Research perspectives. *International Journal of Bilingualism* 8 (4), 427–448.

Verschik, A. (2004b) Estonian compound nouns and their equivalents in the local variety of Russian. *Scando-Slavica* 50 (1), 93–109.
Verschik, A. (2005) Russian–Estonian language contacts, linguistic creativity, and convergence: New rules in the making. *Multilingua* 24, 413–429.
Verschik, A. (2006) Convergence in Estonia's Russian: Directional vs. static vs. separative verb. *International Journal of Bilingualism* 10 (4), 383–404.
Verschik, A. (2007) Multiple language contact in Tallinn: Transfer B2 > A1 or B1 > A2? *The International Journal of Bilingual Education and Bilingualism* 10 (1), 80–103.
Vihalemm, T., Masso, A. and Vihalemm, P. (2004) Eesti kujunev keeleruum. In V. Kalmus, M. Lauristin and P. Pruulman-Vengerfeldt (eds) *Eesti elavik 21. sajandil algul: ülevaade uurimuse Mina. Maailm. Meedia tulemustest* (pp. 57–73). Tartu: Tartu Ülikooli Kirjastus.
Viitso, T-R. (1998) Estonian. In D. Abondolo (ed.) *The Uralic Languages* (pp. 115–148). London: Routledge.
Wardhaugh, R. (2006) *An Introduction to Sociolinguistics* (5th edn). Malden, MA: Blackwell.
Williams, G. (1999) Sociology. In J.A. Fishman (ed.) *Handbook of Language and Ethnic Identity* (pp. 164–180). New York: Oxford University Press.
Zabrodskaja, A. (2006) Eestivene keel(evariant): kas samm segakoodi poole? (Estonian (variety of) Russian: A step towards a mixed code?). *Keel ja kirjandus (Language and Literature)* 9, 736–750.

7 A Small National Language and its Multilingual Challenges: The Case of Latvian

Uldis Ozolins

Introduction and Theoretical Basis

The Baltic language of Latvian is spoken as a first language by just over one million speakers, largely in Latvia but with a scattering of speakers around the world, principally in Europe, North America and Australia. Almost 500,000 people speak it as a second language, with varying degrees of proficiency.

With this number of speakers, Latvian is roughly the 250th largest language in the world (Latvia State Language Agency, 2005: 21). As one of the official languages of the EU, a highly developed literary language, and a language with official status in its nation, the future of Latvian – like neighbouring Estonian and Lithuanian – would appear to be secure. Particularly interesting is that fact that Latvian has not only gained (or more precisely regained) official status for itself through the law, but has also succeeded in increasing the number of people who speak it as a second language, an unusual example of a small language spreading as a lingua franca among speakers of much larger languages.

At the same time, the past, and particularly the recent Soviet past, places constraints upon the spread of Latvian throughout its territory and in all linguistic domains. During the Soviet period hundreds of thousands of Soviet settlers were brought to Latvia, as in the case of Estonia, but were taught nothing about Latvia, its history or culture, and were never encouraged to learn the local language (Agarin, 2010). While, as we shall see, many have now accepted Latvian and are in many cases proficient in the language, there are significant exceptions, and language attitudes from the Soviet period continue to be held.

Moreover, these constraints are not only a relic of the Soviet past but are actively exploited by Russia in seeking to exercise its influence over former Soviet citizens living in what it sees as its 'near abroad'. As a consequence, European organizations have also been drawn into appraisals of Baltic language and citizenship policies.

In the midst of these political pressures, Latvian also needs to be developed as a language, in particular to cope with technological change and European administrative and cultural developments, while also paying attention to its own diversity in terms of regional and dialectical variations. The emphasis on the conflicts between Latvian and Russian has tended to overshadow these other linguistic considerations, and while this chapter pays particular attention to this central issue, it also looks more broadly at other challenges facing the Latvian language today.

Three theoretical perspectives are of particular relevance to the Baltic situation. Bratt Paulston *et al.* (2007) usefully analysed the situation of minorities such as Russians in the Baltic States or Hungarians in Romania as *extrinsic minorities*, minorities that differ from other historical minorities in that they hark back either to a previous era of domination, or to a view of themselves as culturally superior to the host society. Historical examples abound, such as the disposition of many German-speaking minorities in Eastern European countries before World War II. A signal benchmark for such extrinsic minorities is their very high levels of language maintenance and very low rates of assimilation into the host society: 'the norm amongst extrinsic minorities is language maintenance with very slow shift, if at all' (Bratt Paulston *et al.*, 2007: 385). This characterization of the large immigration wave to the Baltic states during the Soviet period is appropriate; however, in the case of Latvia, the attempts to encourage the large extrinsic majority to learn the local language have met with considerable success, but this has been accomplished not with any expectations of shift, but rather the addition of Latvian as L2 in individual repertoires.

The work of Skutnabb-Kangas (1994) adds the dimension of language hierarchy to the notion of extrinsic minorities. She specifically argues that the Soviet period in the Baltic States brought about a paradoxical language situation:

> Russian is thus a majorized minority language (a minority language in terms of numbers, but with the power of a majority language), whereas

the Baltic languages are minorized majority languages (majority languages, in need of protection usually necessary for the threatened minority languages). (quoted in Hogan-Brun et al., 2007: 594)

This characteristic of an extrinsic language gaining such power is typical of colonial or postcolonial situations, and this is how the Baltic states define the period of Soviet occupation and its imposed language hierarchy (Račevskis, 2002).

Rindler Schjerve (2006) has usefully warned against trying to transfer understandings of Western European regional minority languages into the new Eastern European scene. Analysing the need to create new research and policy paradigms in Europe for minority languages, not least because of recent EU expansion, she points out that in Western Europe there are many minority languages that are autochthonous to a particular region or country, but in Eastern Europe most minority languages are the languages of neighbouring states, adding a degree of political complexity to their status:

> For example, three-quarters of the minorities in the New Member States have kin-states and most of these states are also neighbouring countries. (Rindler Schjerve, 2006: 113)

Although some of these Eastern European minorities are in border areas, many are not concentrated in a particular region but are widely scattered, and often heavily represented in major cities. Yet, beyond these demographic differences, Rindler Schjerve also draws attention to the very complex variations of identities that occurred in Eastern Europe, noting

> the shifting and multiple ethnic identities which are common in both the old and especially the new Member States. Data on declared language use and ethnicity in the new Member States where several states have been created or re-created since the 1990s show that ethnic identity and group membership may rapidly shift under the pressure of socio-political changes. This raises the question of as to whether the traditional sociolinguistic concept of linguistic minorities as social groups defined solely on the basis of a common origin and language can be upheld any longer. (Rindler Schjerve, 2006)

Forces of globalization, political pressure from neighbouring countries, widespread use of a lingua franca, the contentious naming of minorities and languages, the claiming of minority status, and attempts at transnational norm enforcement in respect of minorities all create a complex environment in

Eastern Europe, in which the future of the Latvian language needs to be carefully analysed.

However, despite the seeming universality of conflict in such settings, Rindler Schjerve's analysis takes a different path: she argues that the previous sociolinguistic emphasis on language contact, with the presupposition that contact always means conflict, is in fact false in many instances. EU policy now recognizes and encourages linguistic diversity, and many minority language situations are dealt with harmoniously, citing the Catalan example where 'conflict is no longer of interest to Catalan sociolinguistics since the political context of Catalan has moved towards normalisation with the increasing spread of the language' (Rindler Schjerve, 2006: 111). As we shall see, the language situation in Baltic countries is in many aspects a harmonious one, despite political rhetoric to the contrary.

The Latvian Language and its Baltic Context

Latvian is a Baltic language, closely related to Lithuanian. They are the sole survivors of a Baltic language group that included Old Prussian and other related but now extinct languages. They have also been partially influenced by contact with Germanic, Slavic and Finno-Ugric languages. In the case of Latvian, the influence of other language groups is apparent in the following areas:

- word stress (stress on the first syllable, taken from Finno-Ugric);
- grammar (in some aspects similar to Slavic languages, e.g. with a highly active genitive); and
- the numerous loanwords (from all contact languages).

Despite the linguistic similarity between Latvian and Lithuanian, Latvia's sociopolitical history has gone hand-in-hand with that of Estonia over the past 800 years. Known from Antiquity for its amber trade, the Baltic region came to the attention of Western Europe mainly from the 12th century onwards, when, as the result of the unsuccessful Holy War in Palestine, the religious orders looked to the Baltic region as the last non-Christian area in Europe. After finally adopting Christianity, Lithuania, in federation with Poland, built a considerable empire of its own in the 15th to 18th centuries, but the territories of Latvia and Estonia were colonized. The largely German Order of the Sword founded Riga in 1201 and soon controlled most of the territory of present-day Latvia. The Crusaders swiftly abandoned their roles as churchmen and formed a self-appointed landed aristocracy, ruling as the

Livonian Order, introducing serfdom and dominating the countryside until World War I. Meanwhile, the city-based burghers began a flourishing trade as part of the Hanseatic League, of which both Riga and Tallinn were important members, and dominated the cities – and their linguistic hierarchy – again until World War I. The rule of the feudal Livonian Order came to an end in the 16th century, to be succeeded by Swedish rule in the 17th century and by Peter the Great's Russian Empire from the beginning of the 18th century until 1917. During all these regime changes, however, the Germans largely retained their privileges, becoming the 'Tsar's Loyal Germans' who maintained their favoured status under the authoritarian Russian regime (Henricksson, 1983).

Latvian was a peasant language during this long period of German rule, although some German pastors and academics (most notably Herder) recorded the language or folklore and used it to philosophize about nations' cultures. Limited education in the mother tongue was introduced in Swedish times and vernacular literacy spread steadily, but anyone desiring advancement needed to pass as a German. The middle of the 19th century brought a classic Gellnerian national awakening, with the production of the first substantial literary works, a growing awareness of a Latvian identity, and the spread of education in Latvian (Clemens, 1991; Gellner, 1983).

Towards the end of the 19th century, the Russification project of the Tsarist Empire for the first time imposed some constraints on German dominance and limited the use of both the German and Latvian languages, and an intriguing three-way tussle between Russian, German and Latvian influences developed. However, the linguistic scene was not so much a contest between languages as a great mixing and vibrant multinational atmosphere with German, Russian, Latvian, Jewish and other international influences, particularly in *fin de siècle* Riga, which had become an important economic centre. With its outstanding *Jugendstil* architecture, highly literate population and mixing of social groups, Riga embraced modernity and became an international metropolis. Those promoting the Latvian language, given greater status after the 1905 revolution, saw Latvian as a potentially thriving, modern language that could take on a major role in a future Latvian state.

In the confusion of the end of World War I, with both Germany and Russia among the vanquished and the Bolshevik revolution changing all previous allegiances, the three Baltic States – Estonia, Latvia and Lithuania – declared their independence. In this first period of independence (1918–1940) the Latvian language became, for the first time, the dominant official language of its territory.

Latvia has always had a more mixed population than its two Baltic neighbours, and the interwar period saw the Latvian language increase its status and scope, but not necessarily at the expense of other languages.

Latvians constituted around 75% of the population, with sizeable Russian, German, Jewish, Polish and other minorities. Both German and Russian continued to be widely spoken and understood, and English and French were widely learnt. Unlike Estonia and Lithuania, Latvia at this time did not enshrine Latvian in its constitution; however, legislation passed in the 1920s required, among other things, that civil servants (many of whom had been appointed during the Tsarist era) should be fluent in Latvian (Latvia State Language Commission, 2008: 13).

Three features of language policy during this first period of independence (1918–1940) deserve attention:

- *Latvian as an official language.* Although it was not explicitly declared as the country's official language in the constitution, Latvian expanded rapidly in all public and social spheres. As an example, it had become the main language of teaching at the University of Latvia by the end of the 1920s, although extensive use was made of scientific literature in Russian, German, English and French.
- *Latvia, like Estonia, as a forerunner in minority language policy.* The Versailles Peace talks and the rules of the League of Nations demanded that the newly independent Eastern European countries formulate minority policies. These policies were implemented in the Baltic States, often much better than in the rest of Eastern Europe. The policy of cultural autonomy allowed minorities to establish their own schools with state support, and several leading German minority representatives in Latvia and in Estonia were instrumental in establishing the Conference of Nationalities in 1925, a regular meeting of minority representatives from Eastern Europe, until taken over by Nazi Germany in the 1930s to promote its own political objectives (Hiden, 2004; Loeber, 1993).
- *Strengthening of the status of Latvian after 1934.* A bloodless coup in 1934 brought to power a mild authoritarian regime that did a great deal to strengthen the legislative basis of Latvian and particularly to spread Latvian as the language of education, while maintaining essential aspects of the previous policy of cultural autonomy for minorities (Latvia State Language Commission, 2008: 14).

The period of independence ended with the signing of the Molotov–Ribbentrop pact in August 1939, when Germany and the Soviet Union divided Eastern Europe into their spheres of influence, allowing Hitler a free hand to start war with Poland. The Baltic States were incorporated into the Soviet Union, an incorporation never recognized by Western powers, and suffered three occupations in quick succession – by the Soviet

Union (1940–1941), by Germany (1941–1944) and by the Soviet Union again (1944–1991).

The Soviet Period and its Enduring Legacy

The Soviet period brought a radical realignment of language policy and linguistic hierarchy, caused not only by Soviet ideology, but materially influenced by the huge influx of Soviet-period settlers who were never encouraged to learn the local languages. Figure 7.1 shows this radical demographic transformation.

Soviet language policy showed a continual tension between the Leninist principle of equality of all languages of the nations of the Soviet Union (Russian did not have official status until – ironically – Gorbachev's time), and the Stalinist and Brezhnevist support for the spread of Russian at the expense of other languages in the ultimate creation of a *homo sovieticus*. While Latvian had the status of a republican language, Soviet policy brought separate school systems operating in Latvian or in Russian, separate university streams, the ever wider use of Russian in the workplace, and the wider use of Russian in official information and communication. Significantly, no other languages were supported at all. The vast majority of non-Russians who came to Latvia (or to Estonia) during this period and who may have had non-Russian mother tongues were steadily Russified (Agarin, 2010; Knowles, 1989; Kreindler, 1985). What is more, the Baltic States were treated with considerable suspicion as a result of their previous independence and

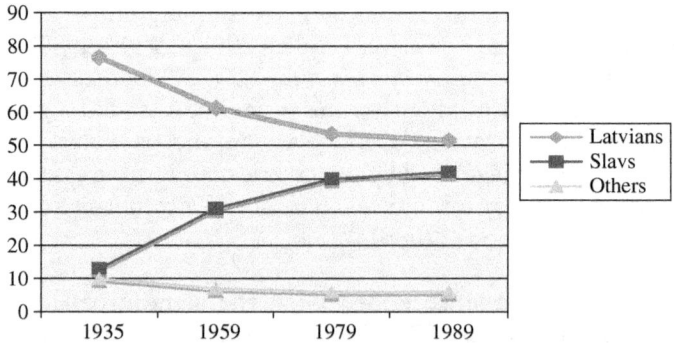

Figure 7.1 Latvia: Changes in national compostion of inhabitants 1935–1989
Source: Census (1935, 1959, 1979, 1989); Latvia State Language Commission (2008: 39).
Slavs: Russian, Ukrainians, Belarusians.
Others: Poles, Lithuanians, Jews, Roma, Germans, Estonians and all other nationalities.

Table 7.1 Non-titulars in the Baltic states claiming proficiency in the titular language

Non-Estonians in Estonia knowing Estonian	15%
Non-Latvians in Latvia knowing Latvian	22%
Non-Lithuanians in Lithuania knowing Lithuanian	35%

Source: Soviet Census (1989).

anti-Soviet attitudes, and publications and activities in the Baltic languages were always closely monitored for alleged nationalist tendencies.

Linguistically, only a small proportion of the Soviet-period settlers ever learnt the local Baltic languages, as shown in the last All-Soviet 1989 Census (Table 7.1). This low level of proficiency of the non-titular populations, and the self-sufficiency of the 'Russian-speaking' population, was in turn to be the major incentive to reverse the direction of language policy from the mid-1980s onwards.

Gorbachev's initiatives of *glasnost* (openness) and *perestroika* (restructuring) were never meant to unleash national forces, but in the non-Russian republics of the Soviet Union this was their unintended consequence. Among the national demands was a reassertion of the importance of republican languages as official languages. In Latvia the desire to promote the native language was also a reaction to demographic trends, as only 52% of the population was now Latvian.

While still part of the Soviet Union, all three Baltic Republic Supreme Soviets passed Language Laws in 1989 that formed the basis of post-independence language policy. Latvian was recognized as the official state language in the territory of the Latvian Socialist Republic. Central to this language policy was a demand that all personnel who had contact with the public, and who had not received education in the Latvian medium school system, should demonstrate a level of proficiency in the language corresponding to their professional status. A limit of three years was given for all such personnel to gain an attestation of their linguistic ability. There was recognition of the need for Russian and other languages during the period of transition until Latvian could achieve its full status in all domains and until competence in Latvian was guaranteed (Latvia State Language Commission, 2008: 47)

These demands, revolutionary in the context of the Soviet system, did not go unopposed. Local pro-Soviet groups backed by Moscow organized a group known as the Interfront to reassert the importance of the integrity of the Soviet Union and the place of Russian, a criticism that has continued in various forms to the present day (Alksnis, 1991; Ramishvili, 1998). However, the policies of the Baltic state have been strongly defended by other international figures (Bildt, 1994).

Just as the Baltic states had gained their independence in the chaos of the end of World War I, they declared their second period of independence in the chaos of the August 1991 anti-Gorbachev putsch in Moscow. One of the few changes to the Constitution in the previous period of independence was to insert a clause stipulating that Latvian was the official state language. The newly recreated Baltic States were faced with overwhelming economic problems and were still occupied by significant Soviet (now Russian) military forces; they had limited experience in foreign relations, and they needed to devise a set of social policies, including language policy, in a demographic situation that was far removed from that of the first period of independence (Karklins, 1994).

In this context, language and citizenship issues came to the fore. In 1992 a series of amendments were made to the 1989 Language Law, declaring an end to a transitional period and beginning a full-scale programme of language attestation, in which hundreds of thousands of employees who had not had a Latvian medium-level education were required to pass tests organized at three levels: the highest level for professionals, managers and public representatives; the second level for those in middle level employment and paraprofessionals (nurses, police officers, clerks and so on); and the lowest level for occupations such as caretakers and manual workers in contact with the public.

Between 1992 and 2000, some 510,000 people were certified at one of the three levels of competence, and around 35,000 have been certified since 2001 (Latvia State Language Commission, 2008: 101). There has also been a steadily growing stream of foreign nationals, employed in Latvia by local or international enterprises, who have also been required to sit the tests. Since 2000 the test has been refined to include six levels, reflecting the European standards of language proficiency, and has been developed with the help of World Bank and EU funds.

An important addition to the attestation process, and one that will see a steady decline in the number of attestations sought, has been the move to make Latvian a compulsory subject in non-Latvian medium schools, and pupils who pass the Latvian examination at the end of primary education (9th grade) and secondary education (12th grade) will be awarded attestation at these respective levels without further testing.

Citizenship

Language was also implicated in the issue of citizenship. Of all the former republics of the Soviet Union, only Estonia and Latvia did not grant automatic citizenship to all residents. Given the proportion of Soviet-period settlers, their limited knowledge of the local national languages and their meagre understanding of the history and culture of local societies, added to the illegality of the occupation of the Baltic states by the Soviet Union since 1940, it was decided that only those who were citizens in 1940 (of whatever nationality) and their descendents could automatically claim Estonian or Latvian citizenship. A naturalization process based on a language and history/constitution test was introduced for non-citizens. This policy again brought heavy criticism from Moscow (Jubulis, 2001).

At the time of independence in Latvia, around 800,000 residents from a total population of 2.5 million were not automatically citizens. After a large-scale emigration of Soviet-period settlers in the early 1990s, the latest figures for January 2011 show just under 325,000 non-citizens still residing in Latvia, constituting around 15% of the population, and around 55,000 persons with other citizenships (mostly Russian) (Latvia Central Statistical Bureau[1]). Just over 135,000 persons have gained citizenship since 1995, when naturalization began, and when the total non-citizen population was around 730,000. So the number of non-citizens in Latvia has almost halved over the past 15 years (Latvia Office of Citizenship and Migration Affairs[2]).

The naturalization tests have seen a pass rate of around 90%. The language part of the examination comprises a 15 minute conversation to assess the candidate's oral Latvian, and a 90 minute written test assessing comprehension of basic written texts including common official communications, and the ability to write a letter in Latvian on an everyday topic. A test in Latvian on the country's history and constitution, which may be taken orally or in written form, complements the language test.[3]

The Language Laws and Related Policy

The period of the mid- to late 1990s and the local and international battles over language policy in the Baltic have given rise to an extensive literature, summarized in Hogan-Brun *et al.* (1997), which is only covered very briefly here. Russia's criticisms of Baltic language and citizenship policies led to a general internationalization of local language issues: European organizations took considerable interest in these issues, especially when the Baltic states applied for membership of a number of European bodies, including the Council of Europe in 1995 and the EU and NATO in 2004.

A leading part was played here by the Organisation for Security and Cooperation in Europe (OSCE), created in Helsinki in 1975 during the Cold War, which continued its activities after the fall of the Iron Curtain. Russia used this as a vehicle to protest against Baltic policy, and the OSCE responded by appointing a High Commission for National Minorities and devised several recommendations on minority policy and minority languages (e.g. OSCE, 1998).

The mid- to late 1990s developed into a continual battle between international organizations pressing their view of minority languages, and the insistence of the Baltic states on their specific needs in language policy. Thus, in contrast to other minority situations where the point of treaties and framework agreements was to allow a wider use of the minority language (e.g. having officials attain fluency in minority languages or using interpreters), in the Baltic the situation was the reverse, because many hundreds of thousands of personnel in public contact did not master the *national* language, in this case Latvian. Moreover, there was a fully operative Russian school system, a vibrant Russian media, close contacts to Russia across the border and wide use of Russian throughout society. At all times the Baltic states resisted the idea of having two official languages, which would have led to a continuation of the linguistic situation of the Soviet era and would have constituted a threat to the national languages (Druviete, 1997).

The Latvian Language Law of 1999, after years of insistent input from the OSCE and others, did eventually make some compromises, particularly by defining more precisely the reasons of public interest for stipulating language requirements in private economic activity, rather than the catch-all earlier provision according to which all those in public contact must have competence in the national language. Other compromises occurred as a result of further lobbying or court actions, including deleting reference to language proficiency for publicly elected representatives, and removing language restrictions on private electronic media. For an outline of this 1999 Language Act and the ensuing debate, see Latvia State Language Commission (2008), Ozolins (1999, 2003) and Hogan-Brun *et al.* (2007).

This use of international instruments to impose language policy on nations has sparked considerable debate. The work of the OSCE has been staunchly defended in some quarters (Zaagman, 1999). However, by examining particular cases studies of the OSCE in the Balkans and elsewhere, Deets (2002) presented a strong critique of the unintended consequences of human rights approaches, suggesting that they often increase ethnic tensions rather than leading to their amelioration. Meanwhile Chinn and Truex (1996) have defended Baltic restrictions on citizenship, while Johns (2003) has highlighted the insistence of the EU on imposing minority policies on Eastern Europe that EU countries do not follow themselves. Wee (2007) has argued that the notion of linguistic human rights has an explicit aim of prioritizing or protecting minority monolingualism, an orientation often at odds with actual language usage or indeed the interests of minorities, while Agarin

(2010), by contrast, has analysed the refusal of the Baltic States to grant citizenship to all (and recognize language rights) as a limitation to democratization in these countries. De Varennes (1995–1996) criticizes the Baltic states for not adhering to international norms, but a more cautious view of the legitimate reach of international instruments is given by Dunbar (2001).

Despite compromises, the 1999 Language Law continued the emphasis of its 1989 and 1992 forerunners, and the central feature remains the requirement that certain occupations demonstrate a specific level of proficiency in Latvian. Significantly, language *use* between individuals is not monitored by these laws (i.e. what language individuals speak to each other), but personnel who deal with the general public must be able to certify their competence. There have also been restrictions on public signs (Latvian always needing to be the only or larger language displayed), which have led to a remarkable change of the streetscape and the 'decyrillization' of the environment.

The Present Status of Latvian and Other Languages

By the end of the millennium, Latvian had recovered to a great extent its former status as the national language, albeit in a difficult, largely bilingual context where Russian was part of a much larger market, particularly as far as the media, sales of goods and services and economic activity were concerned. This uneven situation is demonstrated by Druviete (1998) in a classification (Table 7.2) of the breakdown by domain of the use of Latvian, Russian and English.

A few comments on Table 7.2 are necessary. First, in education since the 1990s there has been a significant decline in the proportion of children attending Russian medium schools. In the mid-1980s, just over 40% of pupils attended Latvian medium schools and the majority attended Russian medium schools. Since independence, this proportion has been reversed: in 1998/1999, 64.95% of pupils attended Latvian medium schools, rising to 73.54% in 2008/2009, with the proportion attending Russian medium schools dropping from 34.71% to 25.83%.[4] This change was initially the result of the emigration of Russian and Soviet-period settlers, but many non-Latvians now willingly send their children to Latvian medium schools, and Russian medium schools have now almost ceased to exist in smaller provincial towns and the countryside, and are concentrated only in the major cities. In the following we look at concerns over the language of instruction in universities, where again the position of Latvian has been considerably strengthened, although more instruction is also now given in English.

Table 7.2 Use of language by sociolinguistic domains and institutions in Latvia

Domain/institution	Latvian	Russian	English
Parliament	****	—	—
Government	****	—	—
Military	***	*	—
Police	**	**	—
Municipalities	****	—	—
Public transport	**	**	—
Public services	**	**	—
Health	**	**	—
Science	**	*	***
Universities	***	**	**
Secondary education	**	**	—
Primary education	**	**	—
Radio/television	**	**	—
Press	**	**	—
Information	***	*	*
Religion	**	**	—
Public sector	***	*	*
Private sector	*	***	—
International affairs	—	*	****
Office administration	***	*	*

Source: Druviete (1998: 124) (original in French, translated by the author).
Note: No. of stars indicates relative use of a language in a domain, from * = some use to **** = preponderant use. '–' indicates the language is not used or is used very insignificantly.

Another aspect of Latvian education policy is the attempt to go beyond the Latvian/Russian language difference to promote the use of *other* languages spoken by residents. Support has been provided for a small number of schools teaching in Ukrainian, Polish or other languages. This is a deliberate attempt to recognize linguistic diversity, and to counter the view that all non-Latvians must be 'Russian speakers'.

Finally, Druviete's table highlights the difference in language hierarchy in the private economic sphere, where Russian continues to dominate as the language of work and business. This is particularly so in the many businesses run by non-citizens, although, as we will see below, this domain too is slowly changing.

In some other domains, Latvian has nevertheless regained its prominence. For instance, there has been a substantial improvement in the proportion of books published in Latvian. In the 1980s less than half of all books published in Latvia were in Latvian, but by 2007 Latvian language books constituted some 85% of all books published (Latvia State Language Commission, 2008: 266). Latvian literature, much sought after by the people during the Soviet era, but in short supply, still attracts an avid readership today. However, the profile of translated foreign literature has changed, with the once total domination of translation from Russian now declining to just over 10%, with translations from German contributing the same proportion, and about two-thirds of all translations into Latvian now being from English texts (Latvia State Language Commission, 2008: 268).

The area of broadcasting media is undergoing considerable turmoil as a result of the global financial crisis. Two public television channels in Latvia broadcast in Latvian, but with occasional material in Russian. Non-Latvian material is generally subtitled in Latvian. A number of private television channels broadcast in Russian, and more Russian programmes are widely available through satellite and cable television; it is here that the market force of Russian is seen at its strongest, with Latvian programmes struggling to present the quality and diversity of the copious Russian material. Latvian public radio has three Latvian stations and one Russian station, and dozens of private stations broadcast in either language.

In other electronic media, Latvian is often included in software development, but its place is not guaranteed:

> Latvian versions of the popular Microsoft Windows and Microsoft Office programmes are available to users in Latvia. And most of the mobile phones available in Latvia have Latvian interfaces or commands and messages. However, the Latvian software versions are a pleasant surprise rather than the norm. (Latvia State Language Commission, 2008: 348)

The need to ensure adequate Latvian software is a constant challenge, and here the alternative is not so much media in Russian as in globalized English. The growing use of English is also highlighted by Porina in her sociolinguistic study, pointing to the changing linguistic profile of a younger Latvian generation:

> A generation shift is occurring since the younger generation (under 15 yr.-olds) no longer has the same command of Russian as the parents. This generation, on account of the internet and other cultural phenomena, is au fait with English which is perceived as a threat to Latvian language purity by the parents since English to a large extent is foreign to them. (Porina, 2009: 185)

Present Language Proficiency, Practices and Attitudes

The present state of the Latvian language is best captured in two publications available in English – *Break-out of Latvian* (Latvia State Language Commission, 2888) and a study available on the internet by the Baltic Institute of Social Sciences, *Language. Report March–April 2008*.[5]

The State Language Commission report gives an historical and contemporary account of the state of Latvian, paying particular attention to the inadequacies in current attempts to strengthen the place of Latvian, and carefully outlining what it sees as the enduring threats to the language.

The historical shifts in language usage, and the increasing knowledge of Latvian among minorities in contemporary Latvia, is well illustrated in Figure 7.2, which traces the Latvian language environment through census years 1935 to 2000 and shows the now declining proportion of minorities without a command of Latvian.

Among the report's most interesting features are its descriptions of the way in which the language hierarchy of Latvian and Russia is changing, illustrated most graphically by the changing demographics of Latvians who know Russian or Russians who know Latvian. Compared with the situation during the Soviet era, when non-titulars were far less likely to know Latvian and Latvians far more likely to know Russian, we are now witnessing the emergence of a younger generation of Russians who know Latvian. This trend reflects changes in school and the public use of Latvian, as illustrated in Figure 7.3.

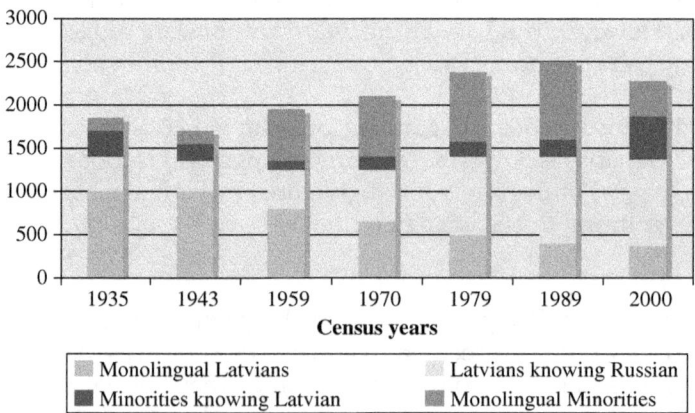

Figure 7.2 Latvian language environment 1935–2000
Source: Latvia State Language Commission (2008: 188).

A Small National Language and its Multilingual Challenges   145

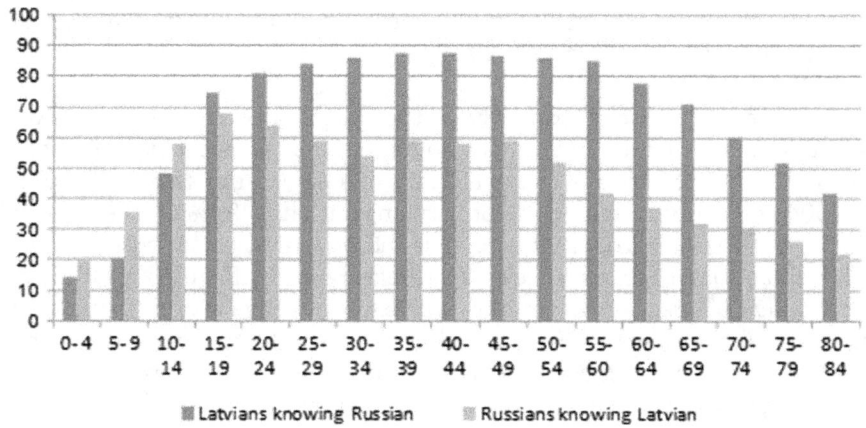

Figure 7.3 Latvians knowing Russian and Russians knowing Latvian, by age group
Source: Latvian census (2000), Latvia State Language Commission (2008: 193).

There has also been more extensive use of Latvian in all public domains, but the Commission is still worried by a much more limited spread of Latvian in the private economic sector and the still dominant place of Russian in many business enterprises as well as in daily life. In many cases, survey results can be read to support a variety of positions. A 2004 survey of the usage of Latvian, for example, asking respondents to assess how much Latvian was used in their place of residence compared to five years previously, found that 53.7% of respondents reported that Latvian was now used more frequently; however, in Riga respondents said that Latvian was used *less* frequently than before (Latvia State Language Commission, 2008: 230).

Several particular concerns over the future of Latvian are expressed in the report. One is that the compromises that Latvia was forced to include in its Language Law by European organizations have undermined the ability to strengthen the position of Latvian, particularly in the private economic sector (Latvia State Language Commission, 2008: 78). A second concern is related more to internal language attitudes – the tendency of Latvians to use Russian when speaking to Russians, even if those Russians know Latvian, which is a clear legacy of the Soviet period (Porina, 2009). The sociolinguist Druviete points to the ambiguous consequences of such a stance:

> The passivity of Latvians in their choice of the language of communication, on the one hand, attests to the linguistic and ethnic tolerance and decreases the possibilities of language conflicts, but on the other hand, it

is a real threat for social integration on the basis of Latvian. (Latvia State Language Commission, 2008: 252)

Third, the report looks explicitly at the question of endangerment, and argues that 'There is no unanimous opinion in the Latvian society about the endangerment to Latvian.' (Latvia State Language Commission, 2008: 255). A 2004 poll showed that 43.9% of Latvians but only 19.1% of Russians and 23.2% of Others consider that Latvian is endangered by some other language. The report does make reference to the threats posed by English – particularly in the areas of science and banking, where it is ousting Latvian (Latvia State Language Commission, 2008: 214) – but it is the still often dominant role of Russian that is of most concern. This concern underlies the insistence that there not be two official languages in Latvia, for

> the fear of the fulfilment of the prediction made by the ethnically Russian mayor of Riga in 2009, that Latvian is bound to disappear in two or three generations if Latvia is to have two official languages. (Porina, 2009: 186)

We will return to this mayor's activities below. The 2008 survey by the Baltic Institute of Social Sciences (BISS) replicates studies conducted since 1996, and thus gives us a unique time series of reported use and attitudes towards various languages over more than a decade. It is on the whole a more positive and less threat-concerned view than the State Language Commission's study, but it is eager to point to the complex dynamics of the language situation. Overall, it stresses the great gains that Latvian has made in securing its status:

> Generally evaluating the dynamics of survey results, a series of positive changes which indicate that the status of the Latvian language is firming up among minority populations should be noted: the skills in state language have improved, the public environment in which Latvian is spoken has expanded, and attitudes towards the speaking of Latvian have improved. (BISS, 2008: 8)

The study outlines many pieces of evidence to support this view:

- The first is the increasing salience and stability of Latvian. 'Almost everyone in Latvia says that the status of the Latvian language is stable and widely recognised. 97% of respondents say that it is important for each and every resident of Latvia to speak the Latvian language', and this

view is held by almost 100% of Latvians and 94% of Russians (BISS, 2008: 15).
- Over the decade, the proportion of Russians who speak only Russian at work has declined from 60% to 28%, while the proportion who speak mostly Latvian has increased from 9% to 32%. The percentage speaking only Russian in shops and on the street has declined a little less – from 40% in 1996 to 31% in 2008. BISS comments that 'The decline of self-sufficiency of minority language can be regarded as significant proof of consolidation of the status of the majority language' (BISS, 2008: 10).
- There is also a broad consensus on the importance of Russian, and in fact the surveys have shown that this view has increased since the late 1990s (BISS, 2008: 15).
- There is also recognition of the importance of English, with nearly 80% of both Latvians and Russians saying it is important to know English (BISS, 2008: 15).

The report gives us very useful statistics on the proficiency in Latvian of those with another mother tongue, breaking it down into proficiency levels that are well understood in the Latvian context as the basis of language attestation. Table 7.3 clearly shows the dramatic fall in those who know no Latvian at all, from 78% in 1989 – a remarkable reduction in two decades.

There are two final items in this report that deserve comment, which are again two sides of the distinctive linguistic tolerance that obtains in Latvia. The first is tolerance from the non-titular side: the survey not only finds positive attitudes towards Latvian among non-Latvians, as shown in similar surveys for many years now, but shows this acceptance of its status even with regard to what are seen as very politically controversial issues. On the issue of secondary school reform, for instance, when in Russian and other

Table 7.3 Changing proficiency in Latvian of persons whose mother tongue is not Latvian

	Level of proficiency claimed			
	Highest (%)	Intermediate (%)	Lowest (%)	Do not know Latvian (%)
June 1996	9	27	44	22
April 2008	26	31	36	7

Source: BISS (2008: 22).

minority stream schools the curriculum was changed in 2004 to a 60:40 balance between Latvian and the other language, a very vocal campaign by some Russian activists who opposed the reform and threatened to boycott the schools was launched. However, this was ignored by the mass of Russian respondents (Galbreath & Galvin, 2005; Hogan-Brun, 2006). The report reflects the strongly divided views of the Russians, but majority support for the reform (Table 7.4).

These results confirm what other authors have also noted – the very fractured nature of the Russian community, with a wide diversity of views, but certainly no majority rejection of Latvian language policy (e.g. Romanov, 2000). Here, a majority of Russian and Other respondents support teaching in Latvian in minority schools, while a sizeable minority of Russians (but far fewer Others) do not support this view.

The second item in the report, as in the State Language Commission report, is the mention of the paradox of linguistic tolerance; this time, it seems to apply to both Latvians and non-Latvians:

> On the one hand, these data indicate competition among languages, because people feel that it is important to speak both languages. On the other hand, data suggest that there are now greater tolerance towards languages, as in both ethnolinguistic groups people are more likely to recognise the importance of the other language. The increase of tolerance towards other languages is indicated also by other data of this survey. For example, the number of respondents admitting that they speak Latvian heartily and with pleasure has increased during the last few years, while the number of people feeling negative emotions while speaking Latvian has decreased. (BISS, 2008: 15)

Table 7.4 What is your attitude towards the teaching of subjects in Latvian in minority schools?

Native language	Do not support at all	Rather do not support	Rather support	Fully support	Hard to say/ not interested
Latvian	1	3	26	69	4
Russian	14	19	31	26	12
Other	—	16	27	47	11
All	6	9	26	52	7

Source: BISS (2008: 50).
Note: By native language (%).

Neglected Issues in Latvian Language Policy

As mentioned previously, the focus on the Latvian–Russian situation has overshadowed other language issues, testifying to the salience of political issues in determining language policy priorities. The issue of Latvian variation and regional varieties, a strong field in historical Latvian linguistics, and even maintained strongly during the Soviet period, has very much receded into the background. An example is the situation of Latgalian, spoken in Latgale in southeastern Latvia; this is recognized as a literary variation of Latvian, and has few resources devoted to its maintenance and cultivation. Currently, there are no schools teaching in Latgalian, and publication in the language is limited. Once more this is an issue mixed up in the Latvian–Russian situation, as Latgale is the part of the country with the highest proportion of Russians. Indeed, the number of Latvian medium schools and institutions fell there during the Soviet period, and re-establishing a Latvian presence has been a priority since 1991. Thus, although Latgalians constitute around one-sixth of the Latvian population, it is only recently that publications and academic conferences have again raised the importance of teaching and maintaining the language (*Mercator Newletter 27*, 2006; Rezekne University, 2008).

By contrast, the Livs, a Finno-Ugric autochthonous group with fewer than a dozen native speakers, are also recognized in the Constitution and have received considerable official interest and visible support. Wicherkiewicz (2009) refers to the distinction between 'welcome' and 'unwelcome' minorities that some countries have resorted to in order to avoid demands from larger minority populations. Instead, symbolic support is given to small, historical and virtually extinct communities that will make few demands for resources or action. Wicherkiewicz (2009) sees a specific instance of this in relation to Latgalian and other regional vernaculars in Latvia. In this way, the interests of even sizeable language minorities may be continually overlooked in favour of the broader political position on the one hand and symbolic attention to chosen minorities on the other.

The Political Challenge of Russian to the Future of Latvian

The continuing challenges to Latvian, as we have outlined, are both political and sociolinguistic. Like its Baltic neighbours, Latvia is committed to an active language policy to both defend its language and extend its use.

The document prepared by the State Language Agency (2005) *Guidelines of the State Language Policy for 2005–2014*,[6] while written largely in a neutral bureaucratic style, does give striking insights into future issues and possible conflicts and their resolution around the language issue. The document takes potential threats to Latvian seriously, and places them in a global context:

> Multilingualism, global systems of information exchange, tendencies of economic integration in the modern world are causing even greater competition of languages and may threaten even languages with relatively high number of speakers. (Latvia State Language Agency, 2005: 19)

The document thus argues strongly that a laissez-faire attitude to language issues would place all small languages at the mercy of the few very large languages that are economically significant:

> Two very big languages are the chief competitors for the Latvian language in the market of languages – Russian and English, both having a very high economic value. The free market principle in the relationships between languages would strengthen even more the positions of these languages in the language situation of Latvia. The only opportunity is to consistently raise the economic value of the Latvian language through a deliberate, purposefully created language policy, also using a legal compensation mechanism in parallel. (Latvia State Language Agency, 2005: 22)

Yet, discussion of market or legal mechanisms cannot take attention away from the overtly political ends that are also being pursued in relation to language policy in Latvia. We have seen the political mobilization around language issues on the part of the Latvian titular population, and mentioned only in passing the responses of those opposing the status of Latvian and supporting the status of Russian as it was during the Soviet era. This opposition to Latvian has taken many, but until recently largely inchoate forms. Romanov (2000) cites the lack of direction and general inability to clearly focus on the language question on the part of the Russian population and their unwillingness to mobilize on this issue. As the studies cited above have shown, there is a marked increase in the capacity in Latvian of the non-titular population, yet paradoxically this has come while there has been a heightened political push to promote Russian. Russian-based political parties have steadily increased their salience in Latvian national and regional politics over the past decade, helped by support from an increased number of naturalized citizens. The largest Russian party, the Harmony Centre (Saskanas centrs), became the largest single party in Parliament in the 2011 elections, and was the largest party in several cities including the capital Riga. In order to also appeal to Latvian voters, it adopted a policy of supporting Latvian as the only official language, but this policy was to be challenged by the events of 2011–2012.

In 2011 a small group of Russian activists, of radical national Bolshevik persuasion, launched a campaign to make Russian the second official language of Latvia through the constitutional process of a referendum. Holding such a referendum needed two rounds of signature-gathering, a process that was going slowly for the proponents until Riga mayor Nils Usakovs (a Russian who was until then popular with both Russian and Latvian electorates) decided to sign up for the referendum. This mobilized a large number of his supporters to then come forward, but he was clearly going against his own party's policy. He argued that the referendum was not about language so much as about self-respect.[7] His action led to a split in his own party, and brought heated debate on language issues to the fore. The proposal to make Russian the second official language never stood a chance of being accepted if voters turned out in any numbers to vote, and this they did. In the referendum on 18 February 2012 it was defeated with:

> 821,722 or 74.8 percent opposed to the motion making Russian the second official state language in Latvia. In favor of the motion were 273, 347 or 24.88 percent of citizens.[8]

The repercussions of the referendum are difficult to assess. The pro vote in some regions of Latvia (particularly in the eastern Latgale and some large cities) will no doubt increase the push for Russian to be recognized as a local regional language and given greater status, although this has been strongly resisted until now. The crush of no votes, however, shows that language is a core element in the Latvian culture and the nation's self-image: the referendum drew a high participation rate (71%) and had a galvanizing effect upon many Latvian politicians who had tended to ignore language issues or who believed the signatures would not be gathered to hold such a referendum. For many this was a clear demonstration of cross-border attempted manipulation of Latvian internal affairs. The Baltic States – as well as many prominent Russians – have often seen the language and citizenship issues as largely foreign affairs matters with Russia, as much as any local issue.[9]

Against this political background, the *Guidelines of the State Language Policy for 2005–2014* might seem to be living in a parallel universe, when they reiterate that the Latvian language is the basis of integration of Latvian society, and predict that Latvian will grow in importance as the number of its speakers and learners rises. While the figures in the referendum would seem to point to a deeply divided society, all other evidence points to this not being the case. As all surveys show, language relations are largely harmonious, with no communal antagonism over the issue, whatever the arguments of politicians, on any side. This pattern of conflict with Moscow but relatively peaceful relations with the Russian population is likely to hold, and recriminations or point-scoring after the referendum have been largely absent.

The *Guidelines* set out not unambitious goals for the next decade:

> The state language policy program is being developed to guarantee the linguistic quality and competitiveness of the Latvian language, to ensure the functioning of the state language, to preserve, protect and develop the traditional environment of the language, to foster the comprehensive study of language and to promote scientifically grounded standardization of literary language and codification of norms. (Latvia State Language Agency, 2005: 20)

The EU's concerns for linguistic diversity and maintaining European languages, as illustrated in its Charter of Fundamental Rights and the Vienna Guidelines, are referred to as the rationale for this policy, at a time when Latvian is just beginning to take its place as an official EU language, with all the attendant language infrastructure needs that this has created.

The heart of the policy is contained in eight 'Directions of action':

5.1 Guaranteeing the legal status of the state language
5.2 Popularization of the need for proficiency in the Latvian language
5.3 Improvement of quality of education in Latvian
5.4 Promotion of acquisition and improvement of the Latvian language in the Latvian diaspora
5.5 Scientific study, cultivation and development of the state language
5.6 Ensuring linguistic aspects for Latvia's integration into the EU
5.7 Ensuring the participation of society in the implementation of the state language policy
5.8 Creative development of the Latvian language and cultivation of the language culture by means of literature and art

The direction 'guaranteeing the legal status of the state language' indicates clearly that the legal and political issues that have come to a head several times in Baltic language policy will not disappear, as the referendum shows. Other than the referendum, since 2005 the legal-political issues have included the following:

- Repeated moves, endorsed by the Cabinet, to increase the number of professions and occupations that deal with the public and that must demonstrate an appropriate level of competence in Latvian.
- In a few instances, changing political fortunes at local government level have brought to power local councils that have pressed for the wider administrative use of Russian in their area. Moves of this kind may well become stronger, although none have so far succeeded in gaining exemption from the Language Law, which states that Latvian is the language of administration (even though Russian may be widely used in face-to-face contact).
- There can also be incentives to cater for the larger linguistic market. A signal example was the campaign in 2008–2009 by a number of Latvia's universities (currently the country has around 60 universities and colleges, public and private) to relax Latvia's language laws to enable universities to offer programmes in Russian to attract fee-paying Russian-speaking international students, a campaign that the government finally did not support. Such incentives may become more alluring if the financial crisis continues and institutions scramble to attract income.

The reform of secondary education in non-Latvian stream schools mentioned above, which foresees a 60:40 division of the curriculum into Latvian and other languages, has certainly strengthened the third stipulated direction, 'Improvement of the quality of education of the Latvian language'. Now, however, the threat comes from another source. The financial crisis of 2008 hit Latvia particularly hard, leading to cutbacks in teachers' salaries, deterioration of the school infrastructure, and a trimming of adult education classes in Latvian attended by those studying for attestation tests. The downturn in the funding of education is matched by even more severe cuts in cultural and arts budgets, placing in jeopardy several of the other directions mentioned, including the scientific study of language and literary and artistic projects that depend upon state budgets.

Finale: Accomplishments and Threats

As this overview of the Latvian situation has shown, the past, particularly the Soviet past, is very much part of the present language situation and still constrains future change. Nonetheless, Latvia has been successful in reasserting the status of its national language, and has doggedly pursued the aim of integrating society on the basis of Latvian in a sometimes hostile international environment, combating local political opportunism, and in spite of the sometimes ambiguous language attitudes among the population.

The future of the Latvian language will thus depend *externally* on

- avoiding a deterioration in the political relationship with Russia;
- Latvia's ability to negotiate and maintain its interests in relation to international organizations (mainly European) regarding issues of language policy, citizenship, human rights and related matters;
- reasonable international assistance in the financial crisis;

and *internally* on
- the continuing recruitment of new Latvians as L2 speakers through the continued growth of the use of Latvian in non-Latvian school systems and wider use of Latvian in society;
- the continual refinement of Latvian language capacity requirements as defined in the Language Act, the interplay between linguistic tolerance and the insistence on Latvian language capacity and its use in critical domains, particularly in employment and in the private economic sector;
- avoiding polarizing politics based on ethnicity or language.

The long struggle to build Latvian into a literary and state language in a relentlessly multilingual environment has come to fruition, but it is a situation that still faces threats. Success or otherwise will be measured by the extent to which the country achieves stable, continuing and harmonious multilingualism, with a leading role for Latvian in its territory.

Notes

(1) See http://data.csb.gov.lv/
(2) See http://www.pmlp.gov.lv/en/statistics/citizen.html
(3) See http://www.pmlp.gov.lv/en/Citizenship/Naturalizacija.html
(4) See http://izm.izm.gov.lv/registri-statistika/statistika-vispareja/3334.html
(5) See www.bszi.lv
(6) See http://www.valoda.lv/index.php?option = com_attachments&task = download &id = 482&lang = en
(7) 'Usakovs pulls an about-face', http://www.baltictimes.com/news/articles/29933/, 9 November 2011.
(8) 'Latvians rejected making Russian an official language', http://www.baltictimes.com/news/articles/30618/, 20 February 2012.
(9) Language referendum in Latvia initiated by Russian secret services – Russian human rights activists...', http://www.baltictimes.com/news/articles/30610/, 16 February 2012.

References

Agarin, T. (2010) *A Cat's Lick. Democratisation and Minority Communities in the Post-Soviet Baltic.* Amsterdam: Rodopi.
Alksnis, V. (1991) Suffering from self-determination. *Foreign Policy* 84, 61–71.
Baltic Institute of Social Sciences (BISS) (2008) *Language. Report March–April 2008.* http://www.bszi.lv.
Bildt, C. (1994) The Baltic litmus test. *Foreign Affairs* 73 (5), 72–85.
Bratt Paulston, C., Haragos, S., Lifrieri Verónic, L. and Martelle, W. (2007) Some thoughts on extrinsic linguistic minorities. *Journal of Multilingual & Multicultural Development* 28 (5), 385–399.
Chinn, J. and Truex, I.A. (1996) The question of citizenship in the Baltic. *Journal of Democracy* 7 (1), 133–147.
Clemens, W. (1991) *Baltic Independence and the Russian Empire.* New York: St. Martin's.
Deets, T. (2002) Reconsidering East European minority policy: Liberal theory and European norms. *East European Politics and Societies* 16 (1), 30–54.
de Varennes, F. (1995–1996) The protection of linguistic minorities in Europe and human rights: Possible solutions to ethnic conflicts? *Columbia Journal of European Law* 2 (1), 107–143.
Druviete, I. (1997) Linguistic human rights in the Baltic States. *International Journal of the Sociology of Language* 127, 161–186.
Druviete, I. (1998) La situation sociolinguistique de la langue lettone. *Terminogramme,* numéro hors série, juillet. Gouvernement du Quebec, Office de la langue française, 105–149.
Dunbar, R. (2001) Minority language rights in international law. *International and Comparative Law Quarterly* 50, 90–120.
Galbreath, D.J. and Galvin, M.E. (2005) The titularization of Latvian secondary schools: The historical legacy of soviet policy implementation. *Journal of Baltic Studies* 36 (4), 449–466.
Gellner, E. (1983) *Nations and Nationalism.* Oxford: Blackwell.
Henricksson, A. (1983) *The Czar's Loyal Germans.* Boulder: East European Monographs.
Hiden, J. (2004) *Defender of Minorities: Paul Schiemann, 1876–1944.* London: Hurst & Company.
Hogan-Brun, G. (2006) At the interface of language ideology and practice: The public discourse surrounding the 2004 education reform in Latvia. *Language Policy* 5 (2), 313–333.
Hogan-Brun, G., Ozolins, U., Ramoniene, M. and Rannut, M. (2007) Language politics and practices in the Baltic States. *Current Issues in Language Planning* 8 (4), 469–631. (Also in Kaplan, R.B and Baldauf, R.B. (eds) (2008) *Language Planning and Policy in Europe* (Vol. 3). Clevedon: Multilingual Matters.)
Johns, M. (2003) 'Do as I say, not as I do': The European Union, Eastern Europe and minority rights. *East European Politics and Society* 17 (4), 682–699.
Jubulis, M.A. (2001) *Nationalism and Democratic Transition: The Politics of Citizenship and Language in Post-Soviet Latvia.* Lanham: University Press of America.
Karklins, R. (1994) *Ethnopolitics and Transition to Democracy. The Collapse of the USSR and Latvia.* Washington: Woodrow Wilson Center Press; London: John Hopkins University Press.
Knowles, F. (1989) Language planning in the Soviet Baltic republics: An analysis of demographic and sociological trends. In M. Kirkwood (ed.) *Language Planning in the Soviet Union* (pp. 145–173). London: Macmillan.

Latvia State Language Agency (2005) *Guidelines of the State Language Policy for 2005-2014.* http://www.valoda.lv/index.php?option = com_attachments&task = download&id =482&lang=en.
Latvia State Language Commission (2008) *Break-out of Latvian.* Riga: Zinatne.
Kreindler, I. (ed.) (1985) *Sociolinguistic Perspectives on Soviet National Languages.* Berlin: Mouton de Gruyter.
Loeber, D.A. (1993) Language rights in independent Estonia, Latvia and Lithuania, 1918–1940. In S. Vilfan (ed.) *Ethnic Groups and Language Rights* (pp. 221–249). Aldershot: Dartmouth.
Mercator Newsletter 27 (2006) International Conference 'Ethnicity in Europe: Sociopolitical and Cultural Processes' held in Rezekne, Latgalia/Latvia 24–26 May 2007. http://www.mercator-central.org/newsletter/newsletter27.htm
OSCE (1998) *The Oslo Recommendations Regarding the Linguistic Rights of National Minorities & Explanatory Note.* The Hague: Foundation on Inter-ethnic Relations.
Ozolins, U. (1999) Between Russian and European hegemony: Current language policy in the Baltic States. In S. Wright (ed.) *Language Policy and Language Issues in the Successor States of the Former USSR* (pp. 6–47). Clevedon: Multilingual Matters. (Also in *Current Issues in Language and Society* 6 (1).)
Ozolins, U. (2003) The impact of European accession upon language policy in the Baltic states. *Language Policy* 2, 217–238.
Porina, V. (2009) *Valsts Valoda Daudzvalodīgajā Sabiedrībā: Individuālais un Sociālais Bilingvisms Latvijā.* [The State Language in Mulltilingual Society: Individual and Social Bilingualism in Latvia.] Riga: Latvian Language Institute, University of Latvia.
Račevskis, K. (2002) Towards a postcolonial perspective on the Baltic States. *Journal of Baltic Studies* 33 (1), 37–56.
Ramishvili, T. (1998) Latvia and Estonia: Human rights violations in the center of Europe. *International Affairs* 44 (4), 116–127.
Rezekne University (2008) *Ethnicity in Europe: Sociopolitical and Cultural Processes. Proceedings of the International Scientific Conference.* Rezekne, Latvia.
Rindler Schjerve, R. (2006) Regional minority language research in Europe – a call for a change in perspectives. *Sociolinguistica* 20, 105–120.
Romanov, A. (2000) The Russian diaspora in Latvia and Estonia: Predicting language outcomes. *Journal of Multilingual and Multicultural Development* 21 (1), 58–71.
Skutnabb-Kangas, T. (1994) Linguistic human rights in education. *Language Policy in the Baltic States. Conference Papers.* Riga: Gara pupa.
Wee, L. (2007) Linguistic human rights and mobility. *Journal of Multilingual and Multicultural Development* 28 (4), 325–338.
Wicherkiewicz, T. (2009) Welcome and unwelcome minority languages. In S. Pertot, M.S. Tom, T.M.S Priestly and C. Williams (eds) *Rights, Promotion and Integration Issues for Minority Languages in Europe* (pp.181–188). Basingstoke: Palgrave Macmillan.
Zaagman, R. (1999) *Conflict Prevention in the Baltic States: The OSCE High Commissioner on National Minorities in Estonia, Latvia and Lithuania.* European Centre for Minority issues. Flensburg: ECMI, Monograph #1.

8 Is Catalan a Medium-Sized Language Community Too?

Emili Boix-Fuster and
Jaume Farràs i Farràs

Introduction

Catalan-speaking territories (including speakers of what is officially designated Valencian) have more than 13 million inhabitants and they represent a socially advanced area, dominated by the service sector, particularly tourism. Their culture is built on a rich heritage steeped in centuries of tradition. The Catalan language, which is a Romance tongue, was codified in the Middle Ages, when it served as the court language of the Crown of Aragon, and began to develop a rich and diverse literature across most literary genres. After a period of decadence from the 16th to the 19th centuries, the Catalan language started to recover in the 19th century and has been remarkably fruitful in the 20th century, in spite of the obstacles posed by Spanish dictatorships and centralizing tendencies, which have besieged it and continue to besiege it (Gustà & Santamaria, 2007). Catalan culture not only draws on a vast literary tradition, but also on a broad dialogue with other cultures, classical and modern, through a determined effort to produce translations.[1]

Catalan is spoken in an area measuring 68,000 square kilometres. From a demographic and linguistic perspective, there is no doubt that the number of Catalan speakers and the numbers of individuals who know Catalan together qualify the Catalan-speaking community as a medium-sized community. With between 5000 and 5800 languages spoken around the world (http://www.ethnologue.com/), Catalan ranks 88th based on the 9 million individuals who speak it (Generalitat of Catalonia, 2009; Querol, 2007) and its total potential of 13 million speakers,[2] far surpassing the great bulk of languages that have 100,000, 10,000, 1000 or only 100 speakers.

In relation to the other medium-sized languages analysed in this volume, the position of Catalan appears peculiar. First, there is a simple comparative effect, in that the Catalan community is in contact with 'central' languages (i.e. Spanish, French and, to a lesser extent, Italian) that have a much greater demographic and political impact. The size of a language is always relative. If the Catalan-speaking community were found, for example, in Eastern and Central Europe (it is no accident that the Czech, Slovak, Croat, Estonian, Latvian, Lithuanian and Hungarian communities are successors to the multinational and multilingual Austro-Hungarian, Russian and Ottoman empires), that is, if Catalan were surrounded by other medium-sized language groups, the dimensions of Catalan would seem more *normal* in the eyes of outside observers and in the eyes of the members of the Catalan-speaking community itself. Second, the Catalan-speaking community has a conflictive relationship with the majority languages, making it weaker and more fragile than most of the other medium-sized languages in Europe. Third, Catalan has a relationship of dependence – like most other languages – in relation to the hypercentral language, English (Calvet, 1999).

Language Security: An Attainable Objective?

Réaume (1991), based on the collective Quebecois experience in defending French against the overwhelming Anglophone dominance in North America, defines language security as the ability of a language community to perform the basic functions of life within its territory in its own language, without worry or suffering, and without having to suffer the 'pain of language' – borrowing a formulation from Larreula (2002). To what extent can Catalan speakers live without impediments in their own language, within their historic territories, in the same way that most members of medium-sized language communities are able to do?

The demographic scale of the Catalan-language community (noted earlier as 9 million speakers; see Vila, 2001, and Pons & Vila, 2004) in theory should enable it to satisfy the needs of cultural production and consumption and to exist as a fully viable cultural community, at least to the same degree as the other communities analysed in this volume. The size should make possible publishing, recording, audiovisual as well as the other kinds of output required to satisfy the needs of a Western citizen. However, the public powers of the various states where Catalan is spoken have, historically, applied all kinds of policies aimed at excluding the Catalan language from use in the public administration, the educational system, the business world and the media. Indeed, shortly before the fall of the Franco dictatorship (1939–1975), Catalan had begun to be compared to a child with a large head (select, minority culture), but with an emaciated body (mass culture). Fortunately, since the reinstalment of democracy, Catalan has made inroads, gaining a mass audience through major radio broadcasters (*Catalunya Ràdio*, Rac1), national and local television channels (TV3, C33, IB3, C9, 8TV, BTV, etc.), daily newspapers (*El Periódico, La Vanguardia, El Punt, Avui, Segre*), a large portion of theatrical productions, sporting events, magazines on travel, cooking and history, most of the commercial catalogues of the big companies such as Carrefour, IKEA and Abacus, and a presence in cyberspace, where a very high number of web pages are in Catalan and there is a domain .cat, which is dedicated to public and private users who express themselves in Catalan on the internet. Publishing in Catalan has attained extremely high levels in terms of number of titles published and continues to grow each year, reaching 10,750 titles in 2008 (according to *Anuari Estadístic de Catalunya*, 2010). The two most prestigious venues in the country (opera house Gran Teatre del Liceu and Camp Nou, the football stadium of FC Barcelona) use Catalan over their public address systems. Government offices of the regional and local administrations normally work in Catalan. As a result, there is a significant mass-audience social and cultural marketplace that must coexist in conditions of inequality with a competing marketplace in Spanish (or French or Italian). Certainly, there are market sectors where Catalan plays an important role (e.g. supermarket chains, newspapers, and radio and television broadcasting), but in general these sectors are secondary with respect to the principal markets that operate in Spanish. Among celebrity magazines, *Lecturas* offers a metaphor for the secondary status of Catalan: *Lecturas* is the only one that publishes a few pages in Catalan (six, to be exact) out of a total issue of more than one hundred pages in Spanish.

One reason why Catalan cultural production still lags behind in a number of areas, including paperback books, celebrity magazines, news programmes, interior design and cooking magazines, sporting newspapers and translations of foreign bestsellers, which are basically output for the mass market, is that Catalan speakers have become bilingual in the language of their dominant neighbour. They have therefore gained a daily familiarity in using Spanish, French and Italian, to the point that they can use these languages with virtually no effort, and consume their cultural products with great ease. At the heart of the issue is the fact that large companies in the marketplace prefer using majority languages because multilingualism and non-majority languages pose a nuisance and a hindrance to the optimization of results and profits. Acting on this preference, large companies are contributing to the accelerating exclusion of medium-sized and small languages, their fields of use and social prestige, with the result that they are sidelined and fall into decadence. For example, the main generalist newspapers are *L'Independant* in Perpignan (in French), *La Vanguardia* in Barcelona (in Spanish, recently in Catalan as well), *Última Hora* in Palma de Mallorca (in Spanish) and *Las Provincias* in Valencia (in Spanish).

In Europe, the case of Catalan is unique for four reasons. The first concerns its legal status. Catalan is the official language of a sovereign state (Andorra) and it is co-official with Spanish in three autonomous communities in Spain. Indeed, the teaching of Catalan is mandatory in the educational system. The second reason relates to its demographics. The number of Catalan speakers is higher than the number of Finnish or Danish speakers, and is equal to the number of Swedish and Czech speakers (Generalitat of Catalunya, 2009). Catalan ranks ninth among the languages spoken within the EU. The third reason concerns its sociolinguistic situation. The language has not been abandoned by its speakers, but is transmitted from parents to children, except in French Catalonia, the city of Alguer on Sardinia (Alghero in Italian), and in some cities in the autonomous region of Valencia (Torres, 2007). With these exceptions, native speakers of Spanish or other languages are largely individuals from other places, either from other parts of Spain or from other countries, and many of them learn Catalan. In terms both of its use and its knowledge, Catalan faces a situation far different from that in communities such as Occitania, Wales or Brittany. The fourth reason relates to its linguistic resources. Catalan is fully codified, with rules and standards and a broad consensus among academics and the general public (except in sectors of the autonomous region of Valencia). The authority on the language (i.e. the Institute of Catalan Studies) is broadly recognized. There are specialized dictionaries and bilingual dictionaries for the most widely spoken languages in the world (e.g. English, French, Chinese, German, Russian, Italian and Swedish). In addition, the Catalan-speaking territories are prepared to create and circulate neologisms of all kinds, relying on a system for standardization (the Termcat centre for terminology, available at http://www.termcat.cat).

Why does the culture and society of the Catalan language suffer from these deficits if, theoretically, its dimensions and resources, as noted above, could be viewed as satisfactory to its needs? To respond to this question, we point to three aspects: (1) the interconnected role of the state and the marketplace; (2) the role of three interlinked macroprocesses, political subordination, immigration and globalization; and (3) a summary of seven challenges facing the Catalan language community.

Importantly, the fragmentation of the language domain across different autonomous communities and states brings into play a variety of differing political and social contexts (for an introduction see Boix, 2008). Catalan speakers are divided among four areas. The first area lies in Spain and includes Valencia (officially *Comunitat Valenciana*), Catalonia and the Balearic Islands, where Catalan enjoys official recognition, in addition to a strip in Aragon (*La Franja*) and the Carxe enclave in Murcia, where Catalan has little or no recognition. The second area is the French region of Pyrénées-Orientales, where recognition is scant. The third area, the enclave of Alguer on the Italian island of Sardinia, also enjoys negligible recognition, while the fourth area is the state of Andorra. In Andorra, Catalan has never ceased being the single official language of the country. (For more information on language policies in the above territories see Strubell & Boix-Fuster, 2011.)

The State and the Marketplace

The state

In Spanish history, the Catalan language community has occupied a marginal position. This is even more so in the French and Italian cases. If we focus on Spain, where 97% of Catalan speakers reside (Vila, 2001), we find that it is essentially Castile that has constructed the Spanish nation, so the dominant language is Castilian, or Spanish. The first Spanish constitution (1812) and the overwhelming majority of its successors did not address the languages of Spain in their articles because it was taken as given that there was only one truly important language: Spanish. Article 3 of the Spanish Constitution of 1978 establishes the duty and right to know Spanish, but it does not say the same thing for the other languages of Spain, which are left unnamed – an absence that has since caused problems. Only the 2006 Autonomous Statute of Catalonia treats the Catalan and Spanish languages equally. However, this equality of treatment was blocked by a ruling of the Spanish Constitutional Court in July 2010 (for the process that led to the rejection of the Catalan Statute of 2006, see Milian, 2009). In Spain, therefore, there is no equal recognition of the languages of its citizens as there is, for example, in Canada, where English and French are considered foundational languages with equal status and recognition in central government bodies. Other examples include Finland and Belgium.

The lamentable history of Spain, the cause of Spain's economic backwardness, has been nearly always accompanied with repression, contempt and neglect directed at languages other than Castilian. In the aftermath of the Reapers' War (1659) and the Spanish War of Succession (1714), with the subsequent ascent of the Bourbon dynasty to the Spanish throne, the Catalan language lost its official status. From that time, all Catalan speakers, save for a few limited exceptions, have suffered repeated assaults and displays of intolerance towards their language (Ferrer i Gironès, 1985). The two most recent Spanish dictatorships (1923–1930 and 1936–1975) excluded the Catalan language from all official public spheres (e.g. government bodies, the educational system, the media and even the Catechism), impeding nearly all Catalan speakers in the pursuit of literacy in their own language. The eradication of Catalan in formal spheres continues to have lasting effects to this day: most citizens do not have a mastery of the written code of the first language of their country. By contrast, the current Spanish democracy upholds more than 200 regulations that mandate the use of the Spanish language,[3] many more than require the use of Catalan alongside Spanish, the official language of all Spain. The prospect is bleak in French Catalonia (officially Pyrénées-Orientales in France), where the French Republic, in spite of its democratic character, sought to impede as efficiently as possible the development of any language that was not French. As a result, the intergenerational transmission of Catalan has been interrupted in this territory, where Catalan first appeared in the High Middle Ages. Only in Andorra, steering a middle course between France and Spain, has the government maintained its official use of Catalan uninterrupted since the Middle Ages. Andorra, as an independent state in the Pyrenees mountains, has representation at the United Nations and it is the only area in the language domain of Catalan where it makes no sense to refer to language normalization (i.e. the process by which an ethnolinguistic community tries to recover the use of its subordinated language in significant public and private domains), because Andorra, a tiny but independent state, has never suffered a traumatic 'denormalization' (i.e. linguistic repression or subordination, see Strubell & Boix-Fuster, 2011).

The marketplace

The marketplace and particularly the regulations governing market makers also work against the Catalan language, as these markets are a crucial factor on a planet almost entirely dominated by a capitalist system. An example of these market regulations arises in free-trade areas, which include language regulations. For instance, EU legislation (Milian, 2003) establishes that product labelling must appear in comprehensible languages, but the wording functions in such a way that Catalan can be excluded, because the Catalan-speaking population has become totally bilingual, also speaking

Spanish, French or Italian. Catalan has become superfluous or is only mandatory on products that carry geographical status labels. Recently passed consumer legislation in Catalonia does establish some obligations on the use of Catalan in product labelling (Law 22/2010, 20 July 2010). In short, as predicted in a manifesto appearing at the start of the Spanish democratic period (Argente et al., 1979), the culture and language of the Catalan-speaking lands – without a state and market that are favourable in our capitalist economy – will always fight an uphill battle, like Sisyphus, against the main powers. The 'recommended dose' of central or hypercentral languages (perhaps similar to the case of medications) tends to be excessive and threatens the survival of medium-sized and small languages (with thanks to Albert Bastardas for the metaphorical comparison). In commercial sectors with little or no regulation, Spanish is usually predominant. Examples include film distribution (Rimbau, 2009) and driving schools (Boix, 2006).

Subordination, Immigration and Globalization

Subordination

Political dependence and marginalization are signs of subordination to a foreign power. The long subordination of the Catalan-language territories has left a lasting effect on the behaviour of Catalan speakers, who have had to adapt willingly or by force to their secondary role as a minority and have interiorized the dominant language and culture. Two interrelated behaviours – two genuine social norms – will have to suffice to demonstrate the residue of this minoritized status: interposition and norms of use applied in language choice.

- *Interposition.* Aracil (1982), one of the pioneers of Catalan sociolinguistics, described the behavioural patterns that are characteristic of minority communities. In a situation of interposition, one of Aracil's patterns, the minority community establishes external relations always through the filter of the dominant culture and language. For example, many Catalan speakers use or once used only their Spanish first names in public life (e.g. José Carreras, Juan Antonio Samaranch, Federico Mayor Zaragoza, Eduardo Punset[4]); broad sectors of the population translate foreign languages through Spanish, incorporating neologisms and other interferences into Catalan via Spanish; people know foreign place-names and citations from standard reference works (e.g. involving the Bible, philosophical texts or set phrases) only in Spanish and generally only gain access to the outside world through the filters of the dominant culture and languages. In short, interposition shows patterns of language use that are, at best, anomalous in nature and could point almost to a dependence or cultural colonialism.

- *Norms of use in language choice.* Another hallmark of subordination is the social norm establishing that the appropriate language to address anyone who is not a member of the same ethnolinguistic group is always Spanish or French. In this way, the language loses its uses in interethnic relations and the opportunity to add new speakers is stymied: because everyone addresses members of other ethnolinguistic groups in Spanish (or French), the latter may perceive that learning and using Catalan is unnecessary and redundant. For example, mixed ethnolinguistic couples (Catalan–Spanish) become strictly Spanish-speaking when following this social norm (Boix, 2009; Boix & Torrens, 2011), except if the Spanish speaker has learned Catalan before forming a family unit. Catalan has a certain power of social appeal. In linguistically homogeneous couples, Catalan usually gains ground, at least in Catalonia. In other words, in these couples, more Catalan is spoken with a couple's children than with the couple's parents (Torres, 2011). Largely unsuccessful campaigns have tried to offset or reverse convergence with Spanish, and some audiovisual media in Catalan show models of this norm of alternative language use, sometimes called 'passive bilingualism', for example, in the case of Catalan public media, CCMA (Boix *et al.*, 2011). One of the basic factors explaining this norm is the long-standing subordination of the Catalan-speaking population, with the obvious result of a deep, internalized bilingualism in Spanish (or French). Finally, a paradoxical factor must be added to this picture of convergence with Spanish: many users of Catalan have Spanish as their first language and, therefore, have no difficulty in using their language of origin when addressing an interlocutor who does not speak Catalan.

Immigration

Despite suffering political subordination, most Catalan-speaking territories have enjoyed a relatively more positive economic situation than the rest of Spain. This gap distinguishes these territories from other European minorities, where their position as minorities in language and culture go hand in hand with relative economic backwardness. As a consequence of prosperity, Catalonia, Valencia and the Balearic Islands have received hundreds of thousands of immigrants from the rest of Spain. Sometimes the newcomers have settled in municipalities that were not inhabited by an earlier native Catalan-speaking population or that were inhabited by immigrants from earlier waves of migration. In those cases, learning and adopting the Catalan language was highly unlikely. Sometimes the newcomers came to municipalities where the native population had already switched to Spanish (e.g. the cities of Valencia and Alacant/Alicante). As a result of these migratory movements, the working classes – particularly in the more marginalized, industrial or metropolitan areas (e.g. Barcelona and Tarragona) – are made up largely of citizens whose families originally came from outside the Catalan-speaking territories. The fact that a majority of these immigrants come from elsewhere in the Spanish state (and speak Spanish as a principal language), together with the fact that many arrived in Catalan-speaking territories in the midst of the dictatorship when the use of Catalan was banned in the public sphere, has impeded a large number of these newcomers from adopting the native Catalan culture and language. In 2008, for instance, 41.3% of people born in Catalonia had Spanish as a first language (EULC, 2008). Most of them belong to families that immigrated to Catalonia in the 20th century. Very few come from native families that have switched to Spanish, although this switch to Spanish is observable in the autonomous region of Valencia. In French Catalonia, approximately half of the population has origins outside the region, a fact that has been crucial to the retreat and abandonment of the language.

No study has yet examined the various degrees of these immigrants' cultural and linguistic integration within Catalan society. The language behaviour and use of the new Spanish middle classes living in the Catalan-speaking territories is not known. Nor has research addressed the role of the Catholic church and its myriad organizations and associations (e.g. schools, youth clubs, parishes, trade unions and so on; see Costa, 1996) or the role of political parties (particularly the leftist PSUC and PSC (PSC-PSOE)) with respect to the process of integration to the Catalan language and culture. A significant number of immigrants, particularly in Catalonia, have moved toward integration, even to the point of promoting the Catalan culture and language. For example, many Spanish-speaking parents have pushed for school immersion programmes in which Catalan is the schools' primary language of instruction.

Since the 1990s, a new group of immigrants has joined immigrants from elsewhere in the Iberian Peninsula or from Latin America. These new immigrants, non-Spanish speakers, come mainly from the Maghreb and sub-Saharan Africa. For many of them, the lingua franca of Catalan society, the most useful language on their arrival, is Spanish. Research is needed to quantify the choices of these immigrants when they are faced with choosing between courses teaching Spanish or Catalan.[5] A description is also needed of the course offering exclusively available to immigrants in Spanish, but not in Catalan. In short, the course offering in Catalan aimed at immigrants appears to run counter to the primary social current that establishes Spanish *de facto* as a pivot language, a principal language. Primary schools, as the main agent of Catalanisation, cannot stand as the only countervailing force against this general trend of Spanish cultural and linguistic domination. Finally, the arrival and establishment of affluent immigrants in the Catalan-speaking territories must not be overlooked. Sastre (2010), after studying the Germans in Mallorca, and Fukuda (2009), after studying the Japanese in Catalonia, are in agreement that these prosperous residents generally have little or no interest in learning Catalan (or Spanish). For individuals who learn Spanish, learning Catalan would require an added burden that they avoid, if possible. They fear that learning Catalan will pose obstacles to learning Spanish well.

Globalization

Finally, in addition to the factors of subordination and migration, the macroprocess of globalization must be added. The dizzying rise in (unequal) relationships across the planet leads to the use, above all, of English as the interlingua. English is also penetrating into society in the Catalan-speaking territories. This occurs in the educational system (i.e. the rise in English learning and usage at all levels of education, from early childhood to university education) and in the economic system (i.e. the requirement for a mastery of English language in a growing number of jobs). The spread of English is highly unequal and creates new cracks of inequality in the population. To date, these new disparities have received very little attention in research.

Together, these three macroprocesses (subordination, immigration and globalization) explain why Catalan speakers sometimes cannot use their language with confidence. Spanish (and, even more so, French and Italian) benefits from strong incoming settlement and its adoption within the Catalan-speaking territories (Vila, 2007). For this reason (although not this reason alone), it is much more unlikely that Spanish speakers will choose Catalan in intergroup conversations than it is for Catalan speakers to choose Spanish. After all, most Catalan speakers have a profound mastery of Spanish and use it regularly in daily life. In the territories within the Spanish-speaking domain, young people have had the opportunity to learn Catalan at school. Even so, proficiency in Spanish is higher because the vast majority of cultural consumption appears more frequently in Spanish (CSASEC, 2008). In Valencia, the Balearic Islands and especially Catalonia, there is a growing phenomenon of code-switching between the two languages: young people of one group resort to the language of the other group (Boix & Sanz, 2008;

Pujolar et al., 2010). However, the situation has not yet reached a mixing of languages similar to the Spanglish typical of Puerto Ricans and other Hispanics in New York (Remeseira, 2010). Nonetheless, the weight of code-switching continues to fall more on Catalan speakers than on Spanish speakers. In addition, the number of bilingual families is on the rise. In EULP (2008), 11.9% of the individuals surveyed in Catalonia responded that Spanish and Catalan were both customary languages in their households. By contrast, only 3.8% responded that they considered both languages to be their mother tongue.

Seven Challenges Facing the Catalan-Language Community

Below, we examine seven challenges facing the Catalan-language community. The analysis will evaluate the similarities and dissimilarities of these challenges in relation to the challenges of other medium-sized communities. Of the seven items, six were put forward by Branchadell (2003), while the seventh item is an addition proposed by the authors of this chapter.

The challenge of disintegration

Disintegration refers to each territory in the language domain developing in an uncoordinated way with respect to the other territories, making it much more difficult or even impossible to establish an 'imagined community' (Anderson, 1983), the perception of a differentiated community. The fragmentation across independent autonomous communities in Spain divides school curricula and can even impede the acknowledgement of belonging to the same language. The Valencian movement to splinter the Catalan language, which has been encouraged by the leading conservative party of Spain (the *Partido Popular*), not only rejects the use of the term of Catalan in favour of Valencian (the traditional, more deeply rooted denomination), but it has also refused to recognize the university degree in Catalan philology and has blocked reciprocity in the transmission of regional television broadcasts in Catalan. The autonomous community of Valencia, with its population of nearly 5.5 million inhabitants, is a principal area in the language domain. This lack of feeling a sense of belonging to the same culture and language entails a lower subjective ethnolinguistic vitality: the language is perceived as less useful, endowed with less prestige.

There are efforts being made to fight against the trend towards disintegration, although they have been insufficient in the face of the secessionist actions of institutions. Two paradigmatic examples of countervailing actions may be given:

- the coordination of all universities in the Catalan-language area through the Joan Lluís Vives University Network, which organizes most of the university summer courses;
- the Ramon Llull Institute, which coordinates the promotion of the Catalan language and culture abroad (e.g. language tutors in universities, presence at the Frankfurt Book Fair) and has representatives from the Balearic Islands, Catalonia, some city halls in Valencia, and Andorra, but not from the regional government of Valencia, which refuses to take part.

Ideally, the necessary coordination of the Catalan-language lands could be reached through an agreement similar to the accord existing between the Flemish and the Dutch for the promotion of the Dutch language. Attempts have been made, but the autonomous government of Valencia has rejected any involvement (Marí, 2006). As long as the primary conservative party of Spain continues promoting policies against the Catalan language (whether it is called Valencian or Catalan), the needed coordination between the inhabitants of Valencia, Catalonia and the Balearic Islands will remain impossible.

The challenge of division

Division refers to the risk of fractures appearing in the Catalan-speaking territories as a result of ethnolinguistic factors. In other words, it is the risk that society might split into different language and cultural groups in confrontation or segregated by means of separate school systems or groups, associations and parties that are ethnolinguistic in nature, for example, a Catalan socialist party splitting from a Spanish socialist party.

In the Catalan-language territories, the balance of this division is different in each territory. In Valencia and Andorra, there are schools with different primary languages of instruction: Spanish and Catalan (Valencian) in Valencia, and Catalan, French and Spanish in Andorra. By contrast, Catalonia, the Balearic Islands and the Catalan-speaking part of Aragon have developed a unitary language model. Schooling is not separated according to language (Spanish and Catalan). The system is linguistically unified, with Catalan used as the core or preferred language of instruction. However, knowledge of both Spanish and Catalan is required by the end of compulsory education and some schools, mainly private ones, give priority to Spanish. Officially, there are no differentiated universities either. With respect to political parties, attempts have been made to manipulate ethnolinguistic differences (e.g. Catalans of Andalusian origin against native-born Catalans; Espasa, 2009) and mobilize action in light of these differences. Two examples are the Andalusian associations at the spring fair in Catalonia *Feria de Abril* (Ros, 2001) and the emergence of a small grassroots political party *Ciudadanos – Partido por la ciudadanía*. Both examples reflect efforts of non-Catalan-speaking natives that call themselves anti-nationalist and presumably offer an alternative, but actually give *de facto* support to Spanish nationalism. Most importantly, these groups favour complete deregulation in the case of Catalan cultural and language policy, leaving the matter to the marketplace, but they uphold state regulation in favour of Spanish.

Signs of mobilization in the native Catalan sector include the formation and actions of *La Crida per la llengua i la cultura catalanes*, and a circular distributed by a minister in the Catalan government, Antoni Comas, who ordered civil servants in Catalan government bodies to use Catalan in their conversations with one another (1991): a flagrant political error, because it could sow division between ethnolinguistic groups. In the recent Catalan political tradition since the second dictatorship (1939–1975), the unity of the population has been emphasized, regardless of its different ethnolinguistic origins. A pervasive bilingualism (Catalan/Spanish) via a common educational system is considered to be a way of breaking down ethnolinguistic boundaries.

The large Catalan political parties, at least verbally, have advocated a union of citizens above and beyond the differences of origin and language, making use of unifying slogans such as 'everyone who lives and works in Catalonia is a Catalan' and 'we are one people'. Research is needed to determine whether these slogans in favour of the civic unity of the Catalan people have a sound basis, and whether they have taken root in today's widely heterogeneous population. For instance, can immigrants from Peru who wish to return to Peru and have no plans to settle in Catalonia, feel Catalan – particularly if their main language is Spanish? Perhaps these natives of Peru would equate Catalan to Quechua, Peru's indigenous and mistreated language, and would therefore dismiss Catalan as useless.

The challenge of dissolution

Dissolution refers to the risk that Catalan, as a minoritized language in intense contact with dominant languages for many years (i.e. Spanish, French and Italian) (see Vila, 2007, for the Spanish case), could eventually suffer so great an adverse influence that it loses the fundamental characteristics of its structure in terms of lexis, morphosyntax, phonetics and discourse.

Catalan went through a modernizing linguistic reform in the first third of the 20th century thanks to the seminal work of Pompeu Fabra (see Costa, 2010). However, it suffers deep and constant erosion from contact with the dominant languages and their powerful influence on cultural consumption. Gradually, the linguistic system of Catalan draws nearer the systems of these neighbouring languages, adopting a vast number of interferences (Boix & Sanz, 2008; Pujolar, 2010). A paradigmatic example is the invasion of slang words from Spanish into Catalan. Imprecations like *joder* have replaced genuine Catalan exclamations like *collons*. In parallel, the standard form of Catalan is undergoing expansion among the population, particularly the versions adopted in each autonomous community: Balearic Islands, Catalonia and Valencia).

Campaigns for language loyalty and purity (e.g. the plethora of language advisors, stylebooks and terminology databases; Nogué *et al.*, 2010) can do little to offset these trends. Even the most seasoned language advisors, facing facts, are forced to allow Spanish elements into the normative model (Pla, 2010). As Pompeu Fabra himself noted, the last word falls to the users of the language. And these users are at the receiving end of powerful pressure to bow to Spanish (or French or Italian) influences.

The challenge of devaluation

Devaluation refers to the lack (or loss) of social functions performed by the language. This particularly includes functions that give prestige to the speaker, such as the use of more technical words. Such functions indicate subjective ethnolinguistic vitality, that is, confidence that the language in question will be useful for the social advancement and competitiveness of its users. Three significant examples of these functions are examined below.

The first point is that it is fundamental to maintain or achieve the function of an anonymous language, that is, a code for use in public spaces that calls on the participation of speakers of different ethnic and cultural groups (Woolard, 2008). In advanced societies, the romantic principle of authenticity that links a language to a given social group, and characterizes and distinguishes it from other groups, is no longer enough: survival requires also the anonymous use of language. Catalan – especially in Catalonia, but also to a lesser extent in the Balearic Islands and to a different extent in Andorra – is in a struggle to become the common language of all social groups. To achieve this aim, widespread campaigns of bilingualism have been promoted. Examples of anonymity arise in the use of Catalan at mass events, such as the public address announcements in Catalan before the hundred thousand spectators at the stadium of FC Barcelona. At a more modest level, there are examples of anonymity in messages addressed to unknown interlocutors: *'qui és l'últim?'* ('Who's the last one') in the queue at the bakery; *'passo?'* ('Can I go in?') at the swimming pool; *'que surt'* ('Are you leaving?') addressed to a car pulling out of a parking space unexpectedly; and *'que baixa'* ('Are you getting off?') at the door exiting from a bus. These messages practically always appear in the dominant language in areas where Catalan is on the verge of disappearing (i.e. French Catalonia, Alguer and Alacant/Alicante), but they can be in Catalan in areas where Catalan has prestige and even some power of social appeal, such as in much of Catalonia and certain neighbourhoods of Barcelona.

A second example of prestigious functions can be found in university education. As noted in an earlier section, no separation of universities by language exists in Catalonia or in the Balearic Islands (although separate language paths do exist in the universities of Valencia, with very low percentages of Catalan use). The universities generally show a very high level of Catalan use, which encourages some new speakers to use it when they begin their studies (Pujolar, 2010). However, globalization threatens to devalue these functions. The arrival of European students (on Erasmus programmes) and Latin American students very frequently leads to the adoption of Spanish or English as the languages of instruction, and the effect is even stronger in the case of research. Grassroots sectors promoting Catalan fear that this setback will also lead a backward slide in earlier periods of education – secondary or even primary education. As always, an agreement will need to be reached that can, as fully as possible, reconcile the mobility and universality of university education with the maintenance and promotion of Catalan as a language of higher learning. The debate on the subject will be long, and it will need to draw on the experience gained from university language policies in other Western countries with medium-sized languages, such as the Netherlands, Denmark and Sweden.

The third example concerns a dilemma facing the Catalan-speaking territories, a dilemma that is well-known in Quebec: which language should be adopted by non-native groups who speak neither Spanish nor Catalan? What is the principal language of integration? In Catalonia, immigration legislation from 2010 establishes Catalan as the primary language of reception. The reasoning is that an individual who learns Catalan first will certainly learn Spanish afterwards, while an individual who learns Spanish first is not certain to learn Catalan afterwards. At present, whatever the rhetoric employed by the government in power, the lingua franca in Catalan society is Spanish. This is supported by the fact that, in the case of the population born abroad (EULP, 2008), in Catalonia 44.3% speak Spanish with their oldest child, 26.6% use other languages, 12.4% make use of a combination of languages, and only 5.6% speak Catalan with their oldest child. Non-natives overwhelmingly lean towards using Spanish. However, it must be remembered that the oldest children are usually born in the country of origin and most immigrants come from Latin America, arriving with Spanish as their first or principal language.

The challenge of disappearance

Disappearance refers to the interruption of transmission from generation to generation, when the language is no longer passed from parents to children. Fishman's classic book (1991) points to the paramount importance of intergenerational language transmission in every community on the planet.

At present, all homogeneous Catalan-speaking couples pass down Catalan in virtually the entire domain (Torres, 2007). Nearly all mixed Catalan–Spanish couples use the dominant language, Spanish, when they meet and begin a relationship. This fits within the prescribed norms of daily use, as described earlier. It could be said that they 'fall in love' in Spanish. In Catalonia, at least, once a mixed-language couple is formed and has children, Catalan gains some ground: the Catalan-speaking parent usually passes Catalan to their children. This is a behaviour that points to significant subjective ethnolinguistic vitality and a gain for Catalan (Torres, 2011). Factors outside the family (e.g. schooling in Catalan, the presence of Catalan in institutions and the association of Catalan with prestigious jobs) doubtless explain the language loyalty given to Catalan in such cases, which is not seen to the same extent in other parts of the Catalan-speaking territories.

In mixed-language couples in Catalonia and the Balearic Islands, the most common occurrence is for each parent to pass down his or her language to their children. In Catalonia, a modest advance in Catalan can be seen; some Spanish speakers now speak Catalan with their children (Boix, 2009). By contrast, the opposite trend occurs in Valencia, with Spanish gaining ground (Montoya & Mas, 2011). In Valencia, even among homogeneous Catalan-speaking couples, Valencian is receding as a language passed down to children, and Catalan's retreat in the south is clear. The interruption of intergenerational transmission is even more sharply apparent in French Catalonia and Alguer, although the issue requires further in-depth exploration beyond the scope of this chapter.

The challenge of domination

This item refers to the connotations of social power that are conferred on users through their knowledge and use of a language, that is, the benefits derived from language knowledge and skills ('linguistic capital' in Bourdieu's terminology). In this sense, the Catalan-speaking territories are marginal or secondary within the political framework in which they find themselves, despite the relative autonomy that they enjoy within the borders of Spain. Political sovereignty derives from the entirety of citizens in the state (Spain, France or Italy), and the inhabitants of the Catalan-speaking territories do not enjoy sovereignty over their own affairs, starting with language matters. Only Andorra possesses complete self-government, which is nonetheless qualified by the country's limited size, which makes it highly dependent on what happens beyond its borders.

Finally, it should be noted that a greater domination or more power for the Catalan-speaking territories (i.e. effective federalism or a degree of sovereignty) would not automatically solve these sociolinguistic problems or challenges, just as it has not solved the problems of medium-sized language communities in independent states. It would, however, give a greater margin of manoeuvre to manage internal cultural and language diversity and raise the visibility of the Catalan-speaking world within the country and abroad.

The lack of domination poses the following principal problems:

- exclusion from political and governmental areas where there is a hegemony of Spanish, e.g. central organs of power, the legal system and the armed forces;
- lack of state machinery in support of, rather than against, the Catalan language;
- absence of control over one's own audiovisual space and the imposition of regulations that sideline Catalan;
- lack of Catalan in visual displays as the native language of the territory, which would create incentives for foreigners to learn the language, if they wished to integrate;
- negligence on the part of large transnational businesses that operate under the premise 'one state → one language';
- exclusion from European institutions and European financial assistance.

The challenge of demobilization

The seventh and last D, which stands for demobilization, is different in nature. It refers to the failure of society to react and mobilize amid the challenges of the previous Ds. A network of organizations defending the Catalan language draws on the active support of thousands of citizens. Together, they carry out activities that, in part, substitute for the absence or timidity or even fear of the governments of autonomous regions or municipalities that should act as their representatives. Organizations with a considerable number of members include *Acció Cultural del País Valencià*, *Òmnium Cultural* and *Obra Cultural Balear*, in addition to initiatives such as *Plataforma per la Llengua* and *Coordinadora d'Associacions per la Llengua*. In Valencia, given the language-based division of the school system, the *Federació d'Escola Valenciana* draws together and mobilizes many thousands of families, which nevertheless do not reach 30% of the school-age population. This is largely due to the failure of Valencia's government to offer sufficient education in Catalan. Thus, there is a significant movement that channels and gives voice to a feeling of language loyalty, which is the foundation needed to counteract the first six challenges described above. Most of the population takes a negative view of any prohibition. Bilingual as they are (particularly first-language Catalan speakers), they accommodate and adapt easily to situations requiring the use of Spanish (and, to a lesser extent, the use of Catalan). For many, the use of one language or the other is a matter of indifference. Others, in many social contexts, are unaware of the collective effects of individual behaviours. An ideological battle in support of multilingualism, that is, in support of Catalan, must still be waged (Palou & Fons, 2009).

Conclusions

In terms of its social and demographic dimensions, the Catalan-language community is clearly medium-sized and comparable to other medium-sized European language communities. With respect to its historical tradition, it has a tradition of educated and official use dating back to the Middle Ages. Its legal status, its sociolinguistic situation and its resources (i.e. codification, linguistic authorities) all equip the Catalan-language community to thrive.

The challenges facing Catalan are, in part, similar to the challenges facing other medium-sized European communities. What is different is that the entire language area is broadly characterized by a lack of control over its own affairs, although clearly at differing degrees in different areas. The political context of the Catalan-speaking territories is imposed from outside in all cases except for the irreproducible case of Andorra. Therefore, phenomena such as interposition and insufficient ethnolinguistic vitality are common across the territory.

As a whole, the language community faces the seven challenges examined above (disintegration, dissolution, division, devaluation, disappearance, lack of domination and demobilization) and these challenges put the community in a relatively 'defenceless' position. Furthermore, the condition of the language in the Catalan-speaking territories is more fragile than in other medium-sized communities because the forces of the state and the marketplace are largely unfavourable towards it. In short, the Catalan language space is not secure. In comparison with the other languages examined in this volume, Catalan is an atypical medium-sized language that may eventually become a 'normal' one. In other words, it may become a language community no longer focused on survival but able to enjoy its language at ease, without suffering, in daily life.

Acknowledgements

We are grateful to the always intelligent remarks of F.X. Vila, who reviewed the first draft of this text. Of course, any shortcomings are strictly the authors' responsibility. This article is supported by the Spanish Ministry of Science and Innovation research grant FFI2009-10424 'Globalización, intercomunicación y lenguas propias en las comunidades lingüísticas medianas (MLC, Medium-sized Language Communities)' and the group 'Estudi de la Variació' (2009 SGR 521), funded by the Catalan Ministry of Economy and Knowledge.

Notes

(1) Non-Catalan readers may find it useful to consult volumes in English, German or French for more information on the sociolinguistic situation of the Catalan-speaking territories (Boix & Milian, 2002; Hall, 2001; Marí, 1993; Nagel, 2007 (Catalan trans. 2007); Vila i Moreno 2008), for information on Catalonia in particular (McRoberts, 2001) and language policies currently in effect (Strubell & Boix-Fuster, 2011), or on the linguistic reform of Catalan, led by Pompeu Fabra (Costa, 2010). A review of any of these works can help to lessen the excessive invisibility of Catalan.
(2) Obviously, among the 9 million speakers of Catalan and the 13 million individuals living in the Catalan-speaking area, there is a very wide range of competences, uses and language ideologies.
(3) See http://www.plataforma-llengua.cat/media/assets/1583/500lleis_que_Imposen_el_castell__des_2009_DEF.pdf.
(4) A well-known exception to the custom of public introductions in Spanish is offered by the example of Joan Miró, who always gave his first name in Catalan, although Joan could be interpreted as a woman's name in English. Also, in some parts of the domain, many first names exist in Spanish as a result of the church's earlier decision to stop using Catalan. This is particularly the case in Valencia, French Catalonia and the Catalan-speaking part of Aragon.
(5) See, for example, the leaflet (consulted in 2010) asking immigrants which of the two languages they wished to study. Published in Spanish, Catalan and 11 additional languages, the leaflet was sponsored by the autonomous government of Catalonia, the Spanish Ministry of Labour and Social Affairs and Barcelona city hall.

References

Anderson, B. (1983) *Imagined Communities*. London: Verso.
Anuari Estadístic de Catalunya 2010 (2010) Barcelona: Generalitat of Catalonia. Statistical Institute of Catalonia.

Aracil, L.V. (1982) *Papers de sociolingüística*. Barcelona: La Magrana.
Argente, J.A., Castellanos, J., Jorba, M., Molas, J., Murgades, J., Nadal, J.M. and Sullà, E. (1979) Una nació sense estat, un poble sense llengua. *Els Marges* 15, 3–13.
Boix, E. (2006) El català a les autoescoles: el català quasi sense corda. *Llengua i Ús* 32, 32–36.
Boix, E. (coord.) (2008) *Els futurs del català. Un estat de la qüestió i una qüestió d'estat*. Barcelona: Publicacions i Edicions de la Universitat de Barcelona.
Boix, E. (2009) *Català o castellà amb els fills?La transmissió de la llengua en famílies bilingües a Barcelona*. Sant Cugat del Vallès: Rourich.
Boix, E. and Milian, A. (eds) (2002) Aménagement linguistique dans les pays de langue catalane. *Terminogramme* 103–104.
Boix, E. and Sanz, C. (2008) Language and identity in Catalonia. In A. Niño Murcia and M.J. Rothman (eds) *Bilingualism and Identity* (pp. 87–106). Amsterdam: John Benjamins.
Boix, E. and Torrens, R.M. (eds) (2011) *Les llengües al sofà. El bilingüisme familiar als països de llengua catalana*. Lleida: Pagès Editors.
Boix, E., Melià, J. and Montoya, B. (2011) Policies promoting the use of Catalan in oral communication and to improve attitudes towards the language. In M. Strubell and E. Boix (eds) *Democratic Policies and Language Revitalisation. The Case of Catalan* (pp. 150–181). London: Palgrave.
Branchadell, A. (2003) Algunes propostes de promoció del català. El cas de les institucions de l'Estat i el sector privat. *Idees* 18, 32–45.
Branchadell, A. (2005) *La moralitat de la política lingüística. Un estudi comparat de la legitimitat liberaldemocràtica de les polítiques lingüístiques del Quebec i Catalunya*. Barcelona: Institut d'Estudis Catalans.
Calvet, L.J. (1999) *Pour une écologie des langues du monde*. Paris: Plon.
Costa, J. (1996) *Dels moviments d'església a la militància política*. Bellaterra: Universitat Autònoma de Barcelona.
Costa, J. (2010) *Pompeu Fabra. The Architect of Catalan. Selected writings*. Amsterdam: Benjamins.
CSASEC (Consell Superior d'Avaluació del Sistema Educatiu de Catalunya) (2008) *Estudi sociodemogràfic i lingüístic de l'alumnat de 4t d'ESO de Catalunya. Avaluació de l'educació secundària obligatòria*. Barcelona: Consell Superior d'Avaluació del Sistema Educatiu, Generalitat de Catalunya.
Enquesta d'usos lingüístics a la Catalunya Nord 2004 (2008) Barcelona: Generalitat de Catalunya, Secretaria de Política Lingüística.
Espasa, A., Garcia, A., Sastre, P., Zambrano, X. (coord. by Fernández, M.) (2009) *Fabricar l'immigrant. Aprofitaments polítics de la immigració. Catalunya 1977–2007*. Lleida: Pagès editors.
Ferrer i Gironès, F. (1985) *La persecució política de la llengua catalana: Història de les mesures preses contra el seu ús des de la Nova Planta fins avui*. Barcelona: Edicions 62.
Fishman, J.A. (1991) *Reversing Language Shift. Theoretical and Empirical Foundations of Assistance to Threatened Languages*. Clevedon: Multilingual Matters.
Fukuda, M. (2009) *Els japonesos a Catalunya i la llengua catalana: Comunitat, llengües i ideologies*. Doctoral thesis, Universitat de Barcelona.
Generalitat de Catalunya (2009) *El català, llengua d'Europa*. Barcelona: Generalitat de Catalunya.
Gustà. M. and Santamaria, N. (2007) *La literatura catalana, en una perspectiva europea*. Barcelona: Generalitat de Catalunya.

Hall, J. (2001) *Convivència in Catalonia: Languages Living Together*. Barcelona: Fundació Jaume Bofill.
Larreula, E. (2002) *Dolor de llengua*. València: Tres i Quatre.
Marí, I. (1993) *Conocer la lengua y la cultura catalanas*. Palma: Federació Llull.
Marí, I. (2006) L'articulació de la comunitat lingüística catalana: alternatives i processos possibles. In *Mundialització, interculturalitat i multilingüisme* (pp. 103–126). Palma de Mallorca: Lleonard Muntaner.
McRoberts, K. (2001) *Catalonia. Nation Building Without a State*. Oxford: Oxford University Press.
Milian, A. (2003) *La igualtat de les llengües a les institucions de la Unió Europea, mite o realitat?*. Bellaterra: Universitat Autònoma de Barcelona.
Milian, A. (ed.) (2009) *El plurilingüisme a la Constitució espanyola*. Barcelona: Institute of Self-Government Studies (Institut d'Estudis Autonòmics).
Montoya, B. and Mas, A. (eds) (2011) *La transmissió familiar del valencià*. València: Acadèmia Valenciana de la Llengua.
Nagel, K-J. (2007, Catalan trans. 2007) *Katalonien. Eine kleine Landeskunde*. Stuttgart: Messidor.
Nogué, N., Bladas, Ò. and Payrató, Ll. (2010) *L'assessorament lingüístic: funcions i criteris*. Barcelona. PPU.
Palou, J. and Fons, M. (2009) Actituds dels docents davant les noves situacions escolars multiculturals i multilingües: Qüestions recurrents. *Zeitschrift für Katalanistik* 22, 151–169.
Pla, A. (2010) *Això del català*. Barcelona: Columna.
Pons, E. and Vila i Moreno, F.X. (2005) *Informe sobre la situació de la llengua catalana (2003–2004)*. Barcelona: Observatori de la Llengua.
Pujolar, J., Gonzàlez, I., Font, A. and Sanmartí, R. (2010) *Llengua i joves. Usos i percepcions lingüístics de la joventut catalana*. Barcelona: Secretaria de Joventut, Generalitat of Catalonia.
Querol, E. (ed.) (2007) *Llengua i societat als territoris de parla catalana a l'inici del segle XXI. L'Alguer, Andorra, Catalunya, Catalunya Nord, la Franja, Illes Balears i Comunitat Valenciana*. Barcelona: Generalitat de Catalunya.
Réaume, D. (1991) The constitutional protection of language. Survival or security. In A.D. Schneiderman (ed.) *Language and the State: The Law and Politics of Identity* (Langage et État: Droit, politique et identité). Cowansville: Yvon Blais.
Remeseira, C. (ed.) (2010) *Hispanic New York. A Sourcebook*. New York: Columbia University Press.
Rimbau. E. (2009) La futura llei de cinema. *El Temps* 116, 119.
Ros, A. (2001) *Being Andalusian in Catalonia: A challenge to nation state construction*. PhD thesis, University of California, San Diego.
Sastre, B. (2010) *Integració lingüística de la població alemanya resident a Mallorca*. Doctoral thesis, University of Hamburg.
Sorolla, N. (2011) Context demogràfic i econòmic. L'evolució de la comunitat lingüística. In M. À. Pradilla and N. Sorolla (eds) *Informe sobre la situació de la llengua catalana* (2010, pp. 8–38). Barcelona: Observatori de la Llengua. Online version: http://observatoridelallengua.cat/observatori.php?llengua=ca
Strubell, M. and Boix-Fuster, E. (eds) (2011) *Democratic Policies for Language Revitalisation: The Case of Catalan*. London: Palgrave.
Torres, J. (2011) Explotació de l´Enquesta d´usos lingüístics de Catalunya 2008. In Secretaria de Política Lingüística. *Anàlisi Sociolingüística de l´EULC 2008*. Barcelona: Generalitat de Catalunya.

Torres, J. (2011) Explotació de l'enquesta d'usos lingüístics de Catalunya 2008. In Secretaria de Política Lingüística, *Anàlisi Sociolingüística de l'EULC 2008* (Vol. 1, pp. 82–100). Barcelona: Generalitat of Catalonia.

Vila i Moreno, F.X. (2001) Demografia lingüística. In F. Vallverdú (dir), *Enciclopèdia de la llengua catalana*. Barcelona: Edicions 62.

Vila i Moreno, F.X. (2008) Catalan in Spain. In G. Extra and D. Gorter (eds) *Multilingual Europe: Facts and Policies* (pp. 157–183). Berlin: Mouton de Gruyter.

Vila, R.M. (2007) Sociolinguistics of Spanish in Catalonia. *International Journal of the Sociology of Language* 184, 59–77.

Woolard, K.A. (2008) Language and identity choice in Catalonia: The interplay of contrasting ideologies of linguistic authority. In K. Süselbeck, U. Mühlschlegel and P. Masson (eds) *Lengua, Nación e Identidad. La regulación del plurilingüismo en España y América Latina* (pp. 303–323). Frankfurt am Main: Vervuert.

9 Challenges and Opportunities for Medium-Sized Language Communities in the 21st Century: A (Preliminary) Synthesis

F. Xavier Vila

Do Numbers Really Matter?

Applying a variety of perspectives, the chapters in this volume have shed light on the challenges faced by a selection of medium-sized language communities (MSLCs). Although the review of each individual case is undoubtedly of great interest, a cross-comparative review may also be useful not only to these communities, but also to other MSLCs around the world. Indeed, much is to be learnt in terms of opportunities and challenges from this selection of reasonably successful MSLCs. In the following pages we will try to extract as many lessons as possible from the cases dealt with here.

It should be remembered that the language communities analysed in this volume were selected on the basis of three main structural premises of demolinguistic and socioeconomic nature (see the introduction to the volume). First, the project focused on language communities with a sizeable number of L1 speakers, between 1 and 25 million. The second basic criterion was that the communities under scrutiny should show a relatively healthy intergenerational transmission. The third criterion was socioeconomic: the communities chosen for analysis were taken to be advancing relatively successfully towards a post-industrial, informational socioeconomic paradigm (Castells, 2003).

Beyond these basic criteria, the MSLCs analysed here demonstrated similarities and differences that deserve a closer examination – first of all, in demolinguistic terms. According to Ethnologue, language communities in the world range in size from those that have a handful of speakers to those with 845 million speakers (Mandarin Chinese) – or indeed the 1213 million speakers of all Chinese languages (Table 9.1). In such a context, the demographic bracket adopted to define MSLCs – between one and 25 million speakers – may appear very strict. In reality, however, it includes around 350 languages.[1] As a consequence, the number of speakers of each MSLC analysed in this project varies dramatically between Dutch, with more than 20 million speakers, and Estonian and Latvian, each with slightly over one million speakers.[2]

Interestingly, in spite of the considerable demographic differences between these communities – the largest one is more than 20 times the size of the smallest – the number of speakers was not seen as a factor that introduced any great differences between them in terms of their use. From a global, or even just a European point of view, most of them could be described as *small*, *minor* or even *minority* languages. None accounted for even 0.5% of the world population, and most did not even reach 2% of the EU population. This fact notwithstanding, the linguistic communities reviewed were said to fulfil the bulk of societal functions, from interpersonal communication to official uses, from academic discourse to television entertainment, and from popular music to commercial functions, in both oral and written modes. Nor could demography predict why foreign languages/lingua francas were in use

Table 9.1 Numbers of speakers of languages analysed in the MSLCs project (in millions)

Source language	Authors	Ethnologue	Wikipedia in English		Wikipedia in the target language	
			Total	L1	Total	L1
Dutch	22	21.7	28	23	23	23
Czech	9.7	9.5	12	–	11.5	–
Catalan	9	11.5	9.4	–	11.5	7.7
Danish	5–6	5.6	6	–	6	–
Hebrew	7 (+13 users abroad)	5.3	<9	5.2	>8	3.5
Finnish	–	5.0	6	–	5	–
Slovene	2.4	1.9	2.5	1.85	2.2	–
Latvian	1.5	1.5	1.9	1.5	>2	*i*
Estonian	1.1	1.0	1.1	–	1.1	–

–, not mentioned.

in some particular domains and not in others. For example, English was reported to occupy more space in Danish universities than in the rest of the MSLCs, even though several of these were demographically smaller.[3]

Also in spite of the huge demolinguistic differences, and as expected given the selection criteria, all the MSLCs analysed showed encouraging symptoms in terms of language reproduction. Relatively recent histories of language shift notwithstanding, none of them showed signs of imminent *global* interruption of linguistic intergenerational transmission; language transmission seemed to be vibrant in all these communities, with children inheriting their parents' language in a normal fashion. Even in linguistically mixed couples, medium-sized language (MSL) transmission was apparently working well in most cases – at least when the couple lived within the MSLC – as parents seemed to pass on the local language to the next generation, in bilingual or monolingual families. Only in some peripheral areas where the MSLC had become strongly minoritized, and among speakers living outside their historical territories or in linguistic enclaves, did language shift seem likely. This is not to say that future trends were highly promising for all cases. In fact, in raw numbers, some of these communities may face a reduction in their speakers in the mid-term: this may be so in societies with strong emigration patterns, or in societies where younger cohorts are substantially smaller than middle-aged and older cohorts. Most of them will probably lose relative weight in the world's language system, given the differences in birth rates between Europe and other continents. However, it remains to be seen whether any of these trends have a significant impact on the sustainability of these language communities.

In other words, from a demographic point of view, all the MSLCs analysed appeared to be basically viable, with no (or very few) signs of language shift. The lesson is, then, that, in demographic terms, even the smallest medium-sized communities should be regarded as sustainable in a globalized context, provided, of course, that other conditions are met.

Elaborate, Complete, but not Necessarily Exclusive Languages

A second significant characteristic of all the MSLCs reviewed here was that, in general terms, their languages were *elaborate* and *complete* – that is, they can be used in all domains (in the sense of Lamuela, 1994, 2004, or Herslund, 1999, quoted by Preisler, 2009: 20). All the communities possessed a standard variety, codified and sufficiently developed for use in virtually all spheres of life, and were well endowed in terms of language equipment, including bilingual and monolingual dictionaries and both descriptive and prescriptive grammars. Many also had electronic and virtual accessories such as language corpora, automatic translators, and information and communication tools. Of course, the actual nature and position of each standard variety was not exactly the same in every community, either in terms of practices or ideologies. Indeed, several cases of public controversy regarding language codification (e.g. the Danish 'Mayonnaise war') were mentioned. Several languages, such as Slovene, appeared to show strong geolectal diversity, to the extent that speakers only manage to master the standard variety after several years of intense language teaching at school. In contrast, other languages, like Danish, seemed to have almost completely erased their traditional dialects and constitute today a relatively homogeneous linguistic community. All languages were described as experiencing some sort of tension between more *normative* varieties and those varieties actually used by common speakers, although in some communities, such as the Czech community, the opposition seemed to be particularly acute. Linguistic ideologies lie at the heart of these differences: the Danish community appeared to lay great stress on the importance of homogeneity, while the Hebrew and Catalan communities were described as relatively open to internal variation. Linguistic ideologies were also crucial in order to understand how language contact phenomena were accepted into each MSLC, and, while purist trends were detectable in all communities, their proponents held very different positions. In this regard it was interesting to see that the ascendancy of purism could not be predicted by the size of the community, but rather depended on historical factors and especially on the feeling of being threatened by other languages.

The existence of well-developed, elaborate standard varieties derived mostly from the fact that all the languages reviewed here were virtually *complete* in terms of language functions; that is, they were used in virtually all spheres of life in their societies. They were obviously used for interpersonal communication in private relations, but also in public contexts – at all levels of education, from the cradle to the university, for governmental and administrative purposes, the judicial systems and in the health sector. They were used by large and small enterprises for both internal and external purposes, in written and oral communications, as well as in all sorts of mass media (even the smallest communities studied had a large number of television stations broadcasting in their languages) and on the internet, and they all had a significant popular culture. The main exception to institutional completeness was Catalan, which remained – and remains – excluded from certain domains under the control of the monolingual central states, such as the army and much of the judiciary system, but is still widely practised in most domains, at least in Andorra, Catalonia and the Balearic Islands.

It should be kept in mind that institutional *completeness* should not necessarily be understood as *exclusivity*. Indeed, the linguistic ecosystems of these MSLCs were far from monolingual in several respects. Leaving aside the presence of speakers of other languages living side by side with the MSL members themselves (to which we will return later), at least three sources of multilingual practices were repeatedly mentioned.

First, one sphere of life that seemed especially open to the introduction of foreign languages was entertainment and pop culture, namely *imported entertainment*, as described by Anat Stavans. Films, music, video games and so on, in English, but also in other foreign languages, were highly popular in all the societies analysed. Some MSLCs were especially open to foreign television channels in the original version, usually with subtitles, while others accessed them mostly in dubbed form or via the internet. In any case, exposure to foreign cultural products was often seen as a useful way to acquire familiarity with other languages. It should be mentioned that openness to foreign cultural products did not mean at all that MSLs were absent from these spheres of life. Indeed, taking all differences into account, products in these languages were reported to be widely available and even popular in many of these domains, especially in radio, music and television; however, in contrast to other contexts, MSLs did not seem to saturate these spheres of life, but left ample space for productions from elsewhere.

Business and commercial relationships constituted a second area in which multilingualism was evident in most of the communities analysed. Many firms (the majority in several cases) were reported as using more than one language, and linguistic capitals other than the MSLs were systematically reported to be highly valued in business areas. As expected, a substantial number of these multilingual practices were caused by international trade, but *internal* ethnolinguistic diversity also prompted the use of languages other than the MSL in several of the societies reviewed. Again, size was not a good predictor of multilingualism, with examples of high and low levels of multilingualism in both relatively big and small MSLCs.

Last, and importantly one of the domains most *vulnerable* to the encroachment of other languages was the sphere of research and higher education. Higher-level research, such as scientific and academic publications, appeared to be yielding ground to English, especially in Denmark and Israel. English was also making progress as a language of instruction, especially in connection with postgraduate studies. It is worth noting that the debate about eventual *domain loss* (Haberland, 2005; Harder, 2009) was not experienced with the same intensity in all societies: Israel showed less concern about this possibility, while Scandinavian countries have developed the notion of *parallelsproglighed* or 'parallel language use' – a concept that deserves the attention of language managers, as it focuses on how to deal with the potential danger of domain loss while remaining open to international movements.

The MSLCs proved to have elaborate languages that were used in most linguistic domains, although not necessarily exclusively. In some areas, especially in those more open to contact with members of other language communities, such as academic work and pop culture, the presence of other languages was notable. However, in no case was it possible to say that a diglossic distribution occurred between the MSL and any other language. That is to say, perhaps with the exception of written scientific production (which, ultimately, can hardly be described as a MSLC in-group type of communication), no community showed signs of a clear division of work between its language and other languages.

Practising Multilinguals... But Still *Attractive*?

In spite of their wide differences in terms of numbers of speakers, the MSLCs analysed here coincide in being highly bilingualized; that is, most of their members claim to be able to speak at least one language other than their L1. In fact, according to Eurobarometer (2006), all MSLCs in the EU except for Hungary and Romania (so not only the MSLCs analysed here) showed a score of bilingualization higher than the EU mean, while all major languages, with the sole exception of German, were below the EU mean (Table 9.2). Indeed, the actual dimension of the language community seems to be an excellent predictor of second/foreign language proficiency – far better than the nation state or geographical position used by the Eurobarometer to explain its own data (Eurobarometer, 2006: 10).

The origins of the bilingualization of these MSLCs were not necessarily the same, and depended heavily on the historical and present ecolinguistic balance of each society. Widespread bilingualization may be the result of an active, successful educational system combined with a high exposure to English-speaking media that provides significant competence in this language, as is the case in Scandinavian and Dutch-speaking societies. However, bilingualization may also arise as a result of geographical vicinity or the intensity of commercial relationships, as in the Czech Republic, or even as a consequence of past or present sociopolitical circumstances, as in the Baltic countries or the Catalan-language territories. Population movements and mass media regulations are also crucial in providing or restricting access to the second language outside the educational context.

The actual existence of qualitative differences regarding the degree of bilingualization or plurilingualization of each MSLC, and with respect to

Table 9.2 Multilinguals in the EU: 'Which languages do you speak well enough in order to be able to have a conversation, excluding your mother tongue?'

Country	At least one language (%)	At least two languages (%)	At least three languages (%)	None
Luxembourg	99	92	69	1
Slovakia	97	48	22	3
Latvia	95	51	14	5
Lithuania	92	51	16	8
Malta	92	68	23	8
Netherlands	91	75	34	9
Slovenia	91	71	40	9
Sweden	90	48	17	10
Estonia	89	58	24	11
Denmark	88	66	30	12
Catalonia + Valencia + Balearic Islands*	83.1	26.2	7.8	16.9
Cyprus	78	22	6	22
Belgium	74	67	53	26
Croatia	71	36	11	29
Finland	69	47	23	31
Germany	67	27	8	33
Austria	62	32	21	38
Czech Republic	61	29	10	39
Bulgaria	59	31	8	41
Greece	57	19	4	43
Poland	57	32	4	43
European Union – 25 member states	56	28	11	44
France	51	21	4	49
Romania	47	27	6	53
Spain†	44	17	6	56
Hungary	42	27	20	58
Portugal	42	23	6	58
Italy	41	16	7	59
United Kingdom	38	18	6	62
Ireland	34	13	2	66
Turkey	33	5	1	67

Source: Eurobarometer (2006: 9). Data for Catalonia, Valencia and Balearic Islands: our elaboration based on data kindly furnished by Fundacc, corresponding to 2008.

*Aggregate data for all the territories where Catalan is used, or is at least official, were not available. Data for bilinguals only include those able to speak Catalan and Castilian and do not count those able to speak only one of those (usually Castilian) plus a foreign language; that is, the percentage of actual bilinguals is clearly underestimated.

†Including Catalonia, Valencia and Balearic Islands.

each language, is an open question. On the one hand, it is reasonable to assume that the levels of command of L2 are not the same in countries where contact with these languages is an everyday phenomenon in many domains, as in some areas of Catalonia, Estonia or Latvia, and in those where contact is more occasional and/or restricted to very specific spheres of interaction, like English in the Czech Republic or Slovenia. However, it remains to be proved that the traditional opposition between second and foreign languages is still useful in this respect. In fact, cases such as English in the Netherlands or Denmark probably challenge this concept. David Graddol (2006: 110) has claimed that 'In a globalised world, the traditional definition of "second-language user" (as one who uses the language for communication within their own country) no longer makes sense. Also, there is an increasing need to distinguish between proficiencies in English, rather than a speaker's bilingual status'. Ofelia García (2009: 59) argues that these notions should be abandoned altogether and substituted with that of translanguaging bilinguals. In any case, a first conclusion is clear: the MSLCs analysed here have already abandoned the era of societal monolingualism and have entered a phase in which societal bilingualism or even multilingualism is the norm rather than the exception.

One of the consequences of this widespread bilingualization seems to be the willingness, on the part of MSL speakers, to converge linguistically towards members of other linguistic groups. Indeed, MSL speakers were reported to switch to other languages on a regular basis in several of the communities analysed. Most importantly, it is not only speakers of (formerly) minoritized languages like Latvian, Estonian or Catalan that were described as switching to the language of the (former) majority – Slovenes, Danish, and to a lesser extent, Czechs, were reported to switch to other languages in the presence of foreigners, even long-term residents. In fact, all MSLCs seem to share low expectations as far as the learning of their languages by foreigners is concerned. Thus, willingness to adapt to the interlocutor's preferred language as far as one's particular capacities will allow seems to be widespread among MSL speakers.

There are many sides to this readiness to switch to another language. In the first place, it may be perceived and depicted as an open, cosmopolitan attitude, which creates a suitable atmosphere for welcoming foreign visitors and international business. Second, a general inclination to code-switch is probably an invaluable aid to improve competence in second/foreign languages, therefore enlarging the MSLC speakers' linguistic capitals. At the same time, however, a generalized willingness to converge with speakers of other languages has as a collateral consequence a reduced incentive for them to learn the MSL. Finally, in macro terms, the direction of code-switching tends to coincide with inequalities in terms of power relationships, with subordinate communities being forced to converge with their supraordinate counterparts. Depending on a myriad of factors, each MSLC – maybe even each speaker – may emphasize one or another facet of this readiness. In this regard, in some MSLCs communities (although not in all), a concern was detected about the effects of automatic convergence on social cohesion and even on the future of the language, and parallel initiatives encouraging the use of MSLs were found in places as distant as Finland – with the project *Puhu minulle suomea (Speak Finnish With Me)* – and Majorca – with the *Voluntaris per la Llengua (Language Volunteers)*.[4]

In spite of their comparatively high degrees of multilingualism, and in spite of their widely attested willingness to converge to foreigners' languages, most of the MSLCs analysed have significant numbers of L2 speakers (Table 9.1). The origin of these new MSL speakers differs in each case, and their numbers are heavily dependent on the absolute and relative number of non-MSL speakers living in the MSLC in the territory, with Hebrew, Catalan and the Baltic languages showing the highest proportions of non-native speakers. In several MSLCs, most new MSL speakers are immigrants whose native language had only a weak demographic and institutional basis, and who tend to follow the standard pattern of relatively rapid intergenerational language shift (Fishman, 1972). In other cases, it is speakers of languages with greater local, demographic and/or institutional historicity, like historical minorities or speakers of former majority languages, who adopt the MSL. In the case of Hebrew, the language is also widely learnt among the Jewish diaspora. In any case, all the MSLCs analysed proved to be attracting speakers of other languages.

Several of the challenges for MSLCs seem connected to this phenomenon of attracting L2 speakers. Young Danish L2 speakers, for instance, were said to be creating new varieties of their own. Indeed, the large number of second language speakers using the MSL highlights the problem of who is a legitimate speaker of a given language, and how new – deviant? – forms of an MSL should be addressed. In this second sense, the different treatment given to foreign accents in Danish according to the speakers' perceived origin is indicative of power and prestige correlations inside each community.

Invisible Hands? MSLCs' Relationship with the State and the Market

Tuesday 15 February 2011 was a momentous day for Catalan internauts. During the Mobile World Congress celebrated in Barcelona, Dick Costolo,

CEO of Twitter, announced that Catalan would soon be added as a language for use in this social networking service. Catalan thus joined the select club of French, German, Bahasa Indonesia, Japanese, Korean and Castilian,[5] the other languages into which the Twitter interface was being translated from its original English version. However, this good news was not really a novelty for the Catalan public. In fact, in recent years, they have grown used to seeing their language not only in multilingual platforms such as Google – including gmail and Google translator – OpenOffice, Mozilla and Wikipedia, but also in other internet platforms less given to linguistic diversity such as Facebook and YouTube. In fact, Catalan was so vibrant on the internet that on 16 September 2006, ICANN (the Internet Corporation for Assigned Names and Numbers) approved the .cat domain, the only language community domain to date, to serve the needs of the Catalan linguistic and cultural community on the internet. As the PuntCAT Foundation's slogan says,[6] 'We are open for business'. Indeed, although several of the aforementioned initiatives may have the support of language enthusiasts, they are totally unconnected to conventional language activism and are in fact business-oriented.

Conversely, Thursday 18 February 2011 was a sad day for television audiences in the Catalan-speaking territories. After years of pressure, the Valencian government, in the hands of the Spanish conservative party, the *Partido Popular*, forced the cultural association Acció Cultural del País Valencià to close down the television relays that made it possible to watch television channels from Catalonia in Valencia. These relays had been paid for by popular subscription and had been in operation for the last quarter of a century, but the conservative Valencian government had been manoeuvring for years to have them closed down. Finally, taking advantage of new regulations deployed in the transition to digital television, the government deprived its population of the only generalist television channels in Catalan available to them.

One of the most unexpected results of the cross comparison carried out in this study was the almost total absence of criticism of the purported negative effects of markets and globalization. Only one of the chapters, the one on Catalan, emphasized 'the market' as a threat for any of the MSLCs under review. One may wonder to what extent these results are biased by the personal perceptions of the researchers. The chances are that a different combination of authors with different sensitivities might have placed more emphasis on the pressure exerted by markets on the long-term viability of these languages (e.g. Phillipson, 2003, 2009). However, there are also a number of signs that seem to corroborate the general diagnosis that markets do not constitute per se a primary danger for MSLCs. Neither in countries where English used to be a politically dominant language (such as Israel), nor in communities where English is almost everyone's second language (such as Denmark or the Netherlands), and even less so in MSLCs in central or eastern Europe, were criticisms raised against 'the market' as if it were a real danger to the viability of MSLs. In all these communities, the MSL was widely used in economic and commercial spheres, from top to bottom, although not necessarily to the absolute exclusion of other languages. Indeed, a closer look at many globalized enterprises shows that much more use of MSL is made than might be expected. Take, for instance, the field of magazines, and think of the many editions of *National Geographic*, which is published not only in big languages such as (among others) English, Castilian, Chinese, Indonesian, French, German, Japanese and Portuguese, but also in several MSLs, including Bulgarian, Croatian, Czech, Danish, Greek, Hebrew, Hungarian, Finnish, Norwegian, Serbian, Slovak, Swedish and Thai. With a slightly different combination of languages, the same can be said of other international magazines such as *Reader's Digest, Cosmopolitan, Playboy*, to mention but a few. And the trend is not restricted to this field. Many other international enterprises in different sectors – from Ikea to the Coca-Cola Company, from Nestlé to Deutsche Bank, from Nokia to Microsoft – make ample use of MSLs in their activities in most if not all the MSLCs reviewed here.

Does this mean that markets are *necessarily* friendly to linguistic diversity or, at least, to MSLs? Not at all. Commercial firms seek profits, and they will be tempted to avoid investment in any language, irrespective of the number of speakers, if the use of a different language will bring greater profits. To understand the MSL-friendly attitude detected here, it should not be forgotten that this volume has reviewed the position of MSLCs that, in many respects, have already 'done their homework' in terms of linguistic standardization and have attained a considerable degree of official recognition. So it is no surprise that some of the same firms that find it reasonable to use a language spoken by five million people or fewer will ignore other languages with a far greater numbers of speakers.

In fact, when we speak about languages and markets, the specific relationship of each MSLC with the state seems to be crucial (Bastardas & Boix, 1994; Spolsky, 2004, 2009). All the MSLs analysed here are spoken in modernized societies with solid state structures, although in historical terms some of them may be quite recent. The relationships between these communities and their states are far from simple. Some communities are concentrated in one state, such as the speakers of Czech, Danish, Estonian, Hebrew or Latvian. Others are spread among two states – for instance, speakers of Dutch – or even among more than two states, like Catalan and Slovene. The history of state support has differed in each community, and even in each fraction of the community. In the cases of Dutch in the Netherlands and

Danish in Denmark, state support of a language community goes back centuries, but it is relatively recent in all the other cases: less than 100 years in the case of Finnish, Hebrew, Slovene and Dutch in Flanders and Brussels, and just a couple of decades for Latvian and Estonian. In any case, all the MSLs analysed enjoyed clear official support in the form of a state of their own, with or without recognition for minorities, or an egalitarian state, shared with other groups in terms of *at least* juridical equality. The sole exception to this rule was Catalan, which, leaving aside the tiny state of Andorra, has the support of only one autonomous (not sovereign) entity. It is no coincidence that the only language lacking clear state support is used far less in the commercial and economic spheres than all the other languages reviewed here.

In other words, enjoying the support of a *favourably disposed* state – that is, one that promotes or even requires the public use of the language and does not impose another one on the speakers – seems to be a crucial step in guaranteeing linguistic completeness for an MSL not only in official spheres, but also in commercial and economic arenas. A careful review of our cases makes this point clear. A favourably disposed state functions as a *language policy engine*, giving official status to a language, using it in all official domains and making it a requirement in many others, promoting its use by all or most citizens, spreading positive attitudes, encouraging its cultivation, guaranteeing that it has as much presence as possible in the media and in the cultural and entertainment arenas. Remember, in this regard, that several of the states where MSLs are spoken, such as Latvia, Estonia and Slovenia, require applicants for citizenship to demonstrate active knowledge of the national language, and language competence is also actively used in immigrant selection procedures in other cases such as the Netherlands or the Czech Republic (Milian i Massana, 2008). In these conditions, a favourably disposed state works as a *language policy mould*, a framework that promotes certain language choices and not others. One after the other, the cases reviewed here reflect, with varying degrees of clarity, the role of the state in correcting what could be perceived as the markets' *pernicious* influences, for example, by defining the school language models and the foreign language(s) (not) to be learnt, by offering language courses to newcomers, by imposing linguistic quotas in the mass media, by requiring labelling in one given language, or even by imposing the learning of language as a constitutional obligation. Of course, state action is not necessarily omnipotent: English gained ground as a language of education in the Netherlands in spite of the fact that the Universities Act stipulated that Dutch was the only language of higher education. However, even accepting their many limitations, in most cases, the *invisible hand* in public and private language policies does not seem to intervene in the markets themselves, but rather in how these markets are regulated in linguistic terms. Indeed, it is not size per se, but rather the language–state relationship, that best predicts language use in official and para-official domains, as witnessed by the historical changes in the position of Dutch in Flanders, the languages of the Baltic countries or Hebrew in Israel (see below).

Clearly this issue requires much more research, but, in any case, the capacity of a globalized economy to adapt to MSLCs is undoubtedly good news for linguistic diversity. There are literally hundreds of these communities spread around the world, and the data compiled here suggest that they could be perfectly viable in a globalized world economy. The problem seems to lie not in the market, but rather with its regulators.

Dealing with Internal Social Ethnolinguistic Heterogeneity

One factor generating significant differences among the MSLCs analysed here was the degree of ethnolinguistic homogeneity in their societies. Ethnolinguistic heterogeneity arose from a variety of sources, from historical proximity, as in the case of Swedish and Finnish in Finland, to very recent immigration such as the arrival of asylum-seekers in many Western countries in the early 2000s. Most of the MSLCs analysed here received significant numbers of immigrants during the 20th century, some of whom were speakers of superordinate languages, but most of whom spoke languages with no status in the receiving societies. On the whole, however, taking the percentages of native speakers of other languages living in the same societies as the MSLC, we see a continuum going from the most homogeneous societies (Slovenia and Czech Republic) to the most heterogeneous ones, including Israel, Estonia, Latvia and the Catalan-speaking territories, in which we can speak of *fragile majorities* in the sense of McAndrew (2010).

Of course, the current state of affairs should not be taken as necessarily stable (Baggioni, 1997). Only a century ago, Catalan, Latvian and Estonian were situated at the most homogeneous end of this continuum of ethnolinguistic composition, while the society living in today's Czech Republic was far more heterogeneous than it is now. For their part, Dutch and Danish were closer to Slovene in terms of dialectal vitality and therefore much more heterogeneous, and Hebrew was just coming back to life as an everyday language in a handful of kibbutzim. Two main variables, independent but intertwined, changed this picture dramatically. On the one hand, demographic movements and changes, including genocides, deportations and mass migrations, created new ethnolinguistic homogeneities and heterogeneities.

On the other hand, nation state building processes and their associated language policies significantly modified the linguistic repertoires of the populations concerned.

Internal diversity poses an extra challenge to MSLCs, which was summarized as follows by Maja Bitenc in her case study: 'One of the main challenges facing the Slovene language community seems to be the question of how to retain the vitality of the Slovene language, so that it will remain the dominant language in the Republic of Slovenia, without violating (and in fact promoting) democratic principles and the basic human rights of those whose mother tongue is not Slovene but who reside in the Slovene territory.' The same challenge was posed, in slightly different terms, by practically all authors in connection with all MSLs, and two main kinds of solution were proposed with varying degrees of emphasis: first, public language policies (i.e. state action) and, second, a new language culture, more respectful of multilingualism and linguistic rights.

The actual answers to the challenge differed markedly between MSLCs, even within each community. In fact, the gamut of positions with regard to how to manage ethnolinguistic diversity is huge, ranging from blatantly assimilationist discourses refusing any recognition of linguistic diversity wherever it appears, such as the ones reported in some social and political circles in Denmark, to explicitly isolationist, anti-integrationist discourses, such as the ones published by the Director of the Estonian Language Institute. It is not only the authorities, but also the various social actors (including every community) and individuals themselves that make decisions, which may move in different directions. For example, Russian and Ethiopian immigrants to Israel showed different attitudes towards Hebrew and first language retention, and different paths of integration were perceptible in Russian minorities in both Estonia and Latvia.

Some very general trends can be identified in the approach to internal ethnolinguistic diversity. First, a distinction tends to be made everywhere between historical minorities and immigrant communities, with the former often being given more rights than the latter and sometimes even receiving official recognition, and the latter being explicitly urged to integrate completely into the MSLC, with little more than some school assistance. MSLCs seem much more willing to recognize even very small historical minorities like the Hungarians and Italians in Slovenia, the Aranese in Catalonia or the Latgalians and the Livs in Latvia. In most if not all MSLCs one can also identify a vague change in the general appreciation of linguistic diversity, with slogans such as 'More than n hundred languages are spoken in X' being found from Helsinki to Amsterdam or Barcelona. Demographic weight is also a significant factor favouring the recognition of some groups over others.

Indeed, a welcome consequence of the advance of democracy and human rights is that more space for linguistic diversity is emerging in all societies, MSLCs obviously included (cf. Spolsky, 2004). However, none of these general trends can explain, by itself, the huge differences in management of internal diversity in each society: it is only through a precise understanding of local history, society and politics that a clear idea can be obtained why Catalonia now has three official languages with a single system of education, the Baltic countries and Andorra are monolingual states with separate school systems, and Israel is officially bilingual and has linguistically separate schools. In other words, while MSLCs may be more sympathetic to linguistic minorities, no general MSLC approach to internal diversity can be identified.

A Recurrent Problem: The MSL Scale Loss

While size per se was not perceived as a determinant for MSL survival, several participants in the workshops pointed to ongoing processes of reduction of their MSLs' potential for communicability, which could be described as a scale loss. To put it in economic terms, several MSLCs faced the risk of losing parts of their (traditional) markets, due to the fact that administrative and political barriers were unexpectedly becoming transformed into new sociolinguistic barriers.

This scale loss was resented in the case of Catalan, where it was said that some political actors insistently appealed to the narcissism of small differences to deter cross-border linguistic exchanges. However, similar concerns arose in other areas such as Scandinavia, where traditional intercomprehension seemed to be yielding to growing problems in mutual understanding, at least on the side of Danish. In the former Czechoslovakia, younger Slovak and Czech speakers were also reported to be losing the ability to understand one another. This concern was even expressed in connection with Dutch, with the Netherlands and Flanders becoming less interrelated in cultural terms. In all these cases, state and administrative borders and institutions played a crucial role in the sense that they still reproduce the *national language* principle, with its double meaning, on the one hand encouraging homogenization within borders, and on the other hand promoting distinctiveness with regard to neighbouring societies. This estrangement from neighbouring varieties appears to be occurring even in the absence of conscious policies, or even against explicit national policies trying to prevent it. Neither Czech nor Danish institutions seek to separate their languages from neighbouring Slovak or Scandinavian languages, and the Flemish and Dutch authorities have even yielded part of their national sovereignty to the *Taalunie*, a supranational institution created to promote linguistic integration. Nevertheless, scholars from all these societies showed concern regarding this growing distance, for, even in a supposedly border-free Europe, cultural activities and products found it difficult to cross borders. In a way, state and sub-state moulds seemed to be more powerful than explicit language policies.

English, Just a Lingua Franca?

Concerns about the loss of scale appeared strongly associated, at least in some of the societies analysed, with a parallel concern: the diminishing abilities of the (educated) members of the MSLC to operate in foreign languages other than English and, therefore, the growing dependence on English-speaking sources as far as cultural and informational issues are concerned.

It should be taken into account that the position of English in the MSLCs analysed was far from homogeneous. In several cases, the language of Shakespeare was – still? – no more than a distant, though highly prestigious, international lingua franca spoken by a growing though still small fraction of the population in a reduced number of situations mostly involving interactions with foreigners. In fact, in many of these countries, English pop-rock music was highly successful, but understood by hardly anyone. And English did not seem to be making significant inroads in the most basic spheres of language use, that is, in interpersonal, face-to-face communications between local residents. In this regard, the Baltic experiences are particularly interesting. For decades, the Soviet Empire imposed Russian as the lingua franca between locals and immigrants from the rest of the USSR. Since independence, both Estonian and Latvian authorities have encouraged the learning and use of the national languages, but also of English, as a tool to bind their societies to the West. Chances were that English would be adopted as a somehow more 'neutral' lingua franca between speakers of the national language and Russian speakers. Nevertheless, in spite of a few anecdotal examples (Laitin, 1998), this does not seem to be the case: while competence in English is on the increase among all language groups, it does not seem to play a relevant role in interpersonal communications, which remain monopolized by the local varieties.

The progress of English at the expense of other languages was especially clear in some MSLCs with older and stronger relationships with either the UK and/or the USA, namely the Netherlands and Denmark. In all these cases, a solid, ever-growing competence in English was apparently displacing other foreign languages. In these and in some other MSLCs like the Hebrew-speaking community, English had already become the undisputed international lingua franca, generally learnt as the first foreign/second language, and widely present *in situ* thanks especially to cultural products such as pop music or audiovisual products, usually subtitled rather than dubbed. In these communities, English was, to a large extent, assumed to be part of the by defect linguistic repertoire of an increasing number of social circles. In terms of language practices, English was used spontaneously with foreigners, who were often 'excused' from learning the local MSL (especially in high professional positions) in postgraduate courses and as the written language of technical and scientific literature. In fact, as a consequence of this wide presence, English terms infiltrated these MSLs, from the most specialized registers to the slang of the young. To a certain extent, the position of English in these more anglicized MSLCs may recall that of Castilian in Spain's Catalan-speaking territories, or that of Russian in the Baltic States during the Soviet occupation.

Nevertheless, several factors make the two situations qualitatively and quantitatively different. First, in spite of its growing public presence, English remained a non-official language in all these communities, with all the associated consequences. Even in the most anglicized societies it was inconceivable that official, administrative activities should be carried out in English. Second, English speakers did not constitute sizeable percentages of the population in these more anglicized MSLCs, so interpersonal contact with native speakers of the lingua franca remained much less frequent. The MSLCs also retained control of their audiovisual space: local products were produced in the MSL, and English was provided with a (usually subtitled) MSL version. In other words, effective integration into these MSLCs did require the learning of the local MSL, and English was no substitute for it, especially for lower-class immigrants. In fact, English in these MSLCs was mostly used for two main purposes: in language-learning events and as a means to communicate across borders. The sole exception of sustained in-group use of English comprised the expanding experiences of bilingual education, by definition an experience in second language learning.

In other words, although English seemed to have made significant inroads in several MSLCs, and it was probably reaching a percentage of the population and a range of social functions wider than any previous lingua franca in history, its position in these societies remained that of a means of outgroup communication, a complementary linguistic capital that did not threaten the position of each respective MSL as the language with the highest socializing value (Bourdieu, 1982; Boix & Vila, 1998; Lamuela, 1994, 2004). To the extent that it remained a lingua franca without local native speakers, speakers of these MSLs were probably quite right not to perceive it as a danger to their languages (Ostler, 2010), as its position was substantially different from those of post-imperial languages with a sizeable number of native speakers in the midst of the MSLCs. In this respect, it suffices to say that while monolingualism in English was hardly mentioned as a threat for 'anglicized' MSLCs, monolingualism in Castilian or Russian was regarded as one of the most conspicuous challenges for Catalan, Estonian and Latvian.

Some Final Remarks

This book brings good news about linguistic diversity. Even in the midst of globalization, there is plenty of room for sustainable linguistic diversity on Earth, at least as far as MSLs is concerned. We have looked at communities of different dimensions – between 1 and 25 million speakers – and we have realized that, in spite of multiple present and historical differences, there are a large number of relatively successful models of linguistic communities in which non-major languages are in a good state of health. Of course, each community has its own features and no two cases are identical, but enough common ground was found to be able to extract a number of useful lessons that can be applied to other language communities.

The first lesson to be learnt is that there is no need for MSLCs to shift to an international language in most domains in order to thrive economically. Our case studies show that MSLs can be used in administration, education, the business world, the mass media, the internet and virtually all relevant domains, without hampering progress and welfare. Without doubt, the scale of a language community is an objective element to be taken into account in language management, but its importance should not be overestimated. Our examples show that MSLCs of just 1 million speakers are perfectly viable as instruments for developed societies. Other examples of apparently perfectly sustainable languages, such as Icelandic, with fewer than half a million speakers, suggest that the demographic contingent for sustainability may be much lower than the one adopted here. And the use of an MSL should not be regarded in terms of *cost*. All but one of the countries analysed here were described by the 2010 Human Development Index[7] as enjoying very high levels of human development and they do not need to switch to a big language for most everyday lives. One may legitimately wonder whether it is precisely because they have retained this control over their linguistic behaviour that they do so well in other aspects of human activity.

A second point of interest here is that all the MSLCs analysed had developed elaborate, complete languages that are used effectively in most spheres of life, although not always exclusively. Interestingly enough, although they were often placed in a multilingual ecosystem, none of the communities showed a diglossic pattern of language distribution – no fixed distribution of languages was detected, apart from the fact that other languages were used particularly in interactions with outgroup speakers. Sustainability may not require completeness, but completeness almost certainly helps long-term sustainability.

A third lesson from this volume is that linguistic sustainability may not require monolingual societies. Many language revitalization movements in the past thought of monolingualism as the only way to escape language shift, but widespread societal bilingualism also seems to be compatible with language maintenance. This is good news, for, in the long run, a dilemma between language maintenance and societal bilingualism would be lethal for MSLs. In general terms, the MSLCs reviewed here were widely bilingualized in one or even more than one major language. However, generalized, unilateral bilingualism does not *necessarily* lead to language shift: none of the MSLCs analysed here was shifting to a bigger, more international language.

The data compiled suggest strongly that MSLCs need favourable public policies, and public policies are made by states. The most vulnerable community was not one of the smallest ones, but rather the only one that did not enjoy the support of a favourable state. The lesson is clear. In spite of all changes introduced by globalization, and in spite of the loss of autonomy of nation states, to guarantee viability in the 21st century, states and politics are crucial (Bastardas, 2007; Milian i Massana, 2008). States are the engines that create public language policies, and they also set the frames for private language management. Indeed, as Fishman (1991) claims, many things can be achieved in the economic field even without state help, but linguistic completeness is probably impossible without a favourably disposed state. The examples analysed here have shown that economic sectors seem to adapt quite easily to the state requirements as far as MSLs are concerned. In linguistic terms at least, the market seems to be a much tamer animal than we might have expected or, at least, a beast that can be kept at bay if necessary.

While markets appear to be relatively open to MSLs in many spheres of life, market pressures in favour of simplification also exist. In certain circumstances, these pressures push mostly in the direction of English and, depending on the particular linguistic ecosystem, in that of other major languages. English has made objective inroads in certain domains in many of the MSLCs analysed. However, as our reports show, these spheres of life in which English is encroaching are not necessarily so numerous; leaving aside its function as a lingua franca among speakers of different L1s, the progress of English is concentrated around research and technology, higher education and imported entertainment. All these areas deserve particular attention, and it would be rash to predict that the diffusion of English will not enter other domains. However, it should also be remembered that states have many instruments to keep foreign languages at a certain distance when so desired, and they are not slow to use them.

Finally, we have seen that ethnolinguistic diversity is much more important for the sustainability of MSLCs than size alone, but it is not necessarily a fatal circumstance for these communities. Some of the cases reviewed have shown that MSLCs may survive even in contexts of high ethnolinguistic diversity. The question is how to manage these more complicated scenarios democratically so that they do not evolve towards language shift, without simultaneously violating human rights. The volume presents some of the strategies adopted by MSLCs and discusses some of their pros and cons. In the end, democratic principles suggest that the decision to adopt one of these strategies or to follow a new, different way should depend on the will of each linguistic community.

Acknowledgements

The author is grateful to Albert Bastardas, Emili Boix, Vanessa Bretxa and Antoni Milian for their comments on previous versions of this paper, and to Natxo Sorolla (CRUSCAT) and Caterina Masramon (Fundacc) for their help with statistical data from the Catalan language territories. This chapter is supported by the Spanish Ministry of Science and Innovation research grant FFI2009-09968 and the group 'Estudi de la Variació' (2009 SGR 521), funded by Catalan Ministry of Economy and Knowledge.

Notes

(1) Obviously, a different selection of MSLCs would have yielded a different picture. See http://www.ethnologue.com/ethno_docs/distribution.asp?by=size for an idea of the other MSLCs that might have been included in the one to 25 million speaker bracket. The Calvet Observatory (http://www.portalingua.info/fr/poids-des-langues/) is also useful, but only for languages with five million speakers or more.
(2) Remember that the Dutch and Finnish cases were analysed during the conferences, although in the end a chapter about these languages could not be included in the volume.
(3) For the sake of brevity, in this chapter we will not make explicit reference to each chapter of the volume with the names of the author(s). Instead, any mentions of one of the communities analysed in this volume should be understood as referring either to the particular chapter dealing with it, or to the discussions held during the workshops.

(4) See http://www.conselldemallorca.net/?&id_parent=463&id_section=2215&id_son=2230
(5) See http://blog.albertcuesta.com/post/3310905909/el-conseller-delegat-de-twitter-ha and http://twitter.com/jinen/status/37574428061741056
(6) See http://www.domini.cat/en_index.html
(7) See http://hdr.undp.org/en/statistics/ (last accessed 24 April 2011).

References

Baggioni, D. (1997) *Langues et nations en Europe*. Paris: Éditions Payot & Rivages.
Bastardas, A. and Boix, E. (1994) *¿Un estado, una lengua? La organización política de la diversidad lingüística*. Barcelona: Octaedro Universidad.
Bastardas i Boada, A. (2007) *Les polítiques de la llengua i la identitat a l'era "glocal"*. Barcelona: Generalitat de Catalunya, Departament d'Interior, Relacions Institucionals i Participació, Institut d'Estudis Autonòmics.
Boix i Fuster, E. and Vila i Moreno, F.X. (1998) *Sociolingüística de la llengua catalana*. Barcelona: Ariel.
Bourdieu, P. (1982) *Ce que parler veut dire. L'économie des échanges linguistiques*. Poitiers: Fayard.
Castells, M. (2003) *The Information Age: Economy, Society and Culture. Volume I: The Rise of the Network Society*. Cambridge, MA: Blackwell.
Eurobarometer (2006) *Europeans and Their Languages*. European Commission. http://ec.europa.eu/public_opinion/archives/ebs/ebs_243_en.pdf
Fishman, J.A. (1972) *The Sociology of Language: An Interdisciplinary Social Science Approach to Language in Society*. Rowley, MA: Newbury House Publishers.
Fishman, J.A. (1991) *Reversing Language Shift. Theoretical and Empirical Foundations of Assistance to Threatened Languages*. Clevedon: Multilingual Matters.
Fundacc – El Baròmetre de la Comunicació i la Cultura. http://www.fundacc.org/fundacc/ca.html
García, O. (2009) *Bilingual Education in the 21st Century. A Global Perspective*. Oxford: Wiley-Blackwell.
Graddol, D. (2006) *English Next. Why Global English May Mean the End of 'English as a Foreign Language'*. The British Council. http://www.britishcouncil.org/learning-research-english-next.pdf
Haberland, H. (2005) Domain and domain loss. In B. Preisler, A. Fabricius, H. Haberland, S. Kjærbeck and K. Risager (eds) *The Consequences of Mobility* (pp. 227–237). Roskilde: Roskilde University, Department of Language and Culture. http://magenta.ruc.dk/cuid/publikationer/publikationer/mobility/mobility2/Haberland/
Harder, P. (2009) *Angles on the English Speaking World. English in Denmark: Language Policy, Internationalization and University Teaching*. Copenhagen: Museum Tusculanum Press, University of Copenhagen.
Herslund, M. (1999) Dansk som det andet sprog. In N. Davidse-Nielsen, E. Hansen and P. Jarvad (eds). *Engelsk eller ikke engelsk? That is the Question* (pp. 39–64). Copenhaguen: Glyndenal.
Laitin, D.D. (1998) *Identity in Formation: The Russian-Speaking Populations in the Near Abroad*. Ithaca: Cornell University Press.
Lamuela, X. (1994) *Estandardització i establiment de les llengües*. Barcelona: Ed. 62.
Lamuela, X. (2004) Installació o establiment? Encara sobre els objectius de la promoció lingüística. *Caplletra* 37, 217–244.

McAndrew, M. (2010) *Les majorités fragiles et l'éducation. Belgique, Catalogne, Irlande du Nord, Québec.* Montréal: Les Presses de l'Université de Montréal.
Milian i Massana, A. (2008) *Globalización y requisitos lingüísticos: una perspectiva jurídica. Supraestatalidad, libre circulación, inmigración y requisitos lingüísticos.* Atelier: Barcelona.
Ostler, N. (2010) *The Last Lingua Franca. English until the Return of Babel.* London; New York: Allen Lane.
Phillipson, R. (2003) *English-only Europe? Challenging Language Policy.* London: Routledge.
Phillipson, R. (2009) English in higher education: Panacea or pandemic? In P. Harder (ed.) *Angles on the English Speaking World. English in Denmark: Language Policy, Internationalization and University Teaching* (pp. 29–54). Copenhagen: Museum Tusculanum Press, University of Copenhagen.
Preisler, B. (2009) Complementary languages: The national language and English as working languages in European universities. In P. Harder (ed.) *Angles on the English Speaking World. English in Denmark: Language Policy, Internationalization and University Teaching* (pp. 10–28). Copenhagen: Museum Tusculanum Press; University of Copenhagen.
Spolsky, B. (2004) *Language Policy.* Cambridge: Cambridge University Press.
Spolsky, B. (2009) *Language Management.* Cambridge: Cambridge University Press.

Index

academia, 94
academic, 6, 25, 27, 28, 35, 50, 77, 101, 149, 180, 183, 184
accent, 43, 44, 45, 56, 57, 187
activism, 188
administration, 14, 39, 63, 196
administrative affairs, 11, 182
Adrey, J.B., 107, 108, 125
adult education, 38, 100, 124, 153
Afghanistan, 54
Africa, 88, 165
African, 44
after-school programme, 91
Agarin, T., 131, 136, 140, 155
Alacant/Alicante, 165, 171
Albanian, 6, 61, 76
Alguer, 160, 161, 171, 172, 177
Alksnis, V., 137, 155
America, 88
American, 30, 57
Amharic, 86, 89, 90, 91, 92, 97
Andersen, M.H., 50, 55
Anderson, B., 167, 175
Andorra, 13, 160, 161, 162, 168, 170, 173, 174, 177, 182, 190, 193
Anglicization, 52
anglicized, 86, 195, 196
Anglo-Americanisation, 24
Anglophone, 158
anonymity, 170
anti-integrationist discourse / tendency, 114, 117, 192
Arab, 12, 87, 88, 89, 90, 94, 95, 97, 99, 101
Arabic, 6, 12, 39, 46, 47, 52, 53, 54, 74, 82, 83, 85, 86, 87, 89, 91, 92, 93, 94, 96, 97, 98, 99, 100, 101, 102, 103, 113
Aracil, Ll. V., 163
Aragon, 157, 161, 168, 175
Aramaic, 82, 86
Aranese, 192
Argenté, J., 176, 163
Argentina, 73, 77
Argentinian, 95
aristocracy, 133
armed forces, [see army]
Armenia, 22
Armenian, 86
army, 2, 29, 38, 41, 107, 138, 142, 173, 182
Asari, E-M., 111, 112, 116, 125
Ashkenazi, 83
Asia, 88
Asian, 36, 91
Asser, H., 108, 115, 116, 125
assimilation, 131, 192
Assyrian, 86
attestation, 137, 138, 147, 153 [see also evaluation & examination]
attitude, [see language attitude]
audiovisual space, 173, 195
Australia, 13, 38, 73, 106, 126, 130
Austria, 11, 19, 22, 58, 68, 76, 78, 185
Austro-Hungarian, 158
authenticity, 85, 95, 170
autochthonous, 58, 66, 68, 107, 123, 132, 149
automatic translators, 64, 182, 188
autonomous community, 160, 161, 167

Bacher, P., 53, 55
Baggioni, D., 191, 199
Bahasa Indonesia, 188
Baker, C., 5, 15
Balažic Bulc, T, 79
Baldauf, R.B., 37, 155
Balearic Islands, 161, 164, 166, 168, 170, 171, 172, 182, 185
Balkans, 140
Baltic, 114, 128, 130, 131, 132, 133, 134, 137, 139, 140, 144, 146, 149, 154, 155, 156, 194
Baltic countries / Baltic states, 106, 125, 126, 127, 131, 132, 133, 134, 135, 136, 137, 138, 139, 140, 141, 151, 156, 184, 191, 193, 195
Baltic language, 133, 137, 139, 152, 187
Ban, J., 77
banking, 146
Barcelona, 4, 6, 8, 9, 13, 14, 15, 17, 159, 160, 165, 170, 175, 176, 177, 178, 187, 192, 199, 200
Barreña, A., 17, 127
Bastardas, A., 2, 15, 26, 163, 189, 197, 198, 199
Belarus, 22, 125
Belarusian, 107, 111, 136
Belgium, 6, 19, 161, 185
belief, 34, 35,61, 82, 83, 102, 113, 119
Ben Yehuda, 82, 83
Ben-Rafael, E., 84, 87, 103
Berruto, G., 5, 15
Bildt, C., 137, 155
bilingual, 15, 20, 31, 49, 53, 64, 66, 68, 73, 90, 113, 124, 125, 126, 129, 141, 159, 160, 162, 167, 174, 181, 182, 186, 193, 195,199
bilingualism, 13, 33, 34, 37, 47, 53, 67, 170, 186, 197
bilingualization, 184, 186
bilingualized, 14, 184, 197
Bitenc, M., 11, 58, 73, 77, 192
Blommaert, J., 2, 15
Bloomfield, L., 5, 6, 15
Bogatec, N., 78
Boix, E., 2, 13, 14, 15, 17, 157, 161, 163, 164, 166, 170, 172, 175, 176, 177, 189, 195, 198, 199, 200
Bologna Declaration, 70

Bolshevik revolution, 134
book, 6, 9, 12, 14, 28, 43, 73, 91, 93, 99, 143, 159, 172 [see also publishing]
border, 2, 3, 10, 14, 19, 31, 68, 132, 140, 151, 173, 193, 194, 195 [see also frontier]
Bosnia and Herzegovina, 22, 73, 76
Bosnian, 60, 61, 74, 121
Bourdieu, P., 172, 195, 199
Bourne, J., 122, 125
boycott, 148
Boyd, S., 55, 56
Branchadell, A., 167, 176, 177
Bratt Paulston, C., 155
Bretxa, V., 1, 198, 200
Brink, L., 51, 55
British, 16, 82, 86, 89, 199
Brittany, 160
broadcast, 39, 49, 61, 62, 64, 74, 87, 92, 93, 114, 143, 159, 167, 182
Brown, K.D., 123, 125
Bugge, K.E., 55
Bulgaria, 22, 185
Bulgarian, 21, 189
Busch, B., 78
business, 10, 13, 14, 38, 39, 41, 49, 65, 74, 88, 89, 90, 94, 142, 145, 159, 173, 183, 186, 188, 196

Calvet, L.J., 3, 15, 158, 176, 198
campaign, 94, 104, 123, 148, 151, 153, 164, 170
Canada, 73, 83, 106, 161
Cantonese, 46
caretaker, 138
Carxe, 161
Castells, M., 179, 199
Castile, 161
Castilian, 161, 185, 188, 189, 195, 196 [see also Spanish]
Catalan, 6, 13, 14, 17, 133, 157, 158, 159, 160, 161, 162, 163, 164, 165, 166, 167, 168, 169, 170, 171, 172, 173, 174, 175, 176, 177, 178, 180, 182, 184, 185, 186, 187, 188, 189, 190, 191, 193, 195, 196, 198, 200 [see also Valencian]
Catalanisation, 166

Catalan-speaking territories, 157, 160, 164, 165, 166, 168, 171, 172, 173, 174, 175, 188, 191, 195
Catalonia, 128, 157, 160, 161, 162, 163, 164, 165, 166, 167, 168, 169, 170, 171, 172, 175, 176, 177, 178, 182, 185, 186, 188, 192, 193
church, 133, 165, 175
census, 19, 20, 60, 66, 74, 107, 109, 114, 136, 137, 144, 145
central language, 7, 158, 163
challenge, 3, 4, 6, 7, 8, 9, 10, 11, 12, 13, 15, 18, 30, 34, 39, 55, 59, 63, 67, 71, 72, 81, 102, 103, 105, 109, 110, 114, 116, 117, 118, 119, 123, 125, 131, 143, 149, 160, 167, 168, 169, 170, 172, 173, 174, 179, 186, 187, 192, 196
Charter of Fundamental Rights, 152
child, 12, 30, 46, 47, 49, 52, 53, 54, 62, 67, 68, 69, 73, 74, 86, 94, 97, 111, 141, 159, 160, 164, 171, 172, 181
China, 22, 38, 77, 93
Chinese, 74, 98, 99, 160, 180, 189
Chinn, J., 140, 155
cinema, 12, 92, 177
Circassian, 12, 86
citizenship, 22, 74, 87, 109, 115, 116, 131, 138, 139, 140, 151, 154, 155, 190
civil servant, 108, 135, 142, 169
classmates (communication with), 113
Clemens, W., 134, 155
Clemmensen, N., 55
clerk, 138
Čmejrková, S., 36
code-switching, 92, 112, 165, 166, 167, 186, 196 [see also mixing strategy]
codification, 72, 152, 174, 182 [see also standardization]
codified, 157, 160, 181
colleagues (communication with), 113
college, 99, 100, 101, 153
colloquial, 32, 74, 85
colonial language, 124
colonialism, 124, 132, 164
commercial (domain), 180, 183, 184, 190
Common European Framework of Reference for Languages, 30
common language, 13, 74, 83, 84, 105, 170

communication, 11, 12, 14, 26, 27, 28, 29, 31, 32, 33, 49, 53, 54, 59, 60, 61, 65, 66, 67, 68, 74, 84, 85, 87, 98, 99, 100, 107, 115, 136, 145, 176, 182, 184, 186, 195
communicative competence, 21, 67
Communist, 19, 21, 24, 26, 107, 121, 128
community language, 86, 98
company, 159, 160 [see also entreprise & firm]
competence, see linguistic competence
competitiveness, 69, 152, 170
complete language, 181, 182, 197 [see also linguistic (institutional) completeness]
comprehension, 54, 55, 100, 139 [see also mutual intelligibility]
compulsory subject, 21, 66, 87, 138
computer, 49, 94, 100
Conference of Nationalities, 135
confidence, 32, 44, 59, 71, 166, 170
conscious policy, 193
constitution, 6, 29, 66, 69, 75, 76, 82, 110, 135, 138, 139, 149, 161
Constitutional Court, 161
constitutional obligation, 190
constitutional stipulation, 96
contact language, 133
converge, 186, 187
convergence, 129, 164, 187
corporate language, 27
corpus [see language corpus]
Costa, J., 165, 170, 175, 176
Coulmas, F., 1, 120, 126
couple
  linguistically homogeneous couples, 164, 172
  linguistically mixed couple, 172, 181
  mixed ethnolinguistic couples, 69, 164, 172
covert language policy, 86, 98
Croatia, 22, 31, 73, 185
Croatian, 60, 61, 74, 76, 121, 158, 189
Cubberley, P., 107, 121, 128
cultural consumption, 2, 158, 166, 170
cultural production, 2, 14, 158, 159, 183
culture, 11, 12, 17, 22, 23, 33, 43, 54, 62, 67, 69, 73, 77, 92, 93, 100, 102, 131, 139, 151, 157, 159, 160, 163, 164, 165, 167, 168, 182

curriculum, 39, 43, 71, 84, 98, 99, 100, 148, 153, 167
CUSC, 4, 8
customary language, 167
cyberspace, 91, 94
Cyprus, 185
Cyrillic, 121
Czech, 8, 9, 10, 18, 19, 20, 21, 22, 23, 24, 25, 26, 27, 28, 29, 30, 31, 32, 33, 34, 35, 36, 37, 158, 160, 180, 182, 184, 185, 186, 189, 190, 191, 193
Czech Republic, 9, 18, 19, 20, 24, 25, 28, 29, 30, 31, 32, 33, 36, 37
Czechoslovakia, 10, 18, 23, 24, 33, 193

daily life, 86, 112, 145, 166, 175
Dane, 10, 42, 43, 44, 49, 50, 51, 53, 54, 55
Daneš, F., 36
danger, 4, 9, 10, 23, 25, 51, 122, 184, 188, 189, 196
Danish, 8, 10, 11, 38, 39, 40, 41, 42, 43, 44, 45, 46, 47, 48, 49, 50, 51, 52, 53, 54, 55, 56, 57, 160, 180, 181, 182, 183, 186, 187, 189, 190, 191, 193
Dansk Sprognævn, 40, 47, 45
Davidsen-Nielsen, N., 50, 51, 55
decyrillization, 141
Deets, T., 140, 155
default language, 12, 113
degree (university), 39, 77, 101, 108, 112, 167
Delsing, L-O. 54, 55
demobilization, 173, 174
democracy, 159, 162, 193
democratization, 141
demographic, 3, 7, 8, 11, 68, 88, 106, 132, 136, 137, 138, 155, 157, 158, 174, 180, 181, 187, 191, 196
demographics, 87, 144, 160
demolinguistic, 9, 13, 179, 180, 181
demonstration, 118
Demšar, F., 78
Denmark, 10, 17, 38, 39, 40, 41, 42, 43, 44, 46, 47, 48, 49, 50, 51, 52, 54, 55, 56, 57, 106, 125, 171, 185, 186, 189, 190, 192, 194, 199, 200
denormalization, 162
deportation, 107, 191

Dermol-Hvala, H., 78
description, 9, 15, 47, 48, 64, 72, 81, 165
destandardization, 10, 32
de Swaan, A., 3, 7, 15
de Varennes, F., 141, 155
deterioration, 94, 153, 154
devaluation, 24, 25, 170, 174
dialect, 2, 3, 10, 38, 41, 43, 48, 52, 54, 57, 61, 68, 74, 99, 103, 121, 182
diaspora, 11, 54, 81, 83, 84, 85, 103, 126, 152, 156, 187
Dickins, T., 36
dictatorship, 157, 159, 162, 165
dictionary, 17, 38, 40, 45, 64, 75, 160, 182
Diderichsen, P., 38, 55
diglossia, 1, 16, 67, 68, 99
diglossic, 51, 83, 184, 197
disappearance, 43, 48, 54, 172, 174
discourse, 21, 25, 42, 43, 49, 61, 109, 110, 117, 121, 125, 155, 169, 180
discrimination, 65, 116, 118
disintegration, 23, 167, 174
dissolution, 10, 169, 174
diversity, 13, 65, 95, 120, 122, 123, 128, 131, 143, 148, 183, 192, 193, 196, 198
division (social), 33, 103, 116, 119, 168, 169, 174
domain loss, 10, 41, 51, 52, 55, 183, 184, 199
dominant language, 26, 59, 90, 94, 107, 161, 163, 169, 170, 171, 172, 188, 192
domination, 119, 131, 143, 166, 172, 173, 175
Dorian, N., 6, 16
Dovalil,V., 31, 36
Druviete,I., 123, 126, 140, 141, 142, 145, 155
dubb, 62, 91, 183, 195
Dular,J., 63, 75, 78
Dunbar,R.., 141, 155
Dutch, 5, 6, 8, 15, 54, 168, 180, 181, 183, 184, 186, 189, 190, 191, 193, 198

ecological (approach), 1, 122, 127
economic activity, 90, 141, 145, 154, 190, 197
economic value, 118, 150
education, 11, 27, 38, 39, 42, 43, 44, 46, 48, 49, 50, 52, 54, 62, 65, 66, 67, 68,

69, 71, 76, 82, 83, 96, 97, 98, 101,
102, 103, 108, 124, 125, 134, 135,
137, 138, 141, 142, 152, 155, 156,
166, 168, 171, 174, 182, 190, 193,
195, 196, 200
educational language policy, 81, 96
educational system, 11, 12, 38, 39, 43, 45,
46, 50, 52, 84, 96, 103, 104, 159, 160,
162, 166, 184
Edwards, J., 3, 16, 199
Ehala, M., 3, 16
elaborate language, 181, 182, 184, 197
elementary school, 67, 99, 101
elite, 18, 41, 45, 117
emigration, 60, 139, 141, 181
employment, 67, 74, 108, 113, 138, 154
endangered language (community), 3, 4,
16, 37, 59, 84, 85, 86, 104, 146
endangerment, 16, 146
English, 5, 10, 11, 12, 13, 16, 17, 20, 21,
23, 25, 26, 27, 28, 29, 30, 36, 37, 39,
40, 41, 43, 45, 46, 49, 50, 51, 52, 53,
54, 55, 57, 59, 62, 64, 65, 66, 69, 70,
71, 72, 74, 77, 79, 80, 82, 83, 85, 86,
89, 90, 91, 92, 93, 94, 96, 97, 99, 100,
101, 102, 103, 106, 112, 114, 115,
117, 124, 127, 135, 141, 142, 143,
144, 146, 147, 150, 158, 160, 161,
166, 171, 175, 180, 181, 183, 184,
186, 188, 189, 190, 194, 195, 196,
197, 198, 199, 200
enterprise, 91, 138, 145, 182, 189 [see also
company & firm]
entertainment, 91, 93, 180, 183, 190, 198
equality, 42, 48, 65, 87, 119, 124, 136,
161, 190
Erasmus programme, 171
Espasa, A., 169, 176
Estonia, 12, 13, 105, 106, 107, 108, 109,
110, 111, 112, 113, 114, 115, 116, 118,
119, 120, 123, 124, 125, 126, 127, 128,
129, 130, 133, 134, 135, 136, 137, 138,
156, 185, 186, 190, 191, 192
Estonian, 8, 12, 13, 105, 106, 107, 108,
109, 111, 112, 113, 114, 115, 116,
117, 118, 119, 123, 124, 125, 126,
127, 128, 129, 130, 136, 137, 139,
158, 180, 186, 189, 190, 191, 192,
194, 196

Estonianization, 109
Estonianness, 13, 123
Ethiopia, 95
Ethiopian, 11, 86, 90, 91, 95, 96, 104, 192
ethnic, 13, 19, 23, 26, 31, 32, 45, 60, 76,
96, 102, 105, 106, 108, 111, 112, 113,
114, 115, 116, 117, 121, 124, 126,
129, 132, 140, 145, 155
ethnic affiliation / identity, 60, 129, 132
[see also ethnicity]
ethnic community, 66, 67
ethnic group, 16, 20, 26, 31, 83, 113, 122,
156, 170
ethnic language, 20
ethnic minority, 37, 66, 67, 78, 79
ethnicity, 13, 19, 20, 21, 120, 123, 132,
154 [see also ethnic affiliation]
ethnolinguistic, 8, 9, 12, 105, 117, 168,
169, 183, 191, 192, 198
ethnolinguistic community / group, 105,
112, 113, 114, 162, 164, 169 [see also
language community]
ethnolinguistic vitality, 3, 16, 96, 167,
170, 172, 174
Ethnologue, 7, 180
Eurobarometer, 65, 71, 74, 78, 184, 185,
199
Euromosaic, 3, 16
Europe, 2, 13, 14, 16, 19, 21, 37, 48, 55,
59, 73, 77, 81, 83, 84, 106, 108, 115,
121, 126, 130, 132, 133, 135, 139,
140, 155, 156, 158, 160, 178, 181,
189, 194, 199, 200
European, 2, 7, 9, 14, 17, 19, 23, 30, 32,
36, 37, 38, 42, 44, 58, 65, 73, 76, 77,
78, 79, 83, 88, 92, 122, 125, 126, 127,
131, 132, 135, 138, 139, 145, 152,
154, 155, 156, 164, 171, 173, 174,
180, 199
European Commission, 65, 78, 199
European Union (UE), 7, 14, 19, 30, 31,
32, 35, 36, 37, 40, 46, 48, 51, 54, 58,
59, 65, 68, 69, 72, 77, 106, 108, 115,
125, 127, 130, 132, 133, 138, 139,
140, 152, 155, 160, 162, 180, 184, 185
Eurozone, 106
evaluation, 63, 98, 100, 126 [see also
attestation & examination]
exam, 77, 115

examination, 28, 30, 97, 99, 100, 138, 139, 180 [see also attestation & evaluation]
exile, 107
explicit policy, 193
extinction, 4, 85
Extra, G., 2, 16, 178
extrinsic minority, 131

Fabra, P., 170, 175, 176
Fabricius, H., 55, 57, 199
face-to-face communication, 153, 194 [see also interpersonal communication]
family, 37, 43, 45, 68, 69, 83, 87, 89, 93, 106, 164, 165, 167, 172, 174, 181
Faroe Islands, 38, 50
Farràs, J., 13, 14, 157
Farsi, 47
favourably disposed state, 190, 197
Ferguson, C.A., 1, 16
Fernández-Armesto, F., 42, 55
Ferrer i Gironès, F., 162
Filippov, M., 117, 126
film, 163, 183
fine, 117
Finland, 50, 106, 161, 185, 187, 191
Finnish, 8, 15, 50, 76, 106, 128, 160, 180, 183, 186, 187, 189, 190, 191, 198
Finno-Ugric, 106, 133, 149
firm, 75, 183, 189 [see also company & entreprise]
first language 13, 20, 38, 61, 71, 76, 96, 97, 130, 162, 164, 165, 174, 179, 180, 184, 192, 198 [see also mother tongue]
Fischer, E., 3, 16
Fishman, J.A., 3, 8, 16, 98, 103, 129, 172, 187, 197, 199
Flanders, 190, 191, 193
Flemish, 168, 183, 193
folklore, 134
Fons, M., 174, 177
foreign accent, 42, 43, 44
foreign language, 9, 11, 23, 25, 28, 29, 30, 31, 32, 36, 38, 43, 53, 59, 65, 66, 67, 69, 70, 71, 72, 74, 77, 85, 86, 87, 93, 96, 97, 99, 100, 104, 163, 180, 183, 184, 185, 186, 190, 195, 198
foreigner, 9, 20, 26, 28, 29, 30, 31, 33, 35, 43, 59, 62, 70, 72, 73, 75, 77, 89, 91, 138, 173, 186, 187, 194, 195

formal situation, 68, 162
Foucault, M., 109, 110, 111, 126
Fournier, A., 118, 126
fragile majority, 191
fragmentation, 161, 167
France, 22, 49, 73, 113, 162, 173, 185
Francis, B., 109, 126
Francophonie, 6
Franja, la, 161
French, 6, 12, 23, 27, 28, 39, 43, 51, 52, 53, 54, 64, 77, 86, 89, 92, 97, 99, 100, 101, 113, 135, 142, 158, 159, 160, 161, 163, 164, 165, 166, 169, 170, 171, 172, 175, 188, 189
French Catalonia, 160, 162 [see also Pyrénées-Orientales]
frontier, 68 [see also border]
Fukuda, M., 166, 176

Galbreath, D.J., 108, 126, 148, 155
Galvin, M.E., 148, 155
García, A., 186, 199
Gellner, E., 134, 155
genocide, 191
German, 5, 6, 19, 20, 21, 22, 23, 26, 27, 28, 30, 31, 37, 38, 39, 44, 51, 52, 53, 54, 58, 60, 61, 62, 64, 65, 76, 77, 86, 98, 131, 133, 134, 135, 136, 143, 155, 160, 166, 175, 184, 188, 189
Germanic, 27, 44, 58, 121, 133
Germany, 19, 22, 27, 38, 49, 73, 134, 135, 136, 185
Giles, H., 3, 16
globalization, 5, 7, 14, 15, 17, 49, 59, 65, 85, 98, 100, 102, 104, 132, 160, 163, 166, 171, 188, 196, 197
glocalization, 9
Goldzweig, G., 95, 104
Gorjanc, V., 78
Gorter, D., 2, 16, 178
government, 11, 30, 40, 42, 46, 48, 49, 54, 55, 62, 75, 76, 85, 89, 91, 93, 107, 117, 123, 142, 153, 159, 161, 162, 168, 169, 171, 173, 174, 175, 177, 182, 188
Graddol, D., 3, 16, 186, 199
grade school, 44, 45
graduation, 83, 100

grammar, 32, 38, 63, 64, 74, 76, 99, 100, 104, 133, 182
Greece, 185
Greek, 21, 23, 82, 189
Greenland, 38
Grenoble, L.A., 3, 16
Grønnum, N., 43, 55
Grundtvig, N.F.S., 41, 55
guise test, 44, 50
Gumperz, J.A., 1, 16
Gundar, 95
Gustà, M., 157, 176

Haberland, H., 16, 52, 55, 57, 183, 199
Hall, J., 175, 177
Hallel, M., 100, 103
Hanseatic League, 134
Hansen, E., 38, 45, 55, 56, 199
Haragos, S., 155
Harder, P., 17, 183, 199, 200
Harjumaa, 111, 112
Harris, R., 121, 126
Harrison, K.D., 121, 122, 126
Hasil, J., 36
Haskala, 84
Haugen, E., 1, 16, 33, 36
health sector, 142, 182
Hebrew, 8, 11, 12, 81, 82, 83, 84, 85, 86, 87, 88, 89, 90, 91, 92, 93, 94, 96, 97, 99, 100, 101, 102, 103, 104, 180, 182, 187, 189, 190, 191, 192, 195
Hebrew Language Academy, 87
Heidmets, M., 125, 127
Henricksson, A., 134, 155
Herder, 134
heritage language, 10, 12, 81, 82, 85, 86,103
Herslund, M., 51, 55, 181, 199
Hiden, J., 135, 155
High Commission for National Minorities, 140
high school, 38, 39, 49, 50, 77, 86, 99, 100, 101
higher education, 4, 10, 11, 17, 41, 57, 69, 70, 71, 72, 77, 107, 108, 118, 183, 190, 198, 200 [see also university]
Hindi, 46, 121
Hindsgaul, D., 127
historical minority, 66, 131, 192
historical-structural, 12, 109, 110, 118

Hogan-Brun, G., 108, 126, 132, 139, 140, 148, 155
Holmen, A., 50, 52, 55, 56, 57
home, 14, 41, 51, 53, 61, 73, 77, 92, 107, 118, 125
homeland, 81, 83, 84, 103, 115, 116, 118
homogenization, 41, 193
Hornberger, N. 110, 128
host society, 131
Hudson, R.A. 123, 126
human rights, 59, 120, 126, 140, 154, 155, 156, 192, 193, 198
humanities, 28, 71, 77, 93
Hungarian, 21, 33, 35, 58, 60, 61, 62, 65, 66, 68, 74, 86, 92, 106, 131, 158, 189, 192
Hungary, 11, 36, 58, 66, 68, 184, 185
Hymes, D., 5, 16
hypercentral language, 7, 158, 163

iazyk mezhnatsional'nogo obshcheniia, 107
Iceland, 38, 50, 93
Icelandic, 196
Ida-Virumaa, 108, 112, 114, 115, 124, 125
identity, 12, 13, 26, 37, 43, 46, 51, 69, 73, 87, 95, 119, 120, 123, 125, 126, 132, 134, 176
ideological, 2, 10, 42, 49, 62, 83, 95, 99, 174
ideology, 9, 10, 11, 21, 22, 23, 25, 26, 31, 34, 35, 36, 48, 58, 71, 72, 84, 102, 104, 123, 127, 136, 175, 176, 182 [see also language ideology]
Idiazabal, I., 17, 127
immersion, 165
immigrant, 11, 12, 42, 43, 47, 53, 54, 59, 67, 72, 82, 83, 84, 86, 87, 88, 89, 90, 91, 93, 95, 96, 97, 98, 100, 103, 104, 105, 106, 109, 111, 112, 115, 116, 118, 164, 165, 169, 172, 175, 176, 190, 192, 194, 195 [see also newcomer]
immigration, 14, 25, 42, 48, 60, 84, 86, 88, 95, 100, 107, 131, 160, 166, 171, 191
implementation, 63, 66, 67, 75, 84, 100, 152, 155
independence, 11, 13, 58, 59, 62, 67, 71, 105, 107, 108, 109, 111, 112, 115, 116, 118, 134, 135, 136, 137, 138, 139, 141, 194

India, 121
Indian, 91
Indo-European, 106, 121
Indonesian, 189
industry, 12, 51, 100, 107, 108
inequality, 105, 106, 119, 120, 122, 159, 166, 187
informal communication, 14, 30, 67, 91, 107, 113
information, 20, 21, 30, 37, 142, 199
information technology (IT), 39, 115
inscription, see sign
Institute of Catalan Studies, 160
integration, 7, 12, 30, 47, 58, 67, 68, 73, 105, 114, 115, 116, 117, 124, 125, 127, 146, 150, 151, 152, 165, 171, 192, 194, 195
interethnic, 12, 105, 112, 113, 114, 120, 164
interference, 163, 170
intergenerational language transmission, 2, 7, 8, 68, 86, 160, 162, 172, 179, 181
interlingua, 166
internal diversity, 10, 61, 95, 193
international affairs, 13, 71, 73, 142
international language, 28
internationalization, 11, 69, 139
internet, 4, 14, 15, 28, 94, 143, 144, 159, 182, 183, 188, 196
interpersonal communication, 12, 86, 180, 182, 194 [see also face-to-face communication]
interposition, 163, 164, 174
intolerance, 49, 55, 65, 162
Ireland, 37, 185
isolation, 11, 54, 55, 109, 111, 125
Israel, 11, 12, 81, 82, 83, 84, 85, 86, 87, 88, 89, 90, 91, 92, 93, 94, 95, 96, 97, 98, 99, 100, 101, 102, 103, 104, 183, 188, 191, 192, 193
Italian, 6, 23, 54, 60, 61, 62, 64, 65, 66, 68, 74, 158, 159, 160, 161, 163, 166, 169, 170, 192
Italy, 11, 22, 49, 58, 68, 76, 78, 173, 185

Jagose, A., 123, 126
Japan, 22, 38, 77
Japanese, 39, 86, 98, 166, 188, 189
Jarvad, P., 55, 199

Järve, P., 108, 126
Jewish, 11, 82, 83, 84, 85, 86, 87, 88, 91, 92, 97, 99, 104, 134, 135, 187
Jewry, 83, 84
Jews, 11, 12, 83, 84, 86, 87, 89, 92, 136
Johannsen, L., 127
Johns, M., 140, 155
Jones, S.P., 5, 15
Jørgensen, J.N., 10, 30, 39, 40, 50, 52, 55, 56, 57
Juaristi, P., 17, 127
Jubulis, M.A., 139, 155
Judaism, 84
Judeo-Arabic, 86
Judeo-Berber, 86 [see also Tamazight]
judicial systems, 182
Juhuri, 86
Junyent, C., 17, 127

Kachru, B.B., 5, 16
Kalin Golob, M., 78
Kallas, K., 107, 126, 127
Kaplan, R.B., 37, 155
Karker, A., 53, 56
Karklins, R., 107, 126, 138, 155
Kasearu, K., 127
Kaučič-Baša, M., 78
Kazakhstan, 22
Kelley, J.G., 108, 126
Kern, D., 78
Kiełkiewicz-Janowiak, A., 36
kindergarten, 4, 39, 83, 94, 99, 101
kin-state, 132
Kirilova, M., 44, 52, 56
Kiswahili see Swahili
Kjærbeck, S., 55, 57, 199
Kloss, H., 1, 5, 16
Knez, M., 78
knowledge, 20, 21, 25, 26, 27, 33, 47, 49, 50, 52, 53, 54, 59, 68, 74, 98, 108, 109, 110, 112, 113, 114, 122, 123, 139, 144, 160, 168, 172, 190
Knowles, E., 136, 155
Kobos, Z.K., 78
Kolstø, P., 107, 126, 127, 128
Komac, M., 66, 67, 78
Kontra, M., 35, 36
Koplewitz, I., 87, 103
Korean, 188

Kõresaar, E., 118, 126, 127
Kraus, J., 24, 25, 36
Kreindler, I., 136, 156
Kristiansen, T., 39, 43, 44, 45, 48, 49, 50, 56
Kristjánsdóttir, B., 48, 53, 56, 57
Kroskrity, P.V., 35, 36
Kruuse, M., 117, 118, 127
Kržišnik, E., 78
Kulturministeriet, 40, 46, 50, 57
Kymlicka, W., 118, 127

L1 [see first language]
L2 [see second language]
labelling, 162, 163, 190
Labov, W., 5, 16
Ladegaard, H.J., 44, 57
Ladino, 82, 86, 98
Laitin, D., 2, 17, 114, 127, 194, 199
Lambert, R.D., 82, 103, 104
Lamuela, X., 181, 195, 199
language acquisition, 72, 74, 124, 125, 152
language attitude, 5, 13, 22, 33, 45, 46, 50, 52, 55, 88, 98,, 102, 106, 116, 117, 125, 128, 131, 137, 145, 146, 147, 148, 150, 154, 176, 186, 189, 190, 192
language awareness, 52, 63
language behaviour [see linguistic behaviour]
language capacity, 124, 150, 154
language choice, 87, 97, 110, 145, 163, 164
language community, 1, 2, 3, 4, 5, 6, 7, 8, 9, 14, 15, 16, 17, 55, 59, 63, 69, 71, 72, 75, 81, 84, 158, 160, 161, 164, 167, 173, 173, 174, 175, 179, 180, 181, 182, 184, 187, 188, 189, 190, 192, 196, 197, 198, 1, 4, 6, 7, 180, 182, 196
language competence [see linguistic competence]
language conflict, 133, 146, 150, 158
language consultancy, 64, 65
language contact, 79, 129, 133, 182
language corpus, 10, 11, 62, 64, 65, 71, 72, 76, 182, 100
language course, 30, 31, 72, 77, 97, 98, 99, 101, 165, 168, 190

language cultivation, 37, 59, 149, 152, 190
language culture, 61, 71, 152, 192
language diversity [see linguistic diversity]
language domain, 4, 9, 10, 11, 13, 14, 26, 27, 28, 35, 41, 51, 52, 55, 57, 59, 63, 68, 71, 72, 87, 113, 114, 115, 130, 137, 141, 142, 145, 154, 159, 161, 162, 167, 172, 175, 181, 182, 183, 184, 186, 188, 190, 191, 196, 197, 198, 199
language duty, 48, 161
language ecology, see linguistic ecology
language education, see language teaching
language environment, 144
language equipment, see linguistic resources
language hierarchy, 131, 132, 142, 144
language ideology, see linguistic ideology
language instruction see language teaching
language law [see language legislation]
language learning, 4, 8, 9, 11, 12, 14, 16, 21, 23, 26, 30, 42, 43, 44, 59, 65, 66, 67, 71, 72, 73, 77, 84, 98, 99, 103, 107, 113, 118, 124, 126, 131, 135, 136, 137, 160, 164, 166, 165, 166, 171, 173, 179, 186, 187, 190, 194, 195, 196, 199
language legislation, 4, 33, 40, 42, 62, 61, 66, 69, 75, 76, 82, 85, 86, 98, 108, 115, 117, 126, 128, 130, 135, 137, 138, 139, 140, 141, 145, 150, 153, 155 162, 163, 171
language loyalty, 170, 172, 174
language maintenance, 97, 102, 131, 197, 199
language management, 4, 9, 37, 184, 196, 197
language of administration, 153
language of instruction, 4, 29, 39, 50, 66, 68, 69, 70, 76, 84, 86, 87, 97, 98, 99, 101, 135, 141, 142, 148, 149, 165, 168, 171, 183
language of international communication, see language of wider usage
language of origin, 84, 87, 103, 164

language of wider usage, 107, 117
language parallelism [*see* parallel language policy]
language planning, 37, 52, 59, 62, 66, 71, 72, 73, 103, 104, 109, 110, 111, 117, 119, 126, 128, 155
language policy, 2, 4, 8, 9, 10, 17, 29, 33, 40, 47, 49, 54, 59, 62, 63, 69, 72, 73, 77, 79, 81, 82, 83, 85, 86, 100, 102, 103, 104, 109, 110, 112, 119, 123, 125, 127, 128, 135, 136, 137, 138, 139, 140, 148, 149, 150, 151, 152, 154, 156, 161, 169, 171, 175, 176, 190, 192, 194, 197, 199, 200
language practices, 9, 11, 33, 52, 83, 104, 111, 126, 128, 144, 155, 182, 183, 195 [*see also* language use]
language preservation, 24, 59
language proficiency, 72, 100, 108, 112, 130, 137, 138, 140, 141, 147, 152, 184,
language prohibition, 174
language promotion, 10, 65, 75, 114, 117, 118, 119, 123, 168, 171
language protection, 4, 61, 66, 67, 78, 104, 117, 132, 155, 177
language regulation, 40, 48, 62, 76, 83, 109, 162, 173, 184, 188, 191
language requirement, 10, 11, 39, 74, 85, 86, 87, 97, 98, 99, 100, 108, 109, 115, 135, 138, 140, 141, 154, 162, 166, 168, 190, 195, 197
language revival, 11, 13, 22, 23, 26, 32, 81, 82,83, 84, 104, 123
language right, [*see* linguistic right]
language security, 158
language shift, 8, 11, 73, 112, 113, 118, 124, 131, 132, 143, 144, 181, 187, 196, 197, 198
language skills, 44, 87, 115, 137
language system, 5, 9, 12, 25, 181
language teaching, 10, 21, 25, 29, 30, 31, 39, 42, 44, 45, 46, 47, 48, 49, 52, 65, 66, 68, 72, 76, 96, 97, 98, 99, 100, 101, 103, 125, 160, 165, 182
language threat, *see* threat
language usage *see* language use
language use, 2, 4, 5, 7, 10, 11, 12, 13, 15, 19, 20, 25, 27, 28, 29, 30, 31, 32, 33, 34, 35, 38, 39, 40, 41, 42, 43, 44, 50, 51, 52, 61, 62, 63, 65, 67, 68, 69, 70, 71, 72, 73, 74, 75, 76, 77, 82, 86, 87, 91, 92, 94, 98, 99, 102, 105, 106, 108, 110, 111, 112, 113, 114, 115, 117, 118, 120, 122, 127, 132, 134, 135, 136, 140, 141, 142, 143, 144, 145, 146, 149, 153, 154, 159, 160, 162, 163, 164, 165, 166, 167, 168, 169, 170, 171, 172, 174, 175, 176, 180, 181, 182, 183, 184, 186, 187, 188, 189, 190, 191, 194, 195, 196, 197, 198 [*see also* language practices]
language variation, 41, 48
Larreula, E., 158, 177
Latgale, 149, 151
Latgalian, 149, 192
Latin, 23, 28, 49, 51, 89, 94
Latin America, 165, 172
Latin American, 91, 171
Latvia, 13, 106, 108, 126, 127, 130, 131, 133, 134, 135, 136, 137, 138, 139, 140, 143, 144, 145, 146, 147, 149, 150, 151, 152, 153, 154, 155, 156, 185, 186, 190, 191, 192
Latvian, 8, 13, 106, 114, 130, 131, 133, 134, 135, 136, 137, 138, 139, 140, 141, 142, 143, 144, 145, 146, 147, 148, 149, 150, 151, 152, 153, 154, 155, 156, 158, 180, 186, 189, 190, 191, 194, 196
Latvian Socialist Republic, 137
Lauristin, 108, 111, 112, 113, 114, 115, 116, 117, 118, 125, 126, 127, 129
Le Page, R.B., 6, 17
leisure, 92, 93
Lieven, A., 107, 124, 127
Lifrieri, L., 155
lingua franca, 14, 17, 29, 31, 33, 59, 72, 86, 107, 112, 114, 124, 130, 132, 165, 171, 194, 195, 198
Linguamón, 4, 8
linguistic ability, *see* language skills
linguistic authority, 174
linguistic behaviour, 23, 26, 30, 35, 110, 165, 196
linguistic capital, 172, 183, 186, 195
linguistic community [*see* language community]

linguistic competence, 11,12, 59, 63, 65, 71, 72, 74, 112, 113, 114, 115, 124, 137, 138, 140, 141, 153, 184, 186, 190, 194
linguistic diversity, 1, 4, 10, 20, 74, 121, 122, 123, 133, 142, 152, 173, 188, 189, 191, 192, 193, 196
linguistic ecology, 1, 36, 81, 82, 122
linguistic ecosystem, 2, 197
linguistic enclave, 91, 181
linguistic hierarchy, 134, 136
linguistic ideology, 9, 18, 21, 25, 40, 155, 182
linguistic infrastructure, see linguistic resources
linguistic [institutional] completeness, 14, 182, 183, 190, 197 [see also complete language]
linguistic landscape, 89
linguistic marker, 10
linguistic minoriy, 43, 46, 48, 54, 95, 132, 149, 155, 193
linguistic prejudice, 86, 94
linguistic pluralism, 47, 87, 88, 102
linguistic quota, 190
linguistic reform, 170, 175
linguistic repertoire, 3, 5, 112, 192, 195
linguistic resources, 54, 63, 65, 152, 160, 181
linguistic right, 59, 66, 67, 76, 107, 113, 118, 119, 120, 121, 125, 126, 128, 140, 141, 152, 154, 155, 156, 161, 192, 196
linguistic sustainability, 4, 10, 197
linguistic tolerance, 13, 147, 148, 154
linguist, 9, 18, 24, 25, 32, 34, 35, 40, 46, 47, 48, 50, 51, 53, 58, 121, 123
linguistics, 65, 119, 121, 123, 126, 127, 149
literacy, 4, 53, 97, 99, 100, 101, 134, 162
literary language, 74, 82, 99, 130, 149, 152, 154 [see also standard language]
literature, 3, 5, 28, 33, 77, 87, 92, 99, 100, 134, 139, 143, 152, 153, 157
Lithuania, 106, 127, 133, 134, 135, 137, 156, 185
Lithuanian, 130, 133, 136, 137, 158
liturgical language, 84
Livonian, 106, 134

Livs, 149, 192
loan, loanword, 25, 35, 51, 82, 87, 133, 170
local language, 107, 123, 124, 131, 136, 139, 181, 194
Loeber, D.A., 135, 156
Lund, J., 53, 56, 57
Lundin Åkesson, K., 55
Lusofonia, 6
Luxembourg, 185

Macedonia, 22, 73
Macedonian, 61, 74, 76
Madera, M., 5, 17
Madsen, M., 52, 55, 57
magazine, 159, 189
Maghreb, 165
majority community / language, 3, 9, 11, 15, 45, 68, 69, 73, 83, 87, 95, 96, 103, 108, 131, 132, 147, 158, 159, 186, 187
majorized minority, 131
Makoni, S., 121, 127
Mallorca, 160, 166, 177
Malta, 185
Mandarin, 46, 53, 180
Marí, I. 168, 175, 177
market, 10, 33, 45, 104, 116, 141, 143, 150, 153, 159, 162, 163, 187, 188, 189, 190, 191, 193, 197
marketplace, 159, 160, 161, 162, 169, 174
Martí, F., 1, 6, 17, 121, 127
Marušič, F., 65, 80
Masramon, C., 198
mass media, 11, 12, 35, 39, 40, 45, 52, 53, 55, 61, 64, 75, 91, 92, 93, 98, 114, 117, 140, 141, 143, 159, 162, 164, 175, 182, 184, 190, 196
Masso, A., 129
mastery, 59, 162, 166
Mayonnaise war, 40, 45, 182
McAndrew, M., 191, 200
McRoberts, K., 175, 177
means of instruction [see language of instruction]
Meden, A., 78
medium of instruction [see language of instruction]
medium school, 108, 138, 149

medium-sized language (community), 1, 4, 5, 6, 7,8, 9, 11, 12, 13, 14, 15, 18, 26, 72, 81, 85, 102, 103, 157, 158, 160, 163, 167, 171, 173, 174, 175, 179. 180, 181, 182,183, 184, 186, 187, 188, 189, 190, 191, 192, 193, 194, 195, 196, 197, 198
member state (European Union), 2, 14, 31, 73, 132
Mercator, 78, 149, 156
Mexican, 95
Middle East, 88
Middle Eastern, 44
middle generation, 21
middle school, 101
migration, 84, 107, 165, 166, 191
migratory flow, see migration
Miheljak, V., 79
Mikkelsen, K., 38, 57
Milian, A., 161, 162, 175, 176, 177, 190, 197, 198, 200
military, see army
Mills, S., 109, 127, 177
mindset, 107 [see also language ideology]
minority community / language, 3, 8, 9, 11, 12, 13, 15, 16, 33, 37, 38, 42, 43, 44, 46, 47, 48, 53, 54, 58, 61, 62, 65, 66, 67, 68, 69, 76, 78, 79, 83, 86, 87, 88, 93, 95, 96, 103, 104, 112, 116, 123, 125, 126, 131, 132, 133, 135, 140, 144, 146, 147, 148, 149, 155, 156, 163, 164, 180, 187, 190, 192
minoritized / minorized, 132, 163, 169, 181, 186
Mishna, 82, 83
Misiunas, R.J., 107, 127
mixed marriages [see couple]
mixing strategy, 112, 120 [se also code-switching]
mobility, 48, 69, 124, 156, 171, 199
Molas, J., 177
Moldova, 22, 121, 127, 128
Moldovan, 20
Mollà, T., 5, 17
Mongolia, 22
Mongolian, 20
monolingual, 5, 12, 66, 83, 102, 107, 114, 125, 181, 182, 183, 193, 197
monolingualism, 140, 186, 196, 197

Montenegrin, 74, 121
Montenegro, 73
Montoya, B., 172, 176
Moravian, 19, 21
Mørch Jacobsen, K., 55
Moreno Fernández, F., 5, 17
morphology, 48, 83
morphosyntax, 114, 169
Moseley, C., 3, 17
mother tongue, 19, 20, 25, 26, 30, 31, 38, 42, 43, 46, 47, 48, 53, 54, 59, 60, 61, 65, 67, 68, 69, 73, 74, 96, 97, 118, 134, 136, 147, 167, 185, 192 [see also first language]
MSL / MSLC see medium-sized language community
Muchnik, M., 98, 104
Mühlhäusler, P., 1, 121, 122, 127
multilingual, 5, 11, 12, 15, 16, 17, 37, 58, 64, 69, 75, 82, 103, 104, 127, 130, 154, 155, 156, 158, 159, 174, 183, 186, 187, 188, 192, 197
multilingualism, 12, 16, 37, 65, 66, 88, 92, 102, 103, 125, 150, 154, 159, 174, 183, 186, 187, 192
multinational company / institution, 9, 25, 27, 37
Munteanu, I., 121, 127
Murcia, 161, 176
music, 12, 62, 92, 180, 183, 194, 195 [see also pop culture]
mutual intelligibility, 2, 33, 61 [see also comprehension]

Nagel, K-J., 175, 177
Narkiss, D., 82, 87, 88, 104
Narva, 107, 115, 125
nation, 4, 8, 13, 23, 36, 38, 66, 76, 81, 102, 121, 122, 134, 136, 140, 192, 199
nation state [see nation and state]
national awakening, 134
national language, 12, 17, 50, 63, 71, 72, 73, 79, 106, 113, 114, 121, 123, 130, 140, 141, 153, 190, 193, 194
national minority, 67
nationalist, 137, 169
nationality, 30, 43, 84, 115, 118, 123, 139
native language, 99, 107, 137, 148, 173, 187

native speaker, 38, 52, 59, 60, 100, 120, 106, 149, 160, 187, 191, 195, 196
NATO, 106, 139
naturalization, 139
naturalize, 109, 115, 124
Nazi, 23, 135
Nećak Lük, A., 78, 79
Nećak, D., 78
neighbouring country / state, 31, 68, 132, 149
neighbouring language, 58, 170
Nejedlý, P., 25, 29, 37
Nekula, M., 27, 37
Nekvapil, J., 9, 10, 18, 23, 24, 26, 27, 32, 35, 36, 37
neoclassical approach, 110
neologism, 87, 160, 163
neo-Marxist, 110
Netherlands, the, 22, 106, 125, 171, 185, 186, 189, 190, 193, 194
Nettle, D., 121, 122, 127
Neustupný, J.V., 23, 36, 37
Nevo, N., 85, 104
new word, see neologism
newcomer, 11, 164, 165, 190 [see also immigrant]
newspaper, 91, 93, 94, 159, 160 [see also press]
Nidorfer, M., 73, 79
Nietzsche, F., 109, 127
night clubs and bars, 113
Nogué, N., 170
non-citizen, 13, 111, 139, 142
non-native, 45, 171, 187
non-standard, 10, 32, 43, 74
non-titular, 137, 147, 150
Nørgaard, O., 107, 127
norm enforcement, 132
normalization, 128, 160, 162
normative variety, 182
North America, 19, 38, 95, 130, 158
Norway, 43, 48, 50, 106
Norwegian, 38, 39, 43, 49, 53, 54, 189
Novak-Lukanovič, S., 67, 79
number of speakers, 8, 19, 71, 130, 150, 180, 189

obligatory use, 69, 75
Occitania, 160

occupation, 23, 105, 106, 108, 116, 118, 123, 132, 135, 138, 139, 141, 153, 195
official domain & communication, 33, 191
official language, 4, 7, 12, 32, 40, 58, 66, 69, 72, 73, 82, 85, 86, 87, 97, 108, 130, 134, 135, 137, 140, 146, 151, 154, 160, 161, 162, 193, 195
official recognition, 161, 189, 192
official statements, see language legislation
official status, 2, 4, 83, 130, 136, 162, 174, 190
official use, see official status
Old Prussian, 133
older generation, 31, 86, 112
Olshtain, E., 85, 104
online communication, 115
Ortega, P., 17, 127, 40
orthography, 40, 45, 51, 63, 75
OSCE, 108, 139, 140, 156
Ostler, N., 17, 196, 198
Ottoman, 82, 158
overt policy, 81, 99
Ozolins, U., 13, 108, 126, 127, 130, 140, 155, 156

Pakistan, 121
Palestine, 82, 86, 133
Palestinian, 12, 99, 103
Palou, J., 174, 177
parallel language policy, 10, 40, 41, 49, 54, 108, 183
para-official domain, 191
parents, 69, 97, 99, 143, 160, 164, 165, 172, 181
parliament, 38, 62, 75, 87, 108, 142, 151
participation, 116, 151, 152, 170
Pashto, 54
passive bilingualism, [see receptive bilingualism]
passive knowledge, [see receptive competence]
Pedastsaar, T., 125
Pedersen, I.L., 38, 41, 45, 48, 57
Pennycook, A., 110, 111, 119, 121, 122, 127
peripheral language, 3

Peru, 169
Phillipson, R., 17, 119, 127, 188, 200
phonetics, 169
Pirih Svetina, N., 78
PISA, 101
Pla, A., 170, 177
pluralism, 47, 87, 88
plurilingualism, 11, 58, 59, 79, 88
Pogorelec, B., 79
Poland, 19, 22, 31, 36, 133, 135, 185
Poles, 19, 136
Police, 138, 142
Polish, 19, 20, 21, 31, 35, 86, 135, 142
political arena, 90
political identity, 87
political mobilization, 150
political party, 25, 46, 150, 165, 168, 169
politics, 38, 39, 46, 52, 110, 116, 117, 126, 150, 154, 155, 193, 197
polyglot, 92
Pons, E., 158, 177
pop culture, 92, 98, 183, 184 [see also music]
Porina, V., 143, 145, 146, 156
Portugal, 19, 185
Portuguese, 6, 189
postcolonial, 5, 124, 125, 127, 132, 156
postgraduate, 76, 77, 183, 195
post-imperial languages, 196
post-Soviet, 13, 106, 109, 118, 155
poststructuralist, 12, 105, 106, 109, 110, 118, 119, 120, 121, 123
Požgaj-Hadži, V., 79
Prague, 9, 23, 30, 35, 36, 37
Preisler, A., 17, 50, 52, 55, 57, 199
press, 4, 11 43, 46, 61, 62, 93, 114, 128, 142 [see also newspaper]
prestige, 33, 41, 43, 44, 59, 61, 69, 94, 123, 160, 167, 170, 171, 187
prestigious, 31, 60, 73, 171, 172, 194
primary education, 30, 31, 71, 138, 142, 171
private economic activity, see private sector
private sector, 13, 39, 88, 108, 140, 142
private sphere, 51, 65, 87, 108, 182
professional arena, 29, 47, 48, 52, 64, 90, 128, 137, 138, 195, 186
pronunciation, 38, 43, 44, 83, 94
proofreading, 64, 65
propagation, 31, 32

public administration, 38, 108, 159
public communication, 71, 72, 91
public company, 91
public domain, see public language sphere
public employee, see civil servant
public functions, see public sphere
public places, see public sphere
public representative, 138
public sector, 88, 108, 142
public servant, see civil servant
public sign, 141
public space, 88, 91, 94, 111, 170
public sphere, 30, 38, 39, 41, 61, 62, 63, 66, 71, 75, 83, 87, 113, 135, 144, 162, 165, 190
public transport, 142
public use (of language), see public sphere
publishing, 13, 17, 36, 159 [see also book]
Puerto Rican, 167
Pujolar, J., 167, 170, 171, 177
Punjabi, 46, 52
purism, 11, 23, 58, 59, 62, 72, 85, 86, 94, 117, 182
purity, 64, 143, 170
Pyrénées-Orientales, 161, 162 [see also French Catalonia]

quality of language, 24, 61, 69, 94, 124, 152, 153
Quebec, 155, 171, 176
Quebecois, 158
Quechua, 6, 169
queer, 123
Querol, E., 157, 177

Rabin, Ch., 82, 104
Račevskis, K., 124, 127, 132, 156
radio, 4, 39, 61, 62, 64, 74, 87, 91, 93, 114, 142, 143, 159, 183
Ramishvili, T., 137, 156
Ramonienė, M., 126
Rannut, M., 117, 126, 155
Réaume, D., 158, 177
receptive bilingualism, 33, 164
receptive competence, 31, 33, 112
reference book, 59, 63, 64, 65, 75
referendum, 151, 152, 154
regional language, 66, 123, 151
regional minority, 132

Rehovot, 89, 91
religion, 142
Remeseira, C., 167, 177
republican language, 136, 137
research, 1, 3, 4, 5, 6, 8, 10, 12, 14, 16,
  24, 27, 28, 29, 33, 46, 50, 57, 63,
  65, 70, 74, 106, 110, 121, 126, 132,
  156, 165, 166, 171, 175, 183, 191,
  198, 199
re-vernacularization, 84
revitalization, 69, 73, 197
revival, 81, 82, 83, 84
Ricento, T., 110, 128
Riga, 133, 134, 145, 146, 151, 156
Rimbau, E., 163, 177
Risager, K., 55, 57, 199
Robbins, K., 120, 128
Roma, 15, 19, 21, 66, 136
Romaine, S. 16, 121, 122, 127
Romance, 58, 121, 157, 170
Romani, 20, 60, 61, 66, 67, 76
Romania, 22, 101, 121, 131, 184, 185
Romanian, 121
Romanov, A., 148, 150, 156
Ros, A.,169
Russia, 13, 22, 30, 100, 106, 108, 111, 112,
  113, 114, 115, 116, 124, 131, 134,
  139, 140, 144, 151, 154
Russian, 11, 12, 13, 20, 21, 23, 27, 31, 35,
  39, 54, 55, 76, 77, 86, 88, 89, 90, 91,
  92, 93, 95, 96, 97, 98, 99, 100, 101,
  104, 105, 106, 107, 108, 109, 111,
  112, 113, 114, 115, 116, 117, 118,
  120, 121, 123, 124, 125, 126, 127,
  128, 129, 131, 134, 135, 136, 137,
  138, 139, 140, 141, 142, 143, 144,
  145, 146, 147, 148, 149, 150, 151,
  152, 153, 154, 155, 156, 158, 160,
  192, 194, 195, 196, 199
Russification, 108, 124, 126, 134, 136

Saami, 106
Šabec, N., 79
Santamaria, N., 157, 176
Sanz, C., 166, 170, 176
Sardinia, 160, 161
Sastre, B., 166, 177
Šaur, V., 25, 37
scale loss, 193, 194
Scandinavia, 36, 93, 193
Scandinavian, 10, 27, 39, 52, 53, 54, 183,
  184, 193
Scandinavian languages, 10, 39, 52, 53,
  54, 193
Schengen Zone, 115
Schjerve, R., 37, 132, 133, 156
school, 20, 21, 27, 29, 30, 32, 38, 39, 40,
  42, 44, 45, 46, 47, 49, 53, 65, 66, 67,
  76, 79, 83, 84, 97, 98, 99, 100, 101,
  104, 108, 111, 124, 125, 135, 136,
  137, 140, 141, 142, 144, 148, 149,
  153, 154, 163, 165, 166, 167, 168,
  174, 182, 190, 192, 193
school system, 42, 44, 46, 65, 67, 136,
  137, 140, 154, 168,174, 193
science, 10, 13, 14, 28, 29, 35, 41,51, 57,
  69, 70, 71, 72, 77, 93, 103, 122, 142,
  146, 175, 199
scientific, 9, 11, 28, 29, 33, 41, 46, 47, 52,
  70, 77, 100, 135, 153, 183, 184, 195
scientist, 52, 62, 70
secessionist, 167
second language, 10, 11, 12, 13, 21, 29,
  40, 41, 43, 44,46, 48, 59, 66, 67,
  69, 72, 81, 86, 88, 93, 96, 97, 99,
  104, 107, 114, 115, 126, 130, 131,
  138, 145, 148, 151, 154, 160, 161,
  171, 181, 183, 184, 186,187, 189,
  192, 195
secondary education / school, 23, 29, 31,
  71; 99, 108, 138, 142, 147, 153, 155
security forces, *see* army
self-confidence [*see* confidence]
semicommunication, 33
semi-private domain, 87
Semitic, 83
Sephardic, 83
Serbia and Montenegro, 22, 73
Serbian, 21, 60, 61, 74, 121, 189
Serbo-Croatian, 58, 59, 61, 65, 74,
  79, 121
settler, 82, 130, 136, 137, 139, 141
Sherman, T., 27, 35, 37
Shohamy, E., 82, 83, 84, 88, 98, 104,
  111, 128
shop, 74, 113, 147
sign, 43, 87, 88, 89, 90, 92, 94, 151
sign language, 92, 98

Siiner, M., 123, 128
Silesian, 19, 21
Simpson, J.M.Y., 1, 17
Šircelj, M., 61, 74, 79
Skela, J., 65, 66, 77, 79
Skerrett, D.M., 12, 13, 105, 106, 107, 108, 109, 110, 113, 115, 118, 122, 123, 128
Skovholm, J., 43, 57
Skutnabb-Kangas, T., 119, 121, 128, 131, 156
Skvortsova, A., 121, 128
slang, 61, 74, 170, 195
Slavic, 19, 27, 30, 32, 37, 58, 60, 61, 121, 128, 133
Slavic language, 19, 27, 30, 37, 58, 60, 61, 133
Slav, 107, 136
Slovak, 10, 19, 20, 21, 23, 28, 29, 33, 34, 35, 36, 158, 189, 193
Slovakia, 18, 19, 22, 30, 33, 185
Slovene, 8, 11, 35, 58, 59, 60, 61, 62, 63, 64, 65, 66, 67, 68, 69, 70, 71, 72, 73, 74, 75, 76, 77, 78, 79, 180, 182, 186, 189, 190, 191, 192
Slovenia, 11, 24, 25, 31, 58, 59, 60, 61, 62, 65, 66, 67, 68, 69, 70, 71, 72, 73, 74, 75, 76, 77, 78, 79, 185, 186, 190, 191, 192
Slovenian, 24, 60, 68, 75, 78, 79
small language, 24, 25, 26, 31, 34, 130, 150, 160, 163
social cleavage, 87
social cohesion, 124, 187
social exclusion, 111, 125
social norm, 64, 163
socializing value, 195
socioeconomic, 2, 8, 68, 86, 179
sociolinguistic, 1, 2, 4, 5, 8, 10, 37, 39, 57, 58, 59, 60, 63, 67, 78, 103, 106, 128, 132, 133, 142, 143, 149, 160, 173, 174, 175, 193
sociolinguistics, 1, 2, 3, 5, 6, 8, 35, 39, 133, 163
Sorčan, S., 78
Sorolla, N.,177, 198
South Americans, 95
Soviet, 13, 19, 100, 105, 106, 107, 108, 109, 111, 115, 116, 118, 121, 123, 124, 126, 127, 128, 130, 131, 132, 135, 136, 137, 138, 139, 140, 141, 143, 144, 145, 149, 150, 153, 155, 156, 194, 195
Soviet Union, 100, 106, 107, 118, 121, 123, 135, 136, 137, 138, 155
Spain, 49, 160, 161, 162, 164, 167, 168, 173, 178, 185, 195
Spanish, 5, 6, 23, 39, 52, 54, 64, 74, 77, 82, 86, 89, 91, 92, 95, 98, 99, 100, 104, 157, 158, 159, 160, 161, 162, 163, 164, 165, 166, 167, 168, 169, 170, 171, 172, 173, 174, 175, 178, 188 [see also Castilian]
speech community, 5, 16, 68
Špelko, T., 77
spelling, see orthography
sphere (of life), 2, 14, 32, 59, 107, 135, 162, 181, 182, 183, 186, 189, 190, 194, 197 [see also domain]
Spolsky, B., 2, 17, 37, 82, 88, 98, 100, 103, 104, 189, 193, 200
sport, 62, 159
Stabej, M., 78, 79
standard language, 3, 10, 14, 23, 32, 33, 34, 38, 39, 41, 42, 43, 44, 45, 52, 61, 64, 73, 74, 75, 99, 114, 160, 163, 170, 181, 182, 187 [see also literary language]
standardization, 3, 11, 32, 102, 152, 189, 199 [see also codification]
state, 2, 3, 4, 8, 13, 14, 18, 22, 23, 24, 31, 32, 33, 34, 37, 38, 41, 42, 58, 70, 79, 81, 82, 83, 85, 86, 97, 99, 106, 107, 108, 113, 114, 116, 118, 121, 125, 126, 127, 130, 131, 132, 134, 135, 136, 137, 138, 139, 140, 141, 143, 144, 145, 146, 148, 150, 151, 152, 153, 154, 155, 156, 158, 160, 161, 162, 163, 165, 169, 173, 174, 177, 182, 184, 185, 187, 189, 190, 191, 192, 193, 194, 195, 197
state language, 113, 137, 138, 146, 151, 152, 154
stateless, 111, 115, 116
status, 3, 4, 38, 44, 50, 51, 52, 55, 56, 57, 58, 59, 60, 61, 66, 67, 68, 72, 74, 75, 76, 81, 84, 86, 87, 91, 93, 94, 96, 103, 105, 111, 118, 125, 130, 132, 134,

135, 136, 137, 141, 146, 147, 150, 151, 152, 153, 159, 160, 161, 163, 174, 186, 191, 199
Statute of Catalonia, 161
Stavans, A., 11, 81, 82, 87, 88, 95, 104, 183
Stich, A., 24, 25, 37
strangers (communication with), 113
stream, 136, 138, 148, 153
street (name / sign), 30, 88, 89, 93, 94, 116, 147
streetscape, 141
Strubell, M., 17, 161, 175, 176, 177, 200
stylebook, 170
subordination, 14, 160, 163, 164, 166
subtitle, 39, 43, 44, 62, 75, 91, 143, 183, 195
Sulbi, R., 117
supercentral language, 7, 15
supermarket, 159
survey, 13, 36, 116, 145, 146, 147, 148, 152
survival, 8, 14, 86, 163, 175, 193
Sussex, R., 107, 121, 128
sustainability, 4, 5, 7, 181, 196, 197, 198
sustainable, 11, 181, 196
Sutrop, U., 106, 117, 126, 128
Swahili, 6, 52
Swann, J., 5, 17
Swede, 39, 41, 50
Sweden, 39, 50, 73, 106, 171, 185
Swedish, 27, 38, 39, 50, 53, 54, 106, 134, 160, 189, 191
switch, [see code-switching]
syntax, 48, 83
Sztompka, P., 118, 128

Taagepera, R., 107, 127
Tabouret-Keller, A., 6, 17
Tagalog, 46, 52
Tallinn, 108, 111, 113, 116, 117, 125, 127, 128, 129, 134
Tamazight, 6 [see also Judeo-Berber]
teacher, 29, 30, 43, 50, 67, 70, 77, 87, 88, 96, 98, 99, 100, 101, 153
teacher training, 84, 99, 101
teaching, 10, 21, 25, 29, 30, 31, 39, 42, 43, 44, 45, 46, 47, 48, 49, 96, 99, 100, 101, 103, 135, 142, 148, 149, 160, 165
technology, 87, 93, 198

Tel Aviv, 88, 89, 91
television, 4, 39, 43, 44, 61, 62, 64, 74, 87, 91, 92, 93, 94, 114, 142, 143, 159, 167, 180, 182, 183, 188
term, 5, 6,7, 26, 29, 33, 61,, 70, 82, 87, 115, 118, 167,
terminology, 7, 70, 160, 170, 173
test, 75, 138, 139, 153
Thai, 189
theatre, 12, 93, 159
Thomas, F.R., 41, 57
threat, 9, 10, 16, 23, 24, 25, 32, 36, 37, 39, 41, 50, 51, 52, 53, 72, 85, 95, 103, 114, 122, 132, 140, 143, 144, 146, 150, 153, 154, 163, 171, 177, 182, 188, 195, 196, 199
Tigrinia, 95
Tigrinya, 86
TIMM, 101
Togeby, O., 47, 48, 57
Tollefson, J.W., 79, 109, 124, 128
Toporišič, J., 79
Torrens, R.M., 164, 176
Torres, J., 160, 164, 172, 177, 178, 200
tourism, 26, 62, 89, 94, 157
trade union, 165
tradition, 5, 82, 92
translanguaging, 186
translation, 6, 46, 47, 52, 53, 73, 143
transnationalism, 81, 84, 85, 132, 173
Trasberg, K., 125
trilingualism, 87
Trudgill, P., 5, 17
Truex, I.A., 140, 155
Trumm, A., 127
Turkey, 185
Turkish, 39, 42, 45, 46, 47, 52, 53

Ugro-Finnic, 58
Ukraine, 20, 22, 30, 126
Ukrainian, 20, 21, 30, 107, 111, 117, 136, 142
undergraduate, 71
Undervisningsministeriet, 52, 53, 57
uniformity, 10, 11, 54, 55
uniformization, 48, 49, 54
United Kingdom, 22, 37, 100, 126, 127, 128, 185, 194, 199
United States, 22

university, 4, 9, 10, 11, 12, 13, 14, 15, 16, 17, 27, 28, 30, 31, 32, 36, 38, 39, 41, 55, 57, 67, 69, 70, 72, 73, 75, 76, 77, 86, 94, 98, 99, 100, 101, 103, 104, 108, 117, 125, 126, 127, 128, 129, 135, 136, 141, 142, 149, 153, 155, 156, 166, 167, 168, 171, 176, 177, 181, 182, 183, 190, 199, 200 [see also higher education]
unknown interlocutor (communication with an), 171
unwelcome minority, 149
Uralic, 106, 125, 129
urbanization, 48
Urdu, 47, 52, 53, 121
USA, 73, 77, 79, 100, 106, 194, 199
USSR, 126, 155, 156, 194

Valencia, 160, 161, 164, 165, 166, 167, 168, 170, 171, 172, 174, 175, 177, 185, 188
Valencian, 157, 167, 168, 172, 188 [see also Catalan]
variation, 16, 41, 43, 45, 47, 48, 49, 55, 108, 120, 149, 182
Vassilchenko, L., 125
vernacular, 61, 84
Verschik, A., 114, 120, 128, 129
viability, 4, 8, 188, 189, 197
video game, 91, 183
Vidovič Muha, A., 79
Vienna Guidelines, 152
Vietnam, 22, 30
Vietnamese, 20, 21
Vihalemm, P., 113, 115, 127, 129
Vihalemm, T., 113, 115, 127, 129
Viitso, T-R., 106, 129
Vila, F.X., 1, 14, 26, 158, 161, 166, 169, 175, 178, 179, 195, 199, 200
vitality, 3, 8, 16, 59, 60, 71, 123, 167, 170, 172, 174, 191, 192

Vitez, P., 64, 80
Vižintin, M.A, 80
vocabulary, 48, 51, 53
Võro, 13, 106, 123

Wales, 160
Wardhaugh, R., 121, 129
web page, 159
Wee, L., 140, 156
welcome minority, 149
Western countries, 171, 183, 191
Whaley, L.J., 3, 16
Wicherkiewicz, T., 149, 156
Williams, C., 104, 121, 129
Willumsen, H., 127
Wilson, J., 36, 37, 126, 155
Woolard, K., 170
word stress, 133
workplace, 136
World War I, 134, 138
World War II, 42, 106, 131
Wright, S., 156

xenophobic, 42, 48

Yiddish, 12, 82, 86, 92, 93, 98
young (generation / people / age group), 10, 21, 33, 43, 50, 53, 54, 73, 86, 87, 100, 112, 119, 143, 144, 166, 195
youth club, 165
Yugoslav, 58
Yugoslavia, 11, 59, 60, 61, 65, 66, 67, 73, 75, 121

Zaagman, R., 140, 156
Zabrodskaja, A., 120, 129
Zadnikar, G., 78
Žaucer, R., 65, 80
Zuckermann, G., 85, 104
Zupan Sosič, A., 80

For Product Safety Concerns and Information please contact our EU Authorised Representative:

Easy Access System Europe

Mustamäe tee 50

10621 Tallinn

Estonia

gpsr.requests@easproject.com